Bodies and Bones

NEW WORLD STUDIES

J. Michael Dash, *Editor*

Frank Moya Pons and
Sandra Pouchet Paquet,
Associate Editors

Bodies and Bones

FEMINIST REHEARSAL AND IMAGINING CARIBBEAN BELONGING

Tanya L. Shields

University of Virgina Press

Charlottesville and London

THIS BOOK IS MADE POSSIBLE BY A COLLABORATIVE GRANT
FROM THE ANDREW W. MELLON FOUNDATION.

University of Virginia Press
© 2014 by the Rector and Visitors of the University of Virginia
Printed in the United States of America on acid-free paper
First published 2014

9 8 7 6 5 4 3 2 1

Library of Congress Cataloging-in-Publication Data

Shields, Tanya L., 1970–
    Bodies and bones : feminist rehearsal and imagining Caribbean belonging /
Tanya L. Shields.
        pages cm. — (New World Studies)
Includes bibliographical references and index.
    ISBN 978-0-8139-3596-6 (cloth : acid-free paper)
    ISBN 978-0-8139-3597-3 (pbk. : acid-free paper)
    ISBN 978-0-8139-3598-0 (e-book)
    1. Caribbean literature—History and criticism. 2. Feminist litera-
ture—Caribbean area. 3. National characteristics, Caribbean, in literature. 4. Feminism in literature. 5. Gender identity in literature.
6. Caribbean Area—In literature. 7. Caribbean Area—In art. I. Title.
PN849.C3S55 2014
809'.89729—dc23

2013041218

For Agatha E. Barker Stephens and Norbert Shields, two ancestors whose pains never limited their capacity to find joy, a bit of drama, and sweets!

Contents

Acknowledgments

THERE ARE SO MANY PEOPLE to thank because they have made this journey possible with love and dignity.

I thank my parents, June and Aubrey Shields, my aunts Shirley Watts and Hazel Wentt, and my uncles Philip Wentt and Anthony Shields, and my godmother Pauline "Jesse" Ezechiels, all of whom provided for me in material and spiritual ways and encouraged me to pursue dreams of knowing and transforming. My siblings, who never forget and make me laugh and cry and laugh while crying: Tracy, Twain, Tiffany, Renee, Taiwo, and Twanna (and their partners Tanya and Jason, and my nieces and nephews—Alaysia, Jamal, Nasir, Aquil, Gabriel, Gaege, and Cassidy). I am grateful to be part of this tribe! You all have the ability to help me enjoy my own fallibilities. I value the negotiations of community you have, er, encouraged me to make. To my cousins Rondell Shields, Sasha Williams, Sheena Shields, and Steve Browne for computer expertise and sharing brighter days from Georgetown to Brixton! And to Mary and Ken Lehmann, whose constant care and kindness have made my life easier from the first day we met.

Teachers and mentors of all sorts have encouraged, scolded, and made a difference, so therefore I would like to thank my teachers, who, through the years, made me happy to be in school and invited me to explore the world with them. My sincerest thanks to Judith Carroll and the late Patricia Long at Our Lady of Lourdes Elementary School, Hollinger Helliger and Elizabeth McGrath at The Academy of the Holy Names, and Carlos Schröder, Robert Carr, and Virginia Bell at the University of Maryland at College Park, all of whom encouraged me to think critically, reinforced the joy of pushing boundaries, and reminded me of the importance of connecting academic work with struggles for justice. My thanks to Susan Lanser, who envisioned and created a comparative literature program that was too radical for the times but continues to inspire years later. I would not have made it without a trinity of scholars-friends-mentors, all of whom pushed and pulled me through the peaks and valleys of my graduate experience and beyond: Merle Collins (my ever-stoic adviser), whose grace and tact I hope to exemplify one day and whose Zen-like "hmmm" I find myself invoking; A. Lynn Bolles, whose generosity of spirit, intellectual zeal, and energy devotion to showing the ways in which people's lives offer theories rather than imposing theories on their lives make me breathless; and Dorith Grant-Wisdom, whose "Aha, but let me play devil's advocate . . ." showed me the joy of teaching the other side and whose passion for justice and dance continues to influence. And to the quiet negotiator, Louise Clement, who taught me the power of generosity at the office.

There are so many friends and colleagues who have sustained me in meaningful ways. My deep and abiding thanks to those of you who have read versions of this manuscript, or listened to me puzzle out these ideas, you have all demonstrated a generosity of spirit and intellect that I hope to pay forward: The Noqui Collective has been a space of friendship, laughter, irreverence, and pure delight. My thanks to Anthony Blasingame, Kimberly N. Brown, Shelly Brown Cooke, James Cooke, and my godsons Courtland and Logan, Mavourneen Dolor, Charlene Dougall, Carolyn van Es, Kenyatta Dorey Graves, Gia Harewood, Randi Gray Kristensen, Ming Leung, Bob Mondello, Richelle Patterson, Kathrynne Homicile Paul, Patricia J. Saunders, Renee Shea, April and Stan Shemak, Tanya Shirley, Seth Clark Silberman, Audrey Stewart, Detannyia Towner, Belinda Wallace, and Gwyn Weathers. Thank you for discussing, dancing, reading, and reassuring.

In North Carolina, robust friendships and generous colleagues have enhanced the charms of the all-together-forward-not-one-step-back Tar Heel state. William Darity, Jr., has always encouraged and entertained me, especially when there are conversations on speculative fiction or music to be had. My community of scholars and friends (NC Aunties!) continues to mentor and share insights and care, particularly Marlyn Allicock, Kia Lilly Caldwell, Jerma Jackson, Eunice Sahle, Karla Slocum, Karolyn Tyson, Heather A. Williams, Lyneise Williams, and Yolonda Wilson. Words cannot express my deep and abiding gratitude. Michaeline Crichlow, Claudia Milian, and Pat Northover have been particularly generous, tireless, and invaluable supports throughout this process, with raucous *philotudinal* discussions and laughter in the best tradition of Caribbean intellectualism.

To my departmental colleagues, particularly Barbara Harris, who saw my potential, Joanne Hershfield for encouraging me, E. Jane Burns, Karen M. Booth, and Silvia Tomášková for reading and supporting, and Michele Berger for concrete survival strategies, thank you all for your friendship and unwavering encouragement.

Institutionally, the University of North Carolina at Chapel Hill first provided me with support during my two years as a doctoral diversity fellow; most recently, a research grant from Institute of African American Research allowed me to travel to Guadeloupe and Grenada in preparation for this book. Joseph Jordan, director of The Sonja Haynes Stone Center for Black Culture and History, provided space to think and work—the value of which cannot be underestimated. Librarians Shauna Collier and Holly Smith have made my work much easier with their attentiveness and "let me find that" attitudes. Additionally, I greatly appreciate the research support provided by Linesha Joseph, Antonia McDonald Smythe, Cheryl Sylvester, and Lillian Sylvester in Grenada. My very special thanks to Gwenaelle Guengant and La Médiathèque Caraïbe of the General Council of Guadeloupe under the aegis of Maison Schwarz-Bart, Maison des Illustres, who provided a transcript of the *Solitude* exhibition.

At the University of Virginia Press, Cathie Brettschneider has been a gentle and guiding hand, and Raennah L. Mitchell and Ellen Satrom have always responded quickly to my inquiries and eased my anxieties. Their patience, advice, and support made the impossible doable. I am immensely grateful to the anonymous readers who understood this project and its promise and whose careful readings and excellent suggestions have made this the book I envisioned. To cultural producers whose work haunted me, thank you for creating spaces that allowed me to rehearse my biases. My thanks to the visual artists whose work moved me tremendously, particularly Marie-Hélène Cauvin, Jason deCaires Taylor, and Jacky Poulier. Thank you for your willingness to share your ideas, talents, and time.

To those who provided respite and relief along the way, especially Stephan Michelson, who has been on this journey since my first year in college, and Bethanne Knudson, whose spitfire spirit ignites my own. In my Guadeloupean home, love and thanks to Josely Lacroix, Nadia and Jose Galas, and Marie-Claude Lacrosil, who make giving look effortless and who have introduced me to artists and historians and taken me around that island more times than I care to count. Your hospitality is always a balm.

To the many, many students I have worked with over the years whose excitement, ideas, and friendship remain with me, you are too numerous to mention, but I continue to value your insights, your eagerness, and your desire to make the world a more equitable place. Over the years, the Women's and Gender Studies staff—Suzanne Hahn, Lynn Sorrell, and Karen Thompson—have made the mundane aspects of university life easy to negotiate. My thanks.

And most of all, to Peter, Porter, and Tatiana Lehmann, who have lived with my body but not my soul for the many months it took to bring this project to completion. You give meaning to all the work and make the sacrifices bearable.

Portions of Chapter 5 were previously published as "The Amerindian Transnational Experience in Pauline Melville's 'The Ventriloquist's Tale'" in *Constructing Vernacular Culture in the Trans-Caribbean*, edited by Holger Henke and Karl-Heinz Magister, 267–297 (Lexington Books, 2008).

Bodies and Bones

Exodus.
Bone soldered by coral to bone,
mosaics
mantled by the benediction of the shark's shadow,

that was the Ark of the Covenant.
Then came from the plucked wires
of sunlight on the sea floor

the plangent harps of the Babylonian bondage,
as the white cowries clustered like manacles
on the drowned women,

and those were the ivory bracelets
of the Song of Solomon,
but the ocean kept turning blank pages

looking for History.

—Derek Walcott, "The Sea Is History"

Introduction: Reading Caribbean Resistance through Feminist Rehearsal

SUNLIGHT ON THE SEA FLOOR is a familiar image of the Caribbean, but the pages of the region's history run red. "Drowned women's bones fused to coral" underlies a history of the sea, one that subaquatically links the stories of the various territories of the Caribbean. The language of bones permits an examination of the structures of resistance and oppression even as they remind us of the flesh that once clung to them.[1] They remind us of flesh that endured the unspeakable and the unimaginable—flesh, which in Walcott's poem is held together by coral cartilage. Coral as connective tissue is more than a connection between the living and the dead: it interweaves environmental degradation with history. And while chronicles of the region may depict the Caribbean as a pawn in the plans of others, Caribbean people have rebelled, challenged, and undermined what western and northern hegemons have imposed politically and ideologically, most dynamically through culture—literature, music, spiritual practices, and rituals such as Carnival. While these forms of resistance have not substantively changed the relationship between Caribbean nations and imperial centers, they remain critical to the ongoing transformation.

In this project, I explore multiple readings of resistance, rebellion, and challenge in the Caribbean context through a feminist analytical lens, using what I term "feminist rehearsal." Feminist rehearsal is a methodological approach to reading texts that promotes multivalent readings and foregrounds gender, encouraging unity and consensus building through confrontation with overlapping histories of knowledge, power, and freedom. Emphasizing the feminist aspect of rehearsal reveals and confronts the ways in which national belonging has been imagined and privileged as a solely male enterprise. This method encourages the audience to become an actor; or, in the words of Brazilian dramatist Augusto

Boal, the audience becomes a "spect-actor," meaning that it creates not just meaning but solutions.[2] The transactional nature of national belonging has meant interrogating both the aesthetic and sociopolitical manifestations of cultural production that impact Caribbean bodies and bones. Each chapter of *Bodies and Bones* rehearses an event, archetype, or community to show how meaning has several reference points, not just one. In this way, by making the past tangible through repetition and revision, this book invites readers into its sociopolitical project of building more feminist, empathetic communities.

The word "rehearsal" implies several events: (1) repetition until something is mastered, (2) constant reexamination of what has already been done, and (3) the suggestion of orality and physical presence, of the body engaged in rehearsal because of the added inflections, pauses, nuances, and bodily shifts resulting from each repetition or revision.

The etymology of the word "rehearse" includes "hearse" for the carrying of a dead body, an important part of cultivating unrecognized archives and of understanding the bodily implications of Caribbean belonging.[3] The symbol of the hearse emphasizes the effects of beating, torture, and mutilation on the body and of social, political, and economic factors. Caribbean identities have been tied to bodies—sexed bodies, racialized bodies, commodified bodies. I invoke bodies and bones as a vivid reminder of the ways in which Caribbean bodies matter; how the tensions that arise in and between those gendered, classed, colored, and sexualized bodies alter, sometimes disappear, and often are reshuffled, lost, and reclaimed. The process of becoming bone engages with both the silencing of the dead and the erasure of their experiences, while speaking to the contradictory hostilities that bind the Caribbean crucible.

These bodies and bones were once tissue: sinewy flesh that has been silenced. As Toni Morrison's Baby Suggs remarks in *Beloved*, "they"—owners, masters, whites—"do not love our flesh," though perversely they used it for pleasure. Ultimately, Baby Suggs advises her congregation that "we flesh; flesh that weeps, laughs; flesh that dances on bare feet in grass. Love it. Love it hard. . . . Love your heart. For this is the prize."[4] These words, "they do not love your flesh," resonate with me as they reveal that black bodies are never presumed innocent or valuable outside the means of production. The lack of love for black flesh has meant that those bodies have endured unspeakable violence, from birth to death. This flesh has been raped, whipped, lynched, burned, dismembered, and pierced by bullets. This flesh has endured forced sterilization and medical experimentation.

Rebecca Skloot's book *The Immortal Life of Henrietta Lacks* highlights the impermissible use of black flesh at the cellular level.[5] Lacks's cells, known as the HeLa cell line, have "played a part in some of the world's most important medical advances, from the polio vaccine to in vitro fertilization."[6] Lacks's cells were harvested from her body without her knowledge in 1951 while she was being treated for cervical cancer. Before biomedical ethics discourse as we know it, the use of black female tissue without ethical consideration—and certainly without the subject's permission—indicates that bodies, bones, and flesh speak in the moment of life and from the grave. In addition to the numerous medical advances the HeLa cells contributed to, what emerges in Skloot's narrative are the details that make Henrietta Lacks's story: her love of her ancestral home in Clover, Virginia; her marriage to her cousin David "Day" Lacks; her epileptic daughter Elsie; her love of dancing and red nail polish; and her daughter Deborah's desire to know how she smelled. These details emerge alongside ever-present references to Lacks's "womb," which reiterate the compartmentalization of the black female body. Much of Henrietta Lacks's story (for herself and for me) is about her womb: her initial feeling that there was a "knot in her womb,"[7] her desire to have more children after the radium cancer treatment, and her insistence that, if she had known she would be infertile after treatment, she would have remained untreated.

These womb matters have affected black women before Henrietta Lacks; consider the women who were sterilized in gynecological experiments in 1930s Alabama. This mistreatment of women's bodies extends to the Caribbean, where, from the 1930s to the 1970s, one-third of Puerto Rican women were not only used as test subjects for the contraceptive pill[8] but they were subjected to *"la operación"*—the colloquial term for voluntary and involuntary sterilization. *La operación* included a range of medical procedures, from tubal ligations to hysterectomies, that for some was sterilization abuse and for others was a manifestation of their reproductive choices.[9] These womb matters reiterate the ways in which black women's bodies have been compartmentalized, objectified, and valued primarily for their reproductive capacity during slavery and in scientific research, further curtailing the possibilities of their citizenship.

Yet Lacks's embodied story ranges from the physical (her "womb concerns"), to the spiritual (Deborah's insistence that her mother's spirit is eternal through the cells generated in the lab,[10] as there are enough of her cells to circle the earth three or more times[11]), to the economic (her family's inability to access the health-care research her cells have produced), and, now, the ironic (the HeLa cells are described as aggressive and invasive of other cell cultures[12]).

Like Lacks's cells and the ubiquitous investment in national control over women's wombs, the bones of enslaved Africans at the bottom of the Atlantic constantly cause me to consider the lack of value placed on and in black lives. Bones are everywhere—reminding me of the ways silenced lives speak: the skeletal bones that throb during a sinus infection, the skull of a once homeless man that lives on a friend's bookshelf, and the bones that speak to forensic anthropologists. As Clea Koff writes in *The Bone Woman*, "bones can talk"; even when people are dead, their bones tell their stories and carry the history of their experience. According to Koff, "Forensic anthropology is all about 'Before and After.' Forensic anthropologists take what is left after a person has died and examine it to deduce what happened before death. . . . A dead body can incriminate perpetrators who believe they have silenced their victims forever."[13] Technology and new scientific developments allow bones to speak for justice in ways that were not imagined a generation ago.

Artists also use bones and other bodily residue as metaphor and praxis, as with the *One Million Bones* project. The work seeks to bring attention to genocide and serves as a "visual petition to raise awareness of the issue and call upon the government to create change."[14] This visual intervention of "creating" bones to witness lives that were lost and damaged continues to illustrate the power of bones to speak, as the One Million Bones organizers remark: "The bone is a symbol of people lost, and people who survive and struggle. It is a symbol of a fundamental human connection: we all have bones, they are our structure, they hold us up. In creating bones, participants learn about violence in faraway nations and make connections to their own experiences to reveal the commonalities that bind us together as humans."[15] These interventions remind us that murder, genocide, and holocaust are not just about killing the body (in faraway places) but about engendering fear and psychic annihilation in the surviving community, as the history of the Americas demonstrates. The commonalities of bone, flesh, and "the body in pain," to invoke Elaine Scarry's work, disrupt narratives of erasure and easy unity by all parties—the terrorized and the terrorizers.

Black feminists have consistently prompted us to think of this flesh as more than metaphor, more than material substance or residue; it was and is life. To continue to ignore these lives is to continue to consign these experiences to erasure; such absences mean that only one type of body—gendered male, and often white flesh—is universalized as valuable. Hortense Spillers asks us to consider the difference between bodies and flesh, and flesh as theory and praxis: "female flesh 'ungendered'—offers a praxis and a theory, a text for living and for dying, and a method for reading both through their diverse meditations."[16] Attentiveness to the flesh reveals ways of living and dying, ways that are complicated and multifaceted, and that ask difficult questions about national belonging and citizenship. Spillers contends that "before the 'body' there is the 'flesh' . . . that zero degree of social conceptualization that does not escape concealment under the brush of discourse, or the reflexes of iconography."[17] Her primary distinction between the body and flesh is between captivity and freedom. The body seems to be a liberated subject, while the flesh is captive. She argues that "If we think of the 'flesh' as a primary narrative, then we mean its seared, divided, ripped-apartness, riveted to the ship's hole, fallen, or 'escaped' overboard."[18] Flesh cannot be "discoursed" away. Indeed, black subjectivity in the Americas has been tied to black bodies and the use, mutilation, and brutalization of black flesh. I understand this as a call to pay attention to the intersectional and overlapping dimensions of black women's lives and to demonstrate how these experiences are marked on their flesh.[19]

In the process of national belonging, black bodies are public, black flesh is used without recognition, and black bone remains to incriminate those who have devalued the corporeal experiences of black people in the Americas. In contrast to Spillers, I do not distinguish between flesh, body, and bone—all are important gateways to understanding the centrality and intersections of one's body in the process of national belonging. And so I apply feminist rehearsal to reading the common material experiences of black bodies, flesh, and bone to reveal a contested or parallel history of the Caribbean that speaks of aesthetic and sociopolitical resistance and rebellion.[20]

Saidiya Hartman reasons that black female personhood in particular was legally bound to and by violence: "The law constituted the subject as a muted, pained body or as a body to be punished; this agonized embodiment of subjectivity certainly intensified the dreadful objectification of chattel status. Paradoxically, this designation of subjectivity utterly negated the possibility of a non-punitive, inviolate or pleasurable embodiment, and instead the black captive vanished in the chasm between object, criminal, pained body and mortified flesh."[21] These "high crimes against the flesh" (to use Spillers's term) range from sexual violence to economic violation to political disenfranchisement and are obscured by histories that did not and do not recognize the flesh and bones soldered by coral.

Rehearsing the Strategic Placement of the Caribbean

In order to best understand the importance of interrogating the Caribbean past, one must first get a sense of the Caribbean as a space—temporal, imagined, and actual. This space has contracted and expanded with various European incursions. First, Christopher Columbus's journeys claimed the region for the Spanish Empire, a claim soon followed by those of the French, English, Danish, and Dutch. From the fifteenth to the nineteenth century, various European interests battled for control of Caribbean shipping routes, markets, and colonial produce in attempts to enhance their powers.

Haitian independence in 1804 marked the beginning of the end (albeit a long end) of overt European control in and over the region. Haiti's victory for freedom, closely followed by the end of the slave trade in 1807 and the abolition of slavery in British colonies by 1838 (emancipation did not come until 1848 in French colonies, 1863 in Dutch colonies, 1873 in Puerto Rico, and 1886 in Cuba), also marked the emergence of the United States as a global power through the Monroe Doctrine of 1823. This U.S. policy, and the Cuban War of Independence from Spain (1895–1898), which became the Spanish-American War, shifted the balance of power in the region from Europe to the United States and moved that country from a postcolonial backwater to an empire. The Platt Amendment of 1903 gave legal standing to U.S. claims on Cuban territory, in effect negating Cuban sovereignty. At the same time, Puerto Rico became one of several U.S. protectorates through the Spanish-American War. These aggressions were intertwined with U.S. occupations and invasions of several Caribbean states: Haiti (1915–1934), the Dominican Republic (1916 –1924), the continuing blockade of Cuba (1960–), Operation Urgent Fury in Grenada (1983), and Operation Just Cause in Panama (1989). In addition to military overtures buttressed by Teddy Roosevelt's "Big Stick Diplomacy," colonizing nations, particularly the United States, deployed their fiscal and cultural power to influence, undermine, and bamboozle these predominantly sugar-producing islands. The idea of the Caribbean as a global cash cow remains, based not so much on monocrop economies but on its shipping routes. The Caribbean endures today as a site of interest for strategic access, but now for the movement of people—documented and not—and the desire to contain drug trafficking (an endeavor reminiscent of efforts to combat communism in the 1950s).[22]

Feminist rehearsal, through revisiting and revising texts, makes visible and legible the realities of these Caribbean bodies by perceiving the "hieroglyphics of the flesh," bone, and body[23] and relating the many transactions that move these bodies from "fragmented commodities" to the details and nuances of subjectivity.[24]

From the 1983 Caribbean Basin Initiative to the North American Free Trade Agreement of 1994, external economic policies have reinvented the Caribbean region. Challenges to colonialism and neocolonial structures have included slave revolts like the Haitian Revolution (1791–1804), maroonage from Suriname to Cuba, democratic socialism in Jamaica, the New Jewel Movement in Grenada, and the Cuban Revolution. Given these histories and continued power asymmetries, one might understand the Caribbean as a space in routine rehearsal, with national sovereignties and power exchanges subject to various actors or direction.

Bodies and Bones proposes to explore the ways in which rehearsal highlights the gendered and negotiated aspects of belonging. Attending to the *trans-* (i.e., the shifts that go through, over, beyond, outside, and within social norms) and the *action* (that something is happening, something is being performed, a deed or an act that is completed) foregrounds the mechanisms for affective and juridical connections to the community. These trade-offs, bargains, and exchanges that people engage in reveal the complex series of negotiations they make in order to survive within and through structures, symbolic or real. The *transactions* that are part of the gendered relations of belonging are important to feminist rehearsal because they are the mechanisms through which bodies exchange information, share revelations about themselves, and expose prejudices they hold. I use the terms "feminist rehearsal" and "rehearsal" interchangeably to focus on transactions or what Spillers would characterize as "practice of the flesh." While I recognize that nonfeminist projects could also make use of rehearsal (one could, for example, rehearse misogyny), for the cases in which I use "rehearsal" rather than "feminist rehearsal," the context should make it clear that I maintain a feminist analytical lens throughout the book. Through feminist rehearsal, I reveal the ways in which the Caribbean is a site of consumption producing for others in terms of labor and pleasure (tourism).[25] This production for foreign consumption reiterates the externalizing effects of belonging in the region.

The ways in which bodies belong to land, to communities, and to nations manifest in many respects, but the core idea is one of connection. The idea of communion—coming and working together as a unit, a community—is crucial to realizing familial, national, and global salvation. These ideas emerge from the earliest moment of Caribbean *becoming*—on various ships transporting women and men to the region.[26] The Caribbean became a space as such with the coming together of multiple ethnic identities and differing norms for gender and sexual relations from Africa, Asia, Europe, and the Americas. Particularly on ships, people who were unlike each other, who had no linguistic or ethnic connection, first "came together" and had to recalibrate how they understood themselves and their shipmates in terms of gender and every aspect of their identities. Creating expressions of community across the disruptions and disjunctions of trans-Atlantic crossings occurred as women and men developed narratives in which to accommodate their new realities and the structural realities of the plantation. Thus, feminist rehearsal invites the examination of multiple texts that discuss particular historical events, archetypes, or communities from numerous vantage points, with the goal of arriving at communities of consensus. By using the imagination to rehearse in fictional laboratories, all of us can move through understanding the entrenched and systemic nature of elite power. While feminist organizing and movements for social justice attempt to resist white supremacy and imperialism, this work is designed to open up the thinking on these issues to a broader audience; it is about building empathetic communities of consensus.

Communities of Consensus

Empathy is the emotion that facilitates tolerant, feminist communities of consensus.[27] It is a construct for embodying another person's experience, worldview, and contradictions and having that internalization move to action—to a shift in consciousness. The process of fully understanding these aspects of another's experience means movement from simply reading to continual practice and revision—to rehearsal. Reading becomes active; it becomes a performance that audiences use to make change. As Glissant postulates, "We 'know' that the Other is within us and affects how we evolve as well as the bulk of our conceptions and the development of our sensibility; the power to experience the shock of elsewhere is what distinguishes the poet."[28] Thus, it is through the creative text and the artistic space that adversaries inhabit the same orbit of value and worth because the Other is in each of us, in our capacity to exercise the vilest aspects of human nature, or the best, or something in between. The "Web of Relation," as Glissant characterizes it, is one of empathy. It is a network of feeling laden with "fragmentary repercussion" for individuals and eventually for communities.[29] While some scholars, such as Sara Ahmed, emphasize that empathy elicits concern only for those most like us, in terms of race, gender, sexual orientation, and nation, it is empathy's possibility to transcend that most interests me.[30] The conceptual and affective shifts made by rehearsal, which develop empathy and through which communities of consensus emerge, develop from repeated engagements with another's story. In effect, we can all create social change through minute engagements that help us to think critically about our environment. When these incremental moments are compiled, there is transformation. And while my focus here is with Caribbean communities, I believe that all societies interested in accountability and transformation can learn from and change through empathetic consensus.

In "Structures of Feeling," Raymond Williams articulates the fallacy of separating the personal from the social. Williams argues that *the social* is seen as fixed and institutional, while anything that does not comply with this model is characterized as *personal* and idiosyncratic.[31] Williams contends that, ultimately, the alternative to hegemonic messages embedded in fixed forms is "feeling and thinking which is social and material," manifested through a practical or lived consciousness.[32] For Williams, structures of feeling are the relations of experience that "go beyond the systemic beliefs of social institutions and join them with meanings and values that are actively lived."[33] As Omise'eke Natasha Tinsley observes in her research on same-sex desire in the Caribbean, it is "by feeling" that captured Africans resisted commodification.[34] In terms of democratic life and the Caribbean, therefore, *feeling* involves exploring the legacies of the plantation system in cultural production and how those inheritances can foster solidarity, identification, and accountability.

Rehearsal asks readers to reimagine and reflect on their own identities and their past actions in the present. By replaying texts in various spatial and temporal Caribbean contexts, readers can interrogate belonging to the region. Ideally, the process of rehearsal builds communities of consensus, which will disrupt the inherited colonial political processes by producing transformative spaces unafraid of difference and undeterred by historical bias.[35] The seemingly sudden "click" or "aha moment" of rehearsal comes from repetition and revision. The time— the hours of adjustment, tweaking, and harmonizing—develops relation and accountability. Naturally, the delimiting factor here is the necessary openness of the participants to the process and the time needed to participate. Yet, even with those who are resistant, I assert that engage-ment with cultural production, particularly pieces of public art and stat-uary, creates sites of rehearsal. This process engages with the vast web of relations generated by the colonial enterprise but is also mediated through various imperial and independent institutions.

Communities of consensus must necessarily pay attention to gender in imagining belonging in order to rethink citizenship as being primarily male and solely heterosexual. Recasting women so that they move from the backdrop of the national project to center stage means gendering national stories beyond heteronormative constructs to those that include continuous critique of the mechanisms used to represent relations of and to political power, coercion, and violence.[36] Anne McClintock argues that, in the permanently contested space of the nation, nationalisms are always gendered, always violent, and always invented. Those national-isms shaped by gender power from the outset are defined by McClintock as "contested systems of representation enacted through social institu-tions, and [by] legitimizing, or limiting, people's access to the rights and resources of the nation-state: land and water, political and economic power, children, food and housing, the technologies of violence."[37] As McClintock notes, in nationalist discourses, women have been mere appendages—simply supplements to "natural" patriarchy—whose nationalist performances are mired in their roles as nurturers, particu-larly as mothers and wives.

Though I agree in the main with McClintock's assessment of the regressive nature of nationalism, since nationalism is always contested, strategic nationalist interventions may produce more equitable or cer-tainly more nuanced outcomes.[38] By disrupting the naturalization of male power through strategic interventions, feminist rehearsal employs the idea of the nation as the embodiment of people's will, rather than the exclusive reserve of those with official power. Reconceptualizing national belonging in this way propels us toward communities of con-sensus.[39] These communities invoke M. Jacqui Alexander and Chan-dra T. Mohanty's articulation of feminist democracy, which calls for a process of decolonization that moves beyond free-market concepts of individuality.

Constructions of "the individual" have meant that citizenship "is the legal representation of a person's relationship to the rights and resources of the nation-state."[40] This person, or citizen, has always been imag-ined as male and, during the colonial period, white. McClintock persua-sively argues that women "were not incorporated into the nation-state as citizens, but only indirectly, through men, as dependent members of the family in private and public law."[41] In the Caribbean, understandings of what is public, what is private, and which bodies are seen as legitimate and legible determine how citizenship and belonging are performed.[42] By exploring the quotidian aspects of life for the vast majority of citizens, we grasp a sense of the multiple implications of people's negotiations with one another and with state institutions. Fluidity shapes negotiation, belonging, and defining Caribbean identity; it has plagued the region from its inception to its existence in the global psyche. Patricia Saunders, quoting McClintock, explains that nationalism is invented and performed because "[t]he nation, far from being a coherent, mutually compatible space, is composed of individuals and communities struggling for control of images, ideas, and discourse that are foundations of the 'nation' (imagined or otherwise)."[43] Saunders elaborates that there is a need for black subjects to reimagine the implications of "their selves and their being-in-the-world . . . not for [the simple] desire to trace narratives of origin, [but] rather, it is a critical perspective that acknowledges the countless ruptures of history, time, culture, identity, and Being."[44] Reimagining these implications in order to develop a critical consciousness has a long history in Caribbean literature.

Regarding anglophone Caribbean literature from the 1840s to 1940s, Leah Rosenberg has argued that literary production "both documented and participated in fundamental transformations of the British Empire and the Atlantic world. . . . Writers . . . negotiated and helped to shape the transformation from Victorian to modernist aesthetics." Additionally, nineteenth-century intellectuals wrote "to establish legitimacy . . . , [and] since their inception, anglophone Caribbean literature and literary criticism have been the products of nationalist discourses designed to extend the political rights of Caribbeans . . . after independence, . . . became a basis for claiming the right to determine national culture."[45] Creating legitimacy for a political project through literature has been intimately tied to representing Caribbean identities and is part of the process of decolonization.

In fact, culture continues to be a critical component in articulating what it means to belong—from articles of flag-embellished clothing, to music, to literature, and public art. The imagination and the stories told in literature, through paintings, and contained in various memorials play a central role in the ways we "be/come" and "be/long." These stories illustrate what "place" means and explain the relations of space and subjectivity. In other words, these stories are ways in which readers rehearse social relations and reimagine social relations. The significance of rehearsing through cultural production is that it reveals how we are "marked and made."[46]

There are innumerable ways to *be* Caribbean. In fact, a cursory history of the region reveals that this complexity and hybridity, whether racial or cultural, have been integral to regional identities, revealing that Caribbean nationalism's holy grail is to become "one people."[47] Even in places with homogeneous racial populations, national mottos express the work implicit in becoming one people. Despite the implied assumption of heteronormativity in the term "one people," these dictums recognize the process of developing consensus even in what may "seem" a monolithic space.[48]

Transformative Fiction

One way of using the alchemy, or the transformative power, of fiction is to rehearse the past in the present. This means considering new ways of organizing socially and politically and, perhaps, alternatives that resist flattening belonging into a singular and normative construction of the citizen. Rehearsing toward communities of consensus creates options for social and political organizing in which history and colonial inheritances are not sanitized but confronted repeatedly. Rehearsal becomes praxis, that is, a habit for unmasking and decentering binaries of the past and dichotomies of the present.

In challenging and unmasking the gendered assumptions linked to citizenship, it is critical to recognize how gender shapes plantation economies, cultures, and power through discourses and social practices and reveals the disjunctures of belonging in racially monolithic spaces.[49] Feminist rehearsal is a productive method for thinking through multiple Caribbean perspectives, geographies, memories, violence, and power dynamics. Feminist rehearsal is a conscious wielding of power by an audience intended to craft a resistant epistemology and feminist praxis. Throughout this text I draw on literary and visual production and use rehearsal to interrupt the master narratives in the region by providing a way of working through painful and seemingly impossible stories. Three actions are embedded in feminist rehearsal: (1) thinking through the tensions and instabilities of various historical ruptures, (2) exploring the transactions that affect belonging or the processes of negotiated membership, and (3) dealing with the "hearse" elements or visible corporeal implications to the material body created by the commodification of the region and the "fragmented commodification" of black women's bodies.[50] This means interrogating the web of exchanges, connections, and relations made in assigning market value to place, culture, and gender. In short, these multiple readings of key events, archetypes, and communities—both historical and literary—are understood as critical moments in the formation of Caribbean identities.

My construction of feminist rehearsal is the process of moving *toward* an ideal rather than *reaching* a utopic performance.[51] Like feminist praxis, these engagements with the past forge new relationships in the present. Feminism is not merely the recognition of "the feminine," or the betterment of women, or attending to the representation of them; rather, feminism is a refashioning of the role gender plays in all our lives, in our worldviews, in our political presents and presence. It is about constructing a world across, between, among, and in spite of colonial legacies and histories. Feminism is a way of engaging with historical violence and pushing beyond it toward a project of amelioration and justice. Feminist rehearsal questions how the layers of collective identity—race, sex, gender, nation, and so on—interact with one another.

In questioning these layers, gender is a significant factor missing from other engagements of rehearsal. Antonio Benítez-Rojo is one Caribbean scholar who has worked on similar ideas, expressed in a number of ways: repetition, rereading, rewriting, and rehearsal. In *The Repeating Island*, he posits that Caribbean people will move from pragmatism to intuition by rereading, which, he argues, is necessary because the reader reads himself or herself into initial readings. I believe both are critical, but my emphasis is on putting such a process into practice. At the very least, feminist rehearsal is one way of considering the relationships and antagonisms in which we all still participate by revisiting complicated gendered and racialized histories through fictional representations of the cold historical facts.

And as Wilson Harris writes in his novel *The Infinite Rehearsal*: "One may still apprehend the obsessional ground of conquest, rehearse its proportions, excavate its consequences within a play . . . a play that is infinite rehearsal, a play that approaches again and again a sensation of ultimate meaning residing within a deposit of ghosts relating to the conquistadorial body—as well as the victimized body—of new worlds and old worlds."[52] Harris's infinite rehearsal, like Benítez-Rojo's repeating with improvisation, is about the constant interplay with and integration of the past. What is critical in the process of rehearsal is understanding the impact of the past on the present—a political present. This political present enables us to build spaces of consensus bound by an ethical grounding in the material past, even as the present parodies, decenters, and foregrounds the inconsistencies of history. Harris believes that infinite rehearsal "is not simply a replaying of things for the sake of replaying things . . . it is part of the very fabric of the imagination. It does not erase difference between cultures. . . . Thus the quest for wholeness is ceaseless and cannot be structured absolutely on the surface or in the depths."[53] Again, inhabiting and understanding the negotiations of another's truth render (political) ideologies legible and make visible the racialized, classed, gendered, and national histories of plantation societies.

Harris argues that the indigenous Caribs "consumed a morsel of the flesh of their enemy and thought thereby they would understand his secrets, what he was planning to do, how he would attack them, how he would ravage their villages."[54] Since belonging is often constructed oppositionally as "us versus them," there is always a foreigner, an Other, to measure against and, often, to feel superior to. Moreover, because the us/them is gendered, there are times in which masculinist national narratives are deployed against women, and they are consumed in nationalist narratives. Harris gives us a precise depiction of indigenous bone flutes—the instruments of death, imagination, and creation made from the bones of humans and animals. As Harris characterizes it, these flutes hold the contradiction of life and death, art and beauty. They are instruments of pleasure, pain, panic, and rehearsal, particularly through their connection to music and death, and in the visibility of carrying the body, being the hearse, their conflicted death and knowledge origins function as part of a historical framework. The creative text is the morsel that, once ingested, transforms, perhaps regenerates, the one who consumes it—even if it is only in a minute way.[55] Building on that morsel of transformation, encouraging one's reflection and participation in the world, creates viable democratic futures that challenge the reproduction of hegemonic (us versus them) citizenship by remembering and rendering valuable the flesh that performs belonging.

Performance Theories in Rehearsal

In this project, the explicitly political nature of theatrical intervention seduces me and invites me to consider the various ways these theories can transform. Theories of performance provide great insights into culture and civic engagement. Performance studies, which explores the merging of theatrical and anthropological methodologies, takes embodied interactions and corporeal knowledge as central, even if the embodying characteristics can be contradictory.[56] Furthermore, this body of work explicitly proposes "identification" and "participation" as methods by which "to intervene and change the course of action."[57] The Sistren Theatre Collective was one manifestation of this in that it facilitated participation and identification by recognizing that theater that fosters a sense of Caribbeanness arises from Caribbean experiences and realities. This theater of recognition not only reveals Caribbean people to themselves but also exposes the piped-in, satellite-relayed, saturation programming from the West as another arm of control through cultural encroachment. Sistren's collaborative methodology, which is based on personal testimony, improvisation, and role-playing "through games, songs and culturally specific techniques"[58] along with strategies taken from Augusto Boal's *Theatre of the Oppressed*, takes two forward paths of building the self from the deepest places within while simultaneously constructing community.

Sharon Green's observations of the Sistren collective, as its members cope with the pressures of globalization, are instructive for the larger issues at hand. Both Green and Sistren's former artistic director, Honor Ford-Smith, cite the forces and problems associated with the external (international funding requirements) and the internal (domestic function and aspirations) pressures on the collective.[59] Green's notation of dispirited national populations recognizes the commodification of culture in this particular moment of globalization. Green quotes Carl Stone, who maintains that "the end of the decade [the 1970s] saw a pattern of demobilization, political apathy and withdrawal into cynicism and hopelessness as many lost faith in political causes and lowered their expectations."[60] Thus, the combination of psychic national hopelessness and economic penetration by Western conglomerates facilitated the development of a culture that moved "from stories to tell in the 1970s to stories to *sell* in the 1990s" (emphasis added), as Eugene Williams of the Jamaican School of Drama notes.[61] The penetration of video technologies with foreign content has led to less dissemination of folk knowledge, which was a critical building block of Sistren's methodology. The collective therefore found it difficult to stay relevant to its grassroots audience as well as to its funders, which, in turn, created a sense of inadequacy and obsolescence for Sistren. Green's overall assessment reiterates that "grassroots theatre can still be relevant if it continually reinvents itself . . . and shifts while remaining rooted to its guiding principles and context."[62] Continually recognizing the possibility of cooption and thus the need to incessantly refine the process are other aspects of the embedded power of the theater process, as well as the power embedded in the systemic structures under challenge.

Earlier in the twentieth century, C. L. R. James made the same argument regarding the role of Caribbean artists in regional belonging. James recognized that the artists who believe in a Caribbean nation are not only obligated to offer their vision in the public sphere, but they also need to use popular forms to connect their art to the people in order to create a larger discourse. James believed that when the creative/intellectual artist reached the popularity of the calypsonian (specifically the calypsonian Mighty Sparrow), the artist would have "arrived."[63] He opined: "My conclusion, therefore, is this. At this stage of our existence our writers and our artists must be able to come home if they want to. It is inconceivable to me that a national artistic tradition, on which I lay so much stress as an environment in which the artist must begin, it is inconceivable to me that this can be established by writers and artists, however gifted, working for what is essentially a foreign audience."[64] James addresses a critical theme in this context: that the development of a liberating national consciousness is predicated on the artist's connection to the audience's home. A national audience reinforces a liberating national consciousness, and the artist must have a connection to the audience— he or she must speak the people's language, primarily their vernacular.

Dwight Conquergood asserts that the "promiscuous traffic between different ways of knowing—the objective official map versus the practical, embodied, popular story—carries the most radical promise of performance studies . . . because performance studies struggles to open a space between analysis and action."[65] In opening this space between analysis and action—or what I am calling feminist rehearsal—performance studies emphasizes the body, one in tune to the needs of the character, the performance partner, and other co-creators, and I envision these performances as drama, painting, statuary, and novels. This knowledge, situated in bone, flesh, and bodies, fosters empathy, accountability, and solidarity.

Transactional Flesh

In *Undoing Gender*, Judith Butler contends that performing gender is transactional in nature by arguing that it is not only a group performance, one necessarily "done" by someone for/because of/in conversation with Others, but also a play (to extend the metaphor) written well before one takes the stage "even if the other is only imaginary." She writes: "If gender is a kind of doing, an incessant activity performed, in part, without one's knowing and without one's willing, it is not for that reason automatic or mechanical. On the contrary, it is a practice of improvisation within a scene of constraint."[66] In other words, the role of the male hero in Caribbean literature, however conflicted, is seen through the lens of patriarchal assumptions because within the scenes of colonial constraint, men have come to think of inheritance as automatic, because, generally, they were automatically the first to inherit, given the male-centered organization of society.[67]

The value of the rehearsals I explore here is their ability to disrupt hegemonic discourses and to create a praxis of mutual spaces for difficult dialogues and liberatory epistemologies.[68] Joan Dayan understands rehearsal as "vodou history" and defines it "as three superimpositions that reinforce one another, while discouraging a unified point of view. I tell the same story again and again in different ways [because] I intend in this narrative [to be] much like ritual. The more a detail, scene or theme is repeated, the more of its meaning is established."[69] Dayan's pathbreaking work argues that Vodou as a philosophy and way of reading provides a philosophical and theoretical method "that circumvents and confounds any master narrative."[70] This representation of Vodou history, along with Glissant's distinction between historical master narratives of *History* and stories of the masses that linger in the common *history*, point to various repetitions and rehearsals of history, memory, and identity.[71]

As a constructed site, the Caribbean, as Christine Barrow puts it, has never been *pre-capital*. It has always been a place in which the model of "bodies as capital" reigned supreme because of the labor needed for the plantation. In addition to transaction as exchange and negotiation, the critical point I explore is whether transactions are voluntary or coerced, and the performance of will in this process. As Shannon Sullivan argues, thinking of bodies as transactional "is to conceive of bodies and their various environments as co-constituted . . . which means thinking of bodies and their environments in a permeable, dynamic relationship in which culture does not just effect bodies, but bodies also effect culture."[72] Furthermore, thinking of bodies as transactional "emphasizes the significance of the concrete, lived experience of bodies."[73] Sullivan's invocation of bodies as transactional gives an immediacy to the past by recentering the ethics of flesh and bones. Enslavement and indenture crystallize the commodification of bodies as transactional because purchase and exchange are explicit in this process. Various Caribbean contexts signal that the voluntary implication of transaction is often constrained by race, class, gender, sexuality, language, and, at times, history. These components constitute the environments that various skins live through.

Gaiutra Bahadur's "Coolie Women Are in Demand Here," from her forthcoming memoir *Coolie Woman: The Odyssey of Indenture*, is an example of the ongoing invention of belonging that foregrounds the spaces that Indian women occupied in India and their new Caribbean homes.[74] Bahadur traveled to the Indian state of Bihar on a quest to find her great-grandmother Sujaria's story and challenge the muteness of historical records. Negotiating her own journey between Guyana, the the United States, the United Kingdom, and India, Bahadur retraced Sujaria's three-month crossing of the *kali pani*, or "dark waters," on *The Clyde*, the ship on which her great-grandmother was both a passenger and "part of its cargo."[75] Bahadur's rehearsal of ancestral memory emphasizes both her great-grandmother's negotiations of race, class, and gender and the writer's accommodations to place, history, and culture. The double time line of *Coolie Woman* illustrates that although women were in demand as wives and mates, they were also violated if they exercised any independent desires: "Just days before Sujaria landed [in Guyana], a coolie was executed for hacking his wife to pieces with the same machete he used to cut sugarcane in the fields. She had been unfaithful to him. That season, four other women were killed in the same way, for the same reason."[76] Indian women used immigration as a way of voiding their marriages in India, forcing the British to pass the Indian Emigration Act in 1883, which "was meant to stop wives from passing as widowed or unmarried to escape their husbands."[77] Here, the collective nature of the coolie woman's identity—racial, sexual, national, and religious—is negotiated and policed across various locations, histories, and cultural norms that implicate the consequences of plantation slavery and, in this instance, indenture.

The overwhelming representation of Indian women in Caribbean societies veers from passive women, happy with patriarchy, to cunning women, out to undermine and disrupt black Caribbean communities.[78] The slave trade initiated economic transactions in the region, and indenture perpetuated them by producing complex interactions between groups from almost every continent. Bahadur's piece illustrates the epistemological exchanges and production in the nineteenth through twenty-first centuries. In these transactions of desire, knowledge, and power, Sujaria emerges as the subject of several stories: one revealed from the archives, two from Bihar—in the past and of the present, one as told by her great-granddaughter, and one that exists as part of the collective experiences of other women who crossed the dark waters. Bahadur's narrative is a counter to hegemonic control of women and their stories—tenacious women who employed sexual leverage and who left their men and their larger communities to forge new lives for themselves. In becoming a Caribbean woman, Sujaria created the Bahadur family and reinvented herself as mother, worker, and, eventually, wife. Within the British colonial power structure, Sujaria negotiated gender, caste, and national expectations to embrace her own power by disavowing both Indian and English social scripts. The transactions of Sujaria's experience inform Caribbean historiographies, as does Bahadur's desire to find and tell these stories.

In *Bodies and Bones*, I examine multiple media—paintings, monuments, and literature—to illustrate the range of possibilities available to discuss the imagining of Caribbean belonging and of fostering communities of consensus. These genres work across an affective and sensory continuum to reveal the hegemonic narratives, to counter discourses, and to amplify spaces of and for transformation. The visual and often visceral language of paintings engages the senses in ways that are different from reading a book. Monuments represent an artist's vision that is sanctioned by the collective process in some way and are engaged by the public or multiple publics. Literature, in contrast, is generally private, individual, and secluded. These media are engaged in through various degrees of the personal and the public in order to consider new pathways, invoke paradoxes and contradictions, and create the multiplicity of readings that rehearsal invites.

Chapter 1, "Rehearsing with Ghosts," applies the concept of feminist rehearsal to various texts about slavery, neo-slavery, and the Middle Passage. The chapter revisits four texts that I interpret as rehearsals of Marie-Hélène Cauvin's 2002 painting *Vers un destin insolite sur les flots bleus de la Mer des Antilles* (Bound by a Horrific Destiny to the Blue Waters of the Caribbean): the Middle Passage in Fred D'Aguiar's *Feeding the Ghosts* (1997); cruise ship tourism; Caribbean boat migrants; and, the Grenada aquatic park. Cauvin's painting and D'Aguiar's novel afford vivid visual and concrete rehearsals that illustrate how the method is applied. In this way, chapter 1 focuses on the lack of freedom, while chapter 2 examines what is considered the ultimate moment of Caribbean freedom: the Haitian Revolution.

Chapter 2, "Their Bones Would Reject Yours," rehearses the Haitian Revolution as an event represented by non-Haitian men: Aimé Césaire's *The Tragedy of King Christophe* (1963), Alejo Carpentier's *Kingdom of This World* (1949), and C. L. R. James's play *The Black Jacobins* (1968). This chapter contemplates the ways in which different readings of the Haitian Revolution reveal paradoxes in the event's historical moment, as well as in twentieth-century moments of its representation. The tone of the chapter shifts significantly to indicate the disjuncture the Revolution caused in the Americas. These texts rehearse representations of racialized Caribbean masculinity that expose the ways in which the male writers of these texts, significant shapers in articulating "Caribbeanness" and "Caribbean maleness," imagined the Revolution's impact on the region during the contentious and formative postcolonial, independent twentieth century.

Chapter 3, "Hope and Infinity," complicates the work of chapter 2 by situating "the feminine" in these masculinized constructions of national belonging from the perspectives of Haitian women. Here, I read Rose Marie Desruisseau's painting *Vodou Ceremony* (1986) and Edwidge Danticat's short story "A Wall of Fire Rising" as two representations of the Revolution that value the revolutionary masses rather than the heroes who are central in chapter 2 and serve as Haitian counterpoints to the texts in "Their Bones Would Reject Yours." In this way, foregrounding twentieth- and twenty-first-century Haitian women's voices builds on Joan Dayan's work on the Haitian national hero, Défilée, who picked up the pieces of Jean-Jacques Dessalines's mutilated and dismembered body. I place Desruisseau's painting and Danticat's story in dialogue with the representations of the Revolution by non-Haitian men in order to foreground Haitian women's representations of it and to center the domestic consequences and corrupted realities of the Revolution.

Chapter 4, "Signs of Sycorax," explores contemporary representations of Caribbean women by rehearsing Sycorax, an archetypal imported Caribbean figure. Sycorax, characterized as a silent witch and mother to the disfigured Caliban, is voiceless in Shakespeare's *The Tempest*. This chapter builds on the work of other scholars who have explored this character—particularly May Joseph—and whose recuperations reflect on both the absence and silencing of women's experiences in colonial encounters. The second part of the chapter reviews Shakespeare's construct, and the final section rehearses radical appropriations of Sycorax from three sources: Grace Nichols's poem "Ala," which is part of her poetic slave narrative *I is a Long Memoried Woman* (1983); Marina Warner's novel *Indigo* (1992); and Nalo Hopkinson's *The Salt Roads* (2003). Nichols's poem is about a woman who commits infanticide; Warner's novel imagines Sycorax as an indigenous woman who raises an African "whelp"; and, Hopkinson's novel has three female protagonists who are Sycorax-like. Indeed, women reimagine, reshape, and represent belonging in a multiplicity of ways that challenge the fallacy of the nation and nation building as solely male enterprises. Using these texts, I contend that reconstructing symbolic notions of Sycorax as a mother, rebel, victim, and survivor challenges the distortions and uneven manifestations of power in the production of belonging. Additionally, these cultural products foreground the concerns of established and emerging Caribbean artists who struggle with making sense of Caribbean pasts while including issues, such as sexuality, not dealt with as openly in earlier texts in the Caribbean canon.

In chapter 5, "Rehearsing Indigeneity," rehearsal is applied to the idea of the "native" as transnational in order to grapple with the notion of racial, ethnic, and cultural "mixing" within Caribbean belonging. In this chapter, Pauline Melville's *The Ventriloquist's Tale* is used to investigate the avenues by which indigenous women and men have produced, reproduced, and contested belonging in the contemporary Caribbean. The novel uses a contemporary Amerindian experience, specifically that of the Wapisiana people, to explore identities not often acknowledged and generally erased in the annals of "Caribbean" history. This section rehearses indigenous belonging by asking readers to consider the spatial and reproductive mixing generated by the encounter of Europeans and indigenous people, which was a fundamentally gendered and sexualized process. Rehearsing these aspects of conquest puts women's (especially indigenous women's) sexual and reproductive agency at the center of belonging to the region. I contend that the Amerindian experience, particularly in Guyana, can be instructive for imagining the sexual economy of Caribbean transnational experiences because, in this context, indigenous female bodies became sites of reproduction. Belonging is imagined through or against their relationships (coerced or otherwise) with European men.

The conclusion, "Rehearsing and Proxy-formance?" reiterates the argument over layered and paradoxical structures of power by highlighting that rehearsal allows readers and viewers to imagine innumerable forms of Caribbean belonging. In effect, each rehearsal enables the reader to approximate the position of a character or to be a type of proxy. I posit that the types of Caribbean belongings imagined through rehearsal can foster liberatory engagement and reiterate the important distinction between rehearsal and performance. This chapter emphasizes the generative power and possibilities of feminist rehearsal, positioning it not only as a metaphor for the process in which the texts are engaged but also as praxis that demands readers engage in the ongoing invention of the "Caribbean."

In *Bodies and Bones*, the creative text, especially if it is communally experienced, facilitates the process of redefining self-interest from simply an individual perspective to that of a community, and eventually from one community to several, until, like a ripple, it expands throughout a nation. The creative text can help participants apprehend often painful processes in which they are asked to relinquish power and explore benefits that are not necessarily evident to the superficial self or to invoke the most primal "me" in order to work through differences, which are tremendous, terrifying, and often traumatizing. Feminist rehearsal is a multidimensional approach to literature and cultural production that invokes theatrical strategies to collectively open spaces of social change and create communities of consensus. Oppositional poetics (and politics) do not operate in a vacuum; rather, they reference the system from which they work for emancipation. In short, feminist rehearsal uses theater and fiction to confront and accommodate those events, archetypes, ideas, and communities that are uncomfortable, unacknowledged, horrific, and difficult to address. In addition to helping viewers map the colonial past in the Caribbean's neocolonial present, the cover image (discussed in chapter 1) highlights debates on gender, power, and race. Each rehearsal signifies the shifting, floating ground and the search for a way and place to belong. These rehearsals do not suggest a lack of hope for Caribbean people or claim that their destinies are predetermined; rather, each rehearsal reveals the entrenched nature of the plantation and colonial ideology, its impact on belonging, and the ways in which women's contributions must be considered within the story of Caribbean peoples' struggles to resist the manacles of colonialism in all its forms. Each rehearsal subverts the notion of the Caribbean as a space of inadequacy in order to highlight the creative and powerful alternatives it produced in itself. Sunlight on the sea floor can be recovered as a hopeful image once men and women in the Caribbean can reconcile the bodies and bones that make the sea a hearse, whose tides lap the shore with history.

1   Rehearsing with Ghosts

> Soon all those bodies melt down to bones, then the sea begins to
> treat the bones like rock, there to be shaped over time or ground
> to dust. Sea does not stop at death. Salt wants to consume every
> morsel of those bodies until the sea becomes them, becomes their
> memory. So it is from the sea that all 131 souls are plucked. From
> a sea oblivious to time . . . those bodies have their lives written on
> salt water.
>
> —Fred D'Aguiar, *Feeding the Ghosts*

FRED D'AGUIAR'S 1997 NOVEL *Feeding the Ghosts* captures
the horror of enslaved bodies becoming bones. The novel, a poetically
written history, chronicles the 1781 *Zong* Massacre in which medi-
cal-doctor-cum-ship-captain Luke Collingwood threw 132 captured
Africans overboard near the Jamaican coast. Collingwood's desire
to profit from insurance claims rather than risk docking with sick,
dying slaves—who would be valueless and unmarketable—spurred his
conspiracy.[1] In a miraculous twist, one man survived and returned to
the *Zong*.[2] In D'Aguiar's novel, the survivor is imagined as a woman
named Mintah who forges a relationship with Simon, a white working-class cook who sustains her until she foments a short-lived insurrection on the ship. D'Aguiar presents the idea of rehearsal through
the sea, whose geography erases and whose tides silence its archive
of bones: "Accustomed to rehearsal, to repeats and returns, [the sea]
did not care about the abomination happening in its name."[3] Mintah
declares that life on water is an "in-between life"[4] and the monotony
of the sea "repeats and returns" and obscures the lives lost, the histories and stories of those bodies in and on the sea. These lives are made
invisible because of the "constantly shifting geography" of the sea;[5] the
sea's history is not visible given its tidal functions. In this book, feminist rehearsal of artistic Caribbean representations not only enables
the understanding of Caribbean notions of time and space beyond the
monotonous drone of the sea but also helps to analyze aesthetic and
sociopolitical moments in order to achieve reconciliatory readings of
traumatized pasts.

Like D'Aguiar's novel, Marie-Hélène Cauvin's 2002 painting *Vers
un destin insolite sur les flots bleus de la Mer des Antilles* (Bound by a

Figure 1. *Vers un destin insolite sur les flots bleus de la Mer des Antilles* (Bound by a Horrific Destiny to the Blue Waters of the Caribbean), Marie-Hélène Cauvin, 2002. Oil on board, 40 x 48 in. (Courtesy of the artist)

Horrific Destiny to the Blue Waters of the Caribbean) commemorates the Middle Passage and links the rehearsal of memory, gender, and the imagination to notions of Caribbean belonging. It does this by replaying at least four moments critical in historical and contemporary understandings of Caribbean belonging: the Middle Passage as described in the novel *Feeding the Ghosts*, the expansion of cruise ship tourism, the movement of Caribbean "boat" people, and the aquatic park at Moliniere Bay in Grenada, West Indies. Taking her title as a point of departure, I use Cauvin's painting as a structuring device to suggest that violence, memory, geography, and the irresistible urge toward the (im)possible bind events in the Caribbean. Juxtaposing historical events not only reveals the structures of colonialism and neocolonialism that continue to affect the region but also exemplifies the interconnected nature of gender and memory. Using feminist rehearsal, this chapter unpacks gender as a means of reclaiming the material body and challenging repeatedly reproduced master narratives.

In the remainder of the chapter, I examine the Middle Passage and some rehearsals of it as examples of the formation of Caribbean identities, particularly how these identities belong through tidal engagements to the region. Here, I refer to Edward Kamau Brathwaite's idea that Caribbean unity is submarine. Therefore, the subaquatic location of Caribbean linkages means that the "tides" are a significant carrier of Caribbean connection.[6] In completing this exercise, one must consider those rehearsals that are emptied of the historical weight of the Middle Passage, that is, those moments that rehearse it without the visible body component or *hearse* (interestingly, the etymology of the word "rehearsal" substantiates the connotation of hearse as a rake or harrow or temporary vehicle for carrying a dead body). Ultimately, imagining a feminist rehearsal allows me to consider the essential significance of gender to the rehearsals of Cauvin's painting, the cruise ship, migrants at sea, and the underwater park. It enables readers and viewers to recast and replay moments that are critical to the formation of Caribbean identities and to interrogate the transactional nature of belonging to the region. In essence, feminist rehearsal means examining formative moments for the purpose of undoing previous portrayals of gender—both masculinity and femininity—examining memory, and exploring history. Fundamentally, feminist rehearsal focuses on this difference because with each act (i.e., each reading of a perspective that is not our own), we get a broader understanding of, and a greater context for, our own realities, our own complexities, and our own inconsistencies.

The words "rereading with a difference" and "rehearsal with a difference" have many connotations. These are metaphors for shifts in consciousness and shifts in what people actually do and therefore have to do with how material reality is constructed, reconstructed, staged, and restaged. Rehearsal places greater emphasis on a group activity (rather than on one person silently rereading with text in hand) and more emphasis on the body's redoing with a difference and a nuance generated from continuous engagement with a text. Instead of being about one individual, rehearsal is about multiple actors interacting, improvising, and moving themselves and their props into multiple configurations across a stage. Although the term could also take the form of individual rehearsing of a song or a reading, I am most interested in the productive potential of collective rehearsals. In these rehearsals, negotiation is central; trade-off and bargaining are internalized, institutionalized, and regularized. This is the moment to investigate if and how the collective nature of various identities—racial, sexual, national, or otherwise—negotiating with each other, with the histories each has inherited and vis-à-vis the cultural norms that govern their environments, makes rehearsal.

These are the negotiations made in light of unequal power relationships and the ways in which coercive practices inform various "skins" of the experiences of historical Caribbean people, as well as fictional characters in like contexts. By reading about these people and characters, the idea of a monolithic Caribbean experience is ruptured; instead, these multiple perspectives by and about Caribbean people bring us to shifts in consciousness—the decolonizing transformation that is attentive to intersectionality, agency, sexual politics, and transnationalism. In M. Jacqui Alexander and Chandra T. Mohanty's construction of feminist democracy, socialism is critically important because it stresses collective mutually emancipatory engagements rather than democratic projects mired in constructions of private property and rugged individualism. Alexander and Mohanty argue that "the issues of feminist democracy—decolonization as central to self- and collective transformation; the fundamentally pedagogic character of feminist praxis; the profoundly anticaptialist, socialist imperative in imagining and enacting global feminist struggles—constitute the fabric of our action, reflection, and vision of the future. . . . The challenge lies in an ethical commitment to work to transform terror into engagement based on empathy and a vision of justice for everyone."[7] The shifts generated by feminist democracy in ideology and consciousness foreground the material details linked to Caribbean bodies, the violence endured by the flesh, histories, and the particular ways in which men and women have experienced catastrophic events, such as crossing the Atlantic as cargo.

The Middle Passage

Cauvin's image is awash in shades of blue with flashes of purple beneath the flat waves. The vibrant sea colors are overshadowed by the disturbing image of a woman atop another submerged body. The swimmer's configuration creates a connection among all the lines of the frame: the fingers of her large, paddle-like left hand almost touch the white sail of the boat behind her that grazes the upper right-hand corner, her right foot connects with the ladderlike oarlocks (or are they shackles?) that encase the dead, somewhat androgynous body that mirrors her own figure, while the body's right leg hovers over the bottom of the frame; the only canvas edge not encroached upon by the painting's objects is the left one, suggesting an openness, a doorway, a hope. Given her upright position, she does not seem to be engaged in a horizontal swim, particularly when compared to the submerged body's recumbent position; instead, she is running. The idea of a runaway is embedded in this figure and harks back to a strategy employed by men and women attempting to escape enslavement. The painting's central figure is a woman fleeing, running on a dead body, reiterating a history of female survival networks and past and present solidarity.[8] It is unclear if the running woman has been moving on multiple bodies, but her placement in the frame suggests an escape from the ship some distance in the background. Hoisted and buoyed by the dead body beneath the waves, the runner, in the foreground, does not acknowledge the corpse keeping her afloat. Her skyward focus suggests that she is unaware of the remains. She is running on a tomb that is shackled in some way (perhaps another invocation of the detritus of the slave ship), with floating arms extended as if crucified. The narrative expanse of this image challenges the idea of a tranquil Caribbean Sea even as Cauvin encloses the painting in gradations of blue and sun.

Though one is dead and the other alive, here are two people (whom I read as women despite androgynous overtones) tentatively united against the forces aboard the white-sailed ship.[9] This first reading indicates that the ship is a slaver and that the woman has escaped from the plantation machine to an unknown but preferable future.[10] The transactions of the slave trade begin the process—bodies captured, bought, and sold on the African coast, then transported and auctioned in the Americas.

As a progenitor in the plantation machine, this ship, though largely indistinct and dwarfed by the sea, is full of minuscule male figures in a rapidly receding background from which the terrified woman flees. Concentrating on the horizon, this survivor seems to walk on water and focuses on an unseen distance, even as the locks she uses as a ladder fall away, pushing the supporting corpse deeper into the sea.[11] As the memory-body floats down, the already fragile connection between the woman and the the cadaver breaks. With such a disconnection, the horrific past becomes a trace, a ghostly remnant of a material, concrete, and substantive bodily past. The hearse of rehearsal invokes the corpse in the Cauvin image—the carrying, re-carrying, and revisiting of this body. The oarlocks are a type of hearse.

I read Cauvin's image as one that tells a story of desperation, allowing us to read gender in terms of freedom and labor. The Atlantic plantation was a brutal place for both women and men, but women's dehumanization and their interactions with the power dynamics of the plantation began in a very particular way on slave ships. Here, they were initiated into plantation violence and labor through forced and strategic sexual liaisons: "Black women's manual and sexual labor was, in effect, 'pimped' by slaveholders. . . . In some instances, sex was provided by slave women in exchange for weapons that could be used to attack the plantation system."[12] As Kamala Kempadoo notes, enslaved women's work ranged from "service work [to] trading, including sexual transactions," and these "were activities through which women could autonomously improve their economic positions and survival chances."[13] The use of intimacy and sex conditioned enslaved women's relations to the plantation from the outset.

The canvas—like D'Aguiar's text—calls attention to the bodies trafficked across the Atlantic (and for Asians, across both the Atlantic and the Pacific) through the slave trade and indenture, to toil relentlessly in Caribbean climes, and to the bodies that continue to traverse Caribbean landscapes in search of pleasure and (constructed notions of) paradise. From the beginning of a Caribbean forged by plantation slavery, the consequences of bodies as capital and as industrialized capital investments have meant a valuation in which Caribbean bodies are ground up in global economic projects. These rehearsals illustrate the ways in which Middle Passage economies continue to shape Caribbean belonging.[14]

Suggestive of the bodies in Cauvin's image, the living, the dead, and the psychologically damaged are captured in and on the sea in D'Aguiar's *Feeding the Ghosts*. The text commemorates the 1781 carnage aboard the *Zong*, an abolitionist cause célèbre that garnered headlines because it exemplified the excesses of torture, greed, and justification engendered by a slave system that characterized enslaved people as disposable stock. Paralleling Cauvin's image, which makes visible one woman's desperate flight from the ship, D'Aguiar's text is another rehearsal of the triangulations of the slave industry—one in which the ship itself is a hearse as it carries the bodies of dead and dying Africans, and then the sea becomes a hearse for the bodies thrown overboard. Both conveyances render these bodies invisible, lost, erased, making Cauvin's and D'Aguiar's remembrances all the more significant because they rebuild an archive that is critical both to belonging and to performing citizenship.

Though the novel opens with Mintah's sensation of drowning, her journey begins in a free community where her father shares his wood-carving skills with her. Her parents eventually separate because of religious differences, and her mother's desire to practice monotheism means that mother and daughter must leave the village for a coastal mission where Mintah is educated. Ultimately her mother's desire to be a Christian begins a chain of events that lead to Mintah's enslavement. At the mission, she encounters a sick Kelsal, who will become the *Zong*'s first mate. Mintah nurses a delirious Kelsal back to health; after his departure, slavers overrun the mission, and Mintah is captured and shackled in a slavehold. From there, she is packed into the belly of the *Zong* with 439 other souls. Mintah's defiance—challenging the desecration aboard the *Zong* by calling Kelsal's name and talking back—results in her being thrown overboard. Hanging onto a rope, she reboards the ship and leads a failed insurrection. She is kept on board, only to be sold into slavery in Maryland. In the end, Mintah relocates to Jamaica and confronts the hopes and horrors of her life in a free space.

Early in the novel, and while on the ship, Mintah refuses love and biological motherhood by dancing a dance to limit her fertility: "She needed to dance this particular dance . . . to transfer the pain of the whip around her legs to that of her womb."[15] Her performance interrupts the reproduction of new slave bodies, and her womb becomes a cavity. Mintah's rehearsal of this rite emphasizes the hearse element, which she invokes through a performative and creative ritual. She both imagines and believes that this performance siphons off biological motherhood.

From the beginning of the Middle Passage journey, African women's generative capacity was an important aspect of the slave system propagating itself. While plantation owners of the time were invested in women having children, most Caribbean colonies—with the exception of Barbados—had low reproduction rates.[16] In D'Aguiar's construct, although Mintah resists becoming a breeder for the plantation, other women use their sexuality to bargain with the men who wield power. In fact, the pregnant woman who reveals Mintah's return to the *Zong* does so while eating bread given to her by her rapist-lover, a crew member.[17] Still, although Mintah refuses Simon's offer of love on the grounds that "she could not entertain that aspect of love while there was so much cruelty and suffering around her"[18] and rejects childbearing, she does embrace her roles as nurturer and warrior.

Jamaican poet Lorna Goodison theorizes that her country's national hero, Nanny, also rejected biological motherhood so that all Jamaicans could claim her as mother of the nation.[19] Nanny was a Maroon[20] leader who fought the British in the eighteenth century and was known as an "Obeah woman," or spiritual and medicinal healer; she is mother to all and none at the same time. Nanny's move from possible corporeal motherhood to metaphoric maternity is a tangible example of the power of the fictions of national motherhood made real in the layering of history and flesh.

From the moment Mintah rejects motherhood through her anti-fertility dance, she becomes, like Nanny, a leader of the captured Africans. Once she returns to the boat, her enslaved shipmates improvise praise songs in her name and create a mythology of Mintah breaking chains between her teeth,[21] remarkably reminiscent of Nanny's ability to shoot cannonballs from her buttocks. Nanny too led a rebellion against British oppressors, and she ushered her fellow Maroons to freedom. The parallels between these two "mothers" are many: Mintah leads four men into an onboard rebellion and, after buying her freedom in Maryland, joins the Underground Railroad to ferry people to freedom, two for every person drowned on the *Zong*.[22] By the end of her life, using the skills her father taught her, Mintah carves her wooden progeny of 131 figures who surround her in her final years and are engulfed in flames on the night of her death.[23]

Mintah's rejection of the hegemonic roles offered to free and enslaved women—biological motherhood and romantic love—in favor of her decimated and fragmented community indicates the instability of these choices for enslaved women. Whether or not they had children, women were caught in a web of production and reproduction, often not of their own choosing. Enslaved women belonged to the plantation, which existed only for profit through crushing work, yet when these women fractured the bonds of ownership, they began the process of belonging to themselves. Mintah's rupturing of the biological family romance is one rejection of familial and bodily plantation transactions:

> The women would return to the slave hold and wriggle into a space between other women. They would grab what sleep they could. Semen from the crew would seep from them onto the deck; children were at various stages of gestation in their wombs. Or wombs unable to function in these conditions would be recipients of some disease or other. Wombs in abeyance; emptied of their fecundity. Amnesiacal wombs, forgetting to bleed, forgetting their function. Wombs that declared everything that had happened to this body had to end there. There would be no inheritance from these wombs.[24]

D'Aguiar personifies these wombs, these spaces of origination. Unlike Benítez-Rojo's construction of the Caribbean womb that delivered Western capital accumulation,[25] these are active wombs, declaring and forgetting. The transactions end in part because these wombs will not procreate; either by "choice" (coercion) or as a result of trauma, some women opt out of biological parenthood. In each space—the *Zong*, the Maryland plantation, and her Jamaican home—Mintah recalibrates belonging on her terms. Each adjustment is an indication of the socio-political realities of the historical period. However, the trauma of the *Zong* massacre is never far behind, and it conditions her actions to her last breath. In an effort to fight the ever-present salt of the sea, Mintah immolates her wooden children, her home, and herself: "The flames licked the salt from the air and then the air itself until the walls of Mintah's house were sucked into flames. . . . Burning wood perfumed Mintah's body."[26]

Mintah's rejection of romance and maternal narratives is steeped in her desire to never forget. These wood carvings are Mintah's archive and her rehearsal through *re-member-ing* her African home, her family, and motherhood. Mintah remembers by abandoning the expectations mired in women's fertility. Reproduction is one way in which women belong to their tribes, their nations, and their communities; for Mintah, reproduction becomes reproducing children in wood. Her rejection of motherhood in service of the plantation and the state, and of citizenship, reiterates that her membership to the community is negotiated through her history and her own subjectivity, rather than through the structures of power embedded in plantation economies. This reproduction in wood replaces bones, just as coral replaces bones in the sea.

The interwoven symbolism of bones and coral from Walcott's poem "The Sea Is History" provides an entry into D'Aguiar's novel as its epigraph (and likewise for this book): "Flesh welded into coral, . . . African bones ground to powder . . . would lie in unsanctified limbo . . . [and] each spirit would have to find its way over this sea, over a scattered road of bones."[27] D'Aguiar's novel and Cauvin's painting also shine light on this submerged history, foregrounding the sacredness of the hearse and the bodies and bones it carries. Cauvin's runner travels on bodies and bones. The unity and disunity of bodies and bones signal Mintah's emotional and bodily fragmentation; she feels disconnected from her body and her name. They are lost to her and yet captured in Captain Cunningham's ledger: "He has me marked in a ledger as his. Kelsal too thinks I belong to him. He tried to stake his claim. The crew know they can do whatever they please with *it* since it is theirs too before it is mine. My body belongs to everyone but me. I move in it like a thief. I do not belong to it. All this journey it is trying to separate itself from me, to be rid of me once and for all. My body seems to think that if it does it will kill me, the intruder in it" (emphasis added).[28] Those "bodies that melt down to bones and then become rock" are the figurative and literal foundation of the Americas, a place built on the bodies and bones of enslaved

Africans. The question of who "owns" black women's bodies has been a pivotal one in this hemisphere. Mintah's disconnect between body and psyche illuminates an acute plantation dynamic: being owned by someone and having it rationalized by his legal system, yet fully believing and demanding one's dignity and personhood. These contradictory impulses—those of the owned and those of the owner—play out in and on black bodies. Mintah's psychological and physical rupture reveals the contentious mental and physical space of enslaved people. She characterizes both Captain Cunningham and Kelsal as staking their claim to "it," that is, her body, and thereby making her an intruder to herself. In this instance, her negotiation is split between her body and her mind. Additionally, Mintah's mind-body disassociation illustrates the power of such dislocation in and on colonized bodies because these bodies are marked like empty ideological vessels who serve only the power structure.

The warring bodies on the *Zong* and the internal war within each of the captured Africans precede the battle of books in the novel, specifically, Captain Cunningham's ledger and Mintah's diary.[29] These two texts fight for supremacy in an English court as both are witnesses to how murder is often disguised as innocuous death. The books become the key components of the novel's legal arguments because Captain Cunningham loses his ability to speak while on the witness stand, overcome by the very idea that his judgment and honor as a gentleman are in question. Mintah, absent from the proceedings altogether, is represented by her diary.[30] In the captain's ledger there are no names, no humanizing features—just strokes of the pen. Mintah's book is a counterpoint to that text, documenting that people who were either sick or recovering from illness were dumped; her "ghost book . . . directly contradict[s] what the captain claims in his ledger."[31] The ghost book fills the space left by omissions in the crew's testimony, yet Mr. Drummond, the investors' lawyer, claims it is another kind of ghost—a fabrication that should "not [be] admissible in this case, if only because it argued against the law concerning the status of Africans as stock. The woman thought to be responsible for its authorship was nowhere mentioned in the captain's ledger."[32] Mr. Drummond suggests that this second account cannot be admitted into evidence because it confuses "the situation by diverting our attention from the law" since it is through the law that citizenship is conferred,[33] and the law as an arbiter of subjectivity is another vehicle for conferring humanity and belonging. Mintah does not legally exist as a person; she is stock, and her book is dismissed because she cannot be a citizen. Mintah's body and words are disqualified because of her status as enslaved.

The court case, like the voyage itself, calls Mintah's personhood into question. Mintah can exist only if the captain gives her value and life in his ledger. Otherwise, like her ghost book, Mintah becomes a trace, unable to lay claim to legal discourses and archives. The contradictions of female personhood and the law under slavery underscore that laws were not only vehicles for dehumanization but also justification of these transactions. Furthermore, Benedict Anderson and Édouard Glissant argue that, in addition to capitalism, print not only unifies language but also gives language the power it does not have before being fixed on the page.[34] Here, legal language and the captain's ledger (a document of capital production) have supremacy over Mintah's diary. The worldview embedded in British legal, maritime, and financial documents erases Mintah's counternarrative. Additionally, D'Aguiar's text, like Mintah's, is itself a ghost book—another rehearsal of the *Zong* that gives an enslaved woman voice.

Similar to D'Aguiar's novel, Marlene NourbeSe Philip's poetry collection *Zong!* (re)members those murdered on that vessel. A gray sea dominates the cover of Philip's text with a skeletal leg (femur, tibula, and fibula) running the length of the cover. The leg's patella is covered by a red circle with the West African Adinkra symbol Gye Nyame. "Gye Nyame" means "Except for God," and, situated on the only bit of color on the cover, the symbol looks ossified as well. Thus, from its visual beginning, Philip's text captures the idea of bodies, bones, and the spirit. The hearse in this image is the sea, a graphic backdrop to the bones in the foreground. Philip thought the novel too coherent a form for the massacre on the *Zong* because "this story must be told by not telling— there is a mystery here—the mystery of evil."[35]

The court proceedings of *Gregson v. Gilbert*, which D'Aguiar alludes to in his text, are "the tombstone, the one public marker of the murder of those Africans. . . . It is a public moment, a textual monument marking their murder and their existence, their small histories that ended so tragically."[36] Philip uses the legal text and the language of legal discourse to tell the story, and "At no point in the poem does she use her own words: instead, she relies entirely on the words of the reported legal text . . . subjected to various kinds of creative manipulations."[37] Philip randomly selects, obliterates, and mutilates the legal documents, "all in pursuit of finding ways to 'not-tell this story that must be told. . . . Poetry is to be found within the silences of the text, and the fragmenting of the text in the way I do serves to flush out the poems lodged within.'"[38] Philip characterizes this mining as a way of witnessing both the silences of history (in and of the sea) and the (il)logic in the law by using verbs to find the muscle of the poems. She considers these poems "the flesh and the earlier 26 poems [of the "Os" section] are the bones."[39]

The poems throughout the collection, but perhaps most accessibly in the first section of Philip's volume, "Os" ("bone" in Latin), not only rupture poetic forms visually and linguistically but also give readers a sense of the words of the dead bubbling underwater. At the bottom of the pages, in subscript, or what she calls the "footnote that equals a footprint," Philip lists 228 African names that symbolize the living, the dead, and all the Africans caught in this traffic.[40] The submerged voices are underscored by the typeface. The book cover reveals that the poems are an "as told to narrative and is really the story of Setaey Adamu Boateng, the voice of the ancestors revealing the submerged stories of all who were on board the *Zong*." The poem "Zong! #1" in part visually stutters "water was our water good water day/s," with a few clear words and "www . . . a wa . . . t" arranged horizontally and diagonally on the page; it is hard to get a handle on how to make meaning. The text forces the reader to reread and rehearse these words often. It visually and psychically creates the impression that the names at the bottom of the page, under a linear border, are speaking from beneath the waves. *Zong!* is full of verbal and visual dislocations. Philip observes that "in the discomfort and disturbance created by the poetic text, I am forced to make meaning from apparently disparate elements—in doing so I implicate myself. The risk—of contamination—lies in piecing together the story that cannot be told. And since we have to work to complete the events, we all become implicated in, if not contaminated by, this activity."[41] The work of this rereading is a rehearsal one that Philip characterizes as contamination, but one that is deeply relational and one that forces the reader to seek relations and connections within the text.[42] This process of finding history and arranging the story is an active memorial. And as Lee Jenkins suggests, "the ruptured text is a way of bearing witness to and formally reproducing a ruptured history."[43] These poems also signal an insistence on the visual being part of the persuasive argument of the text. Philip modeled her text on the African American dance form crumping (also spelled "krumping"), a free-form dance style, in which dancers undulate, wave, and swivel individual parts of the body—torso, arms, legs—while moving laterally across the dance floor. The poems are in motion, and the ebb and flow of the words channel the sea that is the cemetery for the dead. *Zong!* as a memorial challenges the idea of coherence and the telling of one story. Philip wrests away the possibility

of fully knowing even as she struggles to understand the full dehuman-
izing horror of the massacre.

Both Philip's and D'Aguiar's texts, though different genres, capture
the incomprehensibility of what occurred aboard the *Zong*. Each text, in
its own way, provides a space in which to engage with the horrors of the
past. In *Specters of the Atlantic*, Ian Baucom reads both as texts about
trauma that literalize (*Feeding the Ghosts*) and metaphorize (*Zong!*)
"the possibilities of resuscitation by reviving" a half-dead slave and the
legal transcripts respectively.[44] In closing *Feeding the Ghosts*, D'Aguiar
writes, "Where death has begun but remains unfinished because it
recurs. Where there is only the record of the sea. Those spirits are fled
into wood. The ghosts feed on the story of themselves. The past is laid
to rest when it is told."[45] Baucom suggests that these two texts, particularly the novel, are "the work of [a] witness [whose] labor of resuscitation must be at odds with the burial fantasy of its ending."[46] It is the
struggle to create *relation* (as Glissant would characterize it) or empathy
that might be at odds here. In witnessing the trauma through his novel,
D'Aguiar may also be seeking peace or some space of reconciliation, but
until the interlocking and ever-present reality of the plantation machine
can be rehearsed and interrogated, resolution may feel like fantasy.

Returning to Cauvin's image, we see that she similarly memorializes
the lives of lost Africans but also embodies the metaphorical aspects of
rehearsal in the emblematic use of the systems and tropes at play in the
Caribbean. The image is a symbol of narrative control and a counter to
the hegemonic story of the region as a paradise of rolling blue waves.
It speaks to the promise and perils of the landscape, the imagined uto-
pia mired in ecologically degraded plantation realities. It is ultimately
symbolic of rehearsal as a horizon—in other words, the continual process. The central figure looks with trepidation, torment, and yet—hope,
toward a new possibility away from the ship. Even in this painting, the
dynamics of rehearsal as a metaphor for multiplicity and community are
present.

There are several perspectives from which to view this image: the running woman's, the dead woman's, and that of the people on the ship.
Each would yield a different narrative though they all share overlapping
facts—a woman running and a vessel chasing. The fleeing beleaguered
woman could tell a story of leaving fear and moving toward hope, even
if she is unsure about what awaits her. The dead body, held up on spikes
and supporting the run of a living black woman, would tell a story of
perhaps having lost her life in a similar run to escape from another boat.

Finally, the men might tell a story of a crazy woman running on water, or an insolent slave believing she can escape them. These men might also tell of property, profit, and pleasure delayed or denied.[47]

As Cauvin's runner pushes the submerged body deeper and deeper into the sea, the body's bones embed themselves into the coral: the "sea refuses to grant that body the quiet of a grave in the ground. Instead it rolls that body across its terrain, sends that body down into its depths, . . . swells the body to bursting point, tumbles it beyond the reach of horizons and gradually breaks fragments from that body with its nibbling, dissecting current."[48] As the submerged souls become part of the skeleton of the sea, they, like coral, contribute to the bone-on-bone structuring that builds coral reefs. Bones serve as the critical foundation and architecture for the landscapes (and seascapes) that have made the Caribbean a processing zone for cane, banana, coffee, and indigo, as well as—in contemporary capitalism—tourism.

The Cruise Ship

The second rehearsal, *Vers un destin insolite . . .* , invokes a contemporary one: the thriving cruise ship industry in the Caribbean. It is possible to read Cauvin's painting as an escape from a tourist ship, especially those with sails—the image reminds the viewer of a windjammer—and perhaps seeks to recapture a particular Caribbean past. These cruise ships, whether actually powered by sails or by gas turbines, are endemic to late twentieth- and early twenty-first-century Caribbean economies. The morphing (if not bleeding) of the slave ship into the tourist vessel rehearses the sexual and manual labor Caribbean people provide on the ships and in the ports in which the vessels dock.

Similar to its plantation predecessor, the cruise ship marks Caribbean geography, and its environmental impact reshapes one of the region's few resources: the sea.[49] As Peter Odle, former president of the Barbados Hotel Association, put it, "Cruise ships are using our most precious asset—the sea—polluting it like hell and not making any significant contribution to our economy. And instead of taking a firm stand, the governments are all over the place; there is a lack of political will."[50] Such lack of political will is in many respects a colonial inheritance and the dynamics of twenty-first-century neocolonialism and globalization that keep poor countries in a cycle of economic and psychological indebtedness.

I include the cruise ship—a "real" object among Cauvin's and D'Aguiar's fictional reformulations of the Middle Passage—not only to underscore the "fictions" the industry traffics in but also to highlight the blurring of reality and fiction. Critical to my project is the need to illustrate the utility of fiction for understanding and engaging with "reality." I believe these transgressions between real and not-real create the powerful space of mutuality—a space in which we can fictionally work out real concerns.

Of the two major types of cruise ships, the most well known is the "floating city," which is integrated into both the maritime and hospitality industries. These massive boats are owned by colossal companies that include the Carnival Corporation, with more than eighty-one ships and 140,000 berths to fill, and its nearest competitors, Royal Caribbean, with thirty-four ships and 67,000 berths, and the Norwegian Cruise Line, with twenty-one ships and 32,000 berths.[51] In order to maintain a steady flow of customers, cruise lines often undercut land tourism and "re-create the sea" as *the* destination. Polly Patullo uses a brochure from the Princess line to demonstrate the pampering and excesses cruise ships extol, from "fluffy bathrobes" and petits fours, to gala buffets featuring ice carvings and sugar sculptures, and the "sheer flamboyance of a 600-glass champagne waterfall." She concludes, "Such flourishes have little to do with the Caribbean but if the ship is the destination, the Caribbean itself loses relevance except as a vague and shimmering backdrop."[52]

Beneath the glitz and glamour of the ships' excess and overabundance are the workers. While Caribbean hoteliers provide jobs (such as they are) for locals, "cruise ships operating in the Caribbean are free to employ whom they wish. Their ships are not registered in the United States, their home base, but use flags of convenience to avoid its labour laws, taxes and regulations."[53] The Bahamas has the highest number of flags of convenience for cruise ships, while the rest of the Caribbean and circum-Caribbean have flags of convenience for other shipping interests—a way for them to earn income for their countries while enabling a system that again exploits Caribbean laborers.[54]

Because of the rapid rise of the industry and the need to keep berths filled, cruise lines employ a vast number of people and are looking to employ more. However, the highest-paying jobs go to workers from Europe and the United States, while cabin crew members hail from other parts of the developing world. Like their enslaved and indentured predecessors, cruise ship workers in the hold are subject to the same dangers, such as rape and abuse, as they traverse the Caribbean Sea. The ship has become their plantation. These workers are seduced by the idea of getting paid to travel the world on some of the most modern and beautiful ships, but the image is not the reality. The International Transport Workers' Federation reports that "below decks on virtually all cruise ships, there is a hidden world of long hours, low pay, insecurity and exploitation. Those who work continuously below deck, like in the galleys, rarely see the light of day, let alone the shimmering sea of the Caribbean."[55]

Maintaining the region's role as backdrop, cruise companies employ only a few workers from the Caribbean, and workers from non-Caribbean nations, particularly entertainers such as dancers, are asked to perform "Caribbeanness."[56] At the CruiseLineJobs.com website, those applying for positions as dancers are told that they will "perform on stage and help cruise staff in entertaining passengers offstage as well. Experience performing in front of the public is required. Salaries range from $1600 to $3000 per month."[57] A former African American dancer recounts her story of onstage and offstage performances in which she was asked to "act Caribbean" or "make it [her walk, gestures, dancing] more Caribbean." She understood "more Caribbean" to mean "more erotic and sexualized." And, as noted in the advertisement and in line with her experience, her job continued offstage.[58] Dancers like this woman have to negotiate identity, space, and culture as they juggle entertaining passengers under the guise of "Caribbeanness." Such "masking," while part of the region's culture, as in the pre-Lenten festival of Carnival, buttresses the consumption of the Caribbean on the cruise ship.

In this space, and in other tourist spaces, Caribbeanness is a performance particularly lodged in and on female bodies.[59] In this rehearsal, the female performer of eroticized and sexualized "Caribbeanness" is one without the hearse of the Middle Passage. In fact, this performance is in stark contrast to Mintah's dance, which sought to deny reproduction; the cruise performer reproduces a particular and exotic notion of the Caribbean for consumption and profit. As the ship dancer's experience emphasizes, the transactional and performative aspects of rehearsal are intertwined. Since most cruise ship entertainers are not Caribbean but passing as such, their role-playing is simultaneously theatrical and performative, in Judith Butler's articulation of the term. In other words, the discourse of Caribbeanness—what it means to be from the region— is performed not only in the sense of cultural tourism (like the Big Drum ceremony in Carriacou) but also for external expectations and market value.[60]

The performative acts, or scripts of Caribbeanness, are colonial and gendered. These performative acts are not just speech but bodily signs and symbols, such as "the multi-colored native sarong" and dreadlocks (which are not necessarily related to Rastafarianism, though this is often conflated). Such sartorial displays call to mind Dorothy Dandridge as Margot Seaton dancing the limbo in *Island in the Sun* (1957). In this instance, Dandridge passes for and performs as the exotic and erotic Caribbean woman.[61] Here again rehearsal is useful in understanding performative masking and the ruptures created because of it. Rehearsing Caribbean pasts in this way means rethinking, reimagining, and reinventing Caribbean presents and futures. More specifically, we can reconfigure more inclusive ways of what "Caribbean belonging" might mean. These performances on cruise ships, particularly of female dancing, replay the static caricatures of Caribbean people in terms of race and gender. Such stereotypes reiterate the need for feminist rehearsals to move the collective "us" to a more dynamic understanding of what it means to be a Caribbean woman and how the sociohistorical dynamics of this temporal moment highlight the impact of cultural performance as commodity.

The windjammer cruise ship, modeled after the nineteenth-century merchant ships with three to five huge masts, is another vessel that Cauvin's image invokes. Vis-à-vis the floating cities, these tall sailing ships are marketed as an environmental alternative to the mainstream cruising industry and offer more exclusivity for a higher price. Promoted with the slogan "Set sail for something different," windjammers are making a comeback.[62] Mainstream cruises can offer specials as low as $300 for a four- or five-day excursion (not including airfare); for a similar stay and similar conditions (i.e., airfare not included), specials with the Island Windjammer company start at $1,600.00.[63] Passengers are encouraged to make the cruise "their own" by helping the crew hoist the sails or by listening to the "moving strains of the bagpipes [playing] 'Amazing Grace' as the sails are raised." This song, penned by notorious slaver and evangelical preacher Captain John Newton,[64] is part of transporting these vacationers to another time and place in which they too could dream of navigating a more pristine Caribbean emptied of its history of violence.[65] These travelers replay the work of the Middle Passage ships, "pretending" to be the crew, yet their performances are for the sheer novelty of the experience. They are not the workers whose labor propelled these vessels that were necessary to the colonial project, yet their vacation provides some work to those in the region who are dealing with the ravages of the neoliberal project. Furthermore, the irony of Newton's song as an accompaniment to "work" indicates no historical memory, crisis, or connection. It seems that for these people on holiday, though their bodies now traverse the Atlantic, it is purely for pleasure disconnected from the bodies of enslaved people who were transported for work. They are similarly disconnected from the bodies of current migrants who navigate these waters in less opulent boats seeking better opportunities. The Windjammer brand (and the windjammer concept more generally) is about class and power. Following previous rehearsals, the cruise ship is the latest vessel to cross Caribbean waters for economic gain. Similar to slave ships and the original windjammers, which carried cargo across oceans, cruise ships—whether mainstream, windjammer, or otherwise—are about extracting wealth, pleasure, and labor from the perceived abundant paradise of the region. Cruise ships disrupt any sense of empathy; they make fanciful and fun the historical tragedy of the Caribbean.

Migrants at Sea: "Boat People"

Cauvin's painting also suggests a rehearsal of another distinct Caribbean phenomenon: people fleeing their homelands in small and insubstantial boats. The Middle Passage clearly references one type of historic Caribbean transatlantic experience, but this painting invokes yet another contemporary one.[66] Though the painting's ship seems tied to another era, many skiffs that now carry migrants trying to reach destinations such as Trinidad, Barbados, Puerto Rico, and the Bahamas use sheets as sails as they move from the Caribbean Sea into the Atlantic. People from across the Caribbean are forced out onto the open seas because of squeezed local economies, increased poverty, and political repression. The quest to find a hospitable port extends beyond Cubans, Dominicans, and Haitians attempting to reach the United States and includes a bustling intraregional traffic of Guyanese in Trinidad and Barbados, Haitians in the Bahamas, and Dominicans in Puerto Rico.[67] As sociologist Cecilia A. Green explains, "Since the 19th century, general migration in the Caribbean has not only been outward, to the United States and Europe, but also among the islands themselves, as islanders move to areas of new growth."[68] Intraregional migration has generated its own set of vexing issues, particularly the lack of empathy in light of austerity and economic crises.

Green's analysis distinguishing the experiences of the English-speaking Caribbean (especially Jamaica, Barbados and Trinidad) from Haiti continues, noting that

> conventional wisdom sees migrants as mostly male, mostly unskilled, and somehow "threatening" to the social order. Most migrants are in fact

women, and as a group their educational and skill levels are well above average. Many migrants are trained as teachers and nurses and exercise these professions in their new homes. Green argues that from the point of view of the islands themselves, migration is better viewed as a "brain drain" than as an expulsion of the least fit and least skilled. [She also notes] that migratory flows have decisively shifted over time towards the U.S., [and] there are now more West Indians living in New York than in all of Europe.[69]

These migratory patterns underscore the history of Caribbean labor as transnational and global. I read the image of the runner fleeing the boat in two ways. This is a boat transporting male officials who seek to capture and repatriate this woman to a place to which she does not want to return. Her face reveals the "credible fear" that many refugees are asked to demonstrate to immigration officials.[70] As April Shemak documents in *Asylum Speakers,* "boat refugee narratives suggest that once again we must look to the submerged and submarine spaces to begin to comprehend the complexities of Caribbean history and identity."[71]

While the runner can be read as a migrant, the submerged body can be read as an aspect of the deity Yemaya/Erzulie: "One of [Yemaya's] most singular avatars is that of Olokún [in Santería], herself a deity who lives at the bottom of the sea tied to a chain, the sight of whom can bring sudden death."[72] In Haitian Vodou, La Sirèn, a wife of Agwe, is a mermaid spirit, a seductress, and an aspect of Yemaya; she has a female companion, sometimes referred to as her "shadow side," La Balèn. La Balèn, a whale, inhabits the depths of the ocean and is considered the dark intuitive sister who can be dangerous and aggressive.[73] Similar to these female dualities that emerge in various Afro-Caribbean religions, the runner and the submerged figure are doubled since the runner's survival is directly linked to the dead and sinking body.[74] Another Vodou duality that the image invokes are La Marasa, biological twins who are "associated with the ebb and flow of waters," and, according to VèVè Clark, one that "invites us to imagine beyond the binary."[75]

In the migrant-of-the-sea reading that Cauvin's image calls to mind, the runner has fallen or has been pushed off the boat by her fellow travelers and is using the dead body below as a flotation device to avoid drowning. News accounts abound with stories of the terror and victimization suffered by wayfarers willingly charting a course on the ocean for political and economic reasons. As William R. Doerner reported in October 1987:

> The victims of the carnage were among 150 Dominicans, mostly young women, who had paid up to $600 each for illegal passage to Puerto Rico

aboard a 50-foot wooden fishing boat. The group had set out at 2 a.m. Tuesday from Death's Head Beach in Nagua [and] the ship was only four miles out to sea when, . . . its two outboard motors exploded. . . . [U]nable to swim, many probably drowned within a few minutes of the accident. But others, either swimming or clinging to hastily emptied floating gasoline containers, tried to reach shore. . . . [T]he [rescue] plane, unable to put down in water, . . . could only look on in helpless horror. . . . One witness recalled, "In one instance we saw a shark literally throw someone in the air and then attack the person."[76]

Like the victims in Doerner's account, Cauvin's woman runs on the submerged body perhaps because she cannot swim, and, like these real women, she scrambles and clings to life. The submerged woman can be read as the embodiment of Olokún, a manifestation of Yemaya sometimes embodied as a shark who can bring sudden death. In this case, the shark is encased in the oarlocks killing those who, having been thrown overboard, run on the sea.

Another replaying of this migrants-at-sea trope is Ana Lydia Vega's short story "Cloud Cover Caribbean," which relates the experiences of three men who flee Hispaniola and Cuba. One of these men, the Haitian Antenor, travels solo in his small makeshift vessel and, upon hearing a man drowning, fishes him out of the water and into the boat. Though Antenor and his new passenger, Diogenes from the Dominican Republic, do not speak the same language, "They each told the other, without either understanding, what he was leaving behind—which was very little—and what he was seeking. They told of the endless pain of being black, Caribbean and poor; of deaths by the score; they cursed clergy, the military and civilians; established an international brotherhood of hunger, a solidarity of dreams."[77] Joint suffering secures bonds of solidarity, relation, and empathy until they pull Carmelo, a Cuban, "obviously from Santiago," from the churning waters. Once in the boat, Carmelo and Diogenes use their linguistic power to exclude Antenor and effectively seize his boat.

In this polyglot space, dissension leads to appropriation of resources. Linguistic power allows Carmelo and Diogenes to solidify their bond, which effectively leaves Antenor, their "brother," and "the pain of being black, Caribbean, and poor" in a subordinate position. The earlier equality of poverty and linguistic incomprehension is undermined by Carmelo's presence as he demands that Antenor share his rations: "Quickly forgetting the vows of mutual aid spoken with his fellow islander prior to the Cuban's arrival," Diogenes and Carmelo almost push Antenor overboard to get to his food.[78] In this moment, Antenor's nationality and language put him in the minority and undermine his masculinity by dispossessing him of his resources. As the two enjoy Antenor's unwilling hospitality, they discuss their plans for business in Florida, particularly prostituting women. Their discussion of sex work in Cuba, the Dominican Republic, and Miami illustrates the lucrative nature of selling sex and selling the Caribbean, or a particular version of it—"Hey, in the Dominican Republic we have so many whores we have to export them"—while Carmelo laments Cuban women's independence—"In Cuba the women think they are equal to men and so they don't want to get out and work the streets."[79] As Antenor is feminized by his lack of resources, Diogenes and Carmelo negotiate their hypermasculinity around their desire to traffic women.

In Vega's story, Caribbean masculinity moves from a cooperative space to a place in which hypersexuality and heteropatriarchy reign. This signals, in the parlance of M. Jacqui Alexander, the commingling of heterosexism and patriarchy based on masculine domination. In Vega's story, nationality, language, and, to a lesser extent, religion (she makes several references to Afro-Caribbean religions and the rhythms that emerged from them) illustrate how difference and belonging are articulated. These characters, like the migrants who cross the sea and the runner in Cauvin's painting, replay both the dynamics of the Middle Passage and the economic and political policies that push Caribbean people onto sloops in search of security and stability.[80] The men are in a state of constant negotiation, with each other and with the wider world. As Antenor's gendered identity is destabilized, he is effectively a man without a place—he has left Haiti and his boat is now a linguistically occupied territory. In contrast, the two Spanish speakers belong to the boat's majority, but they too quarrel. National pride undermines the linguistic coup, and the boat capsizes. A U.S. Coast Guard cutter rescues the men,[81] and the captain consigns them, like Middle Passage cargo, to the hold with the "spiks":

> Get those niggers down there and let the spiks take care of 'em. . . . Whereupon the Caribbean brothers were taken, sans tender loving care, down to the ship's hold. There amidst wooden crates and mouldy trunks, they exchanged their first post-wreck glances: a mixture of fright and relief, sautéed in some lightly browned hopes. [Where a Puerto Rican voice growls,] "If you want to feed your bellies here you're going to have to work, and I mean work. A

gringo don't give nothing away. Not to his own mother." Then a black arm thrust through the crates to hand them dry clothes.[82]

Ultimately, these migrants are linked together by their race and their region in the face of U.S. hegemony. Their blackness, Carmelo's "clearly from Santiago" and the crew member's "black arm thrust through the crates," undermines the color hierarchies and linguistic solidarities in their home countries since they will be black and foreign in the United States. Like enslaved travelers, they are tied to a particular architecture on the ship—the hold—which in this story does not become the hearse of the *Zong* or the sea but does emphasize the "cargo" realities of the Middle Passage.

Language aside, the final passage of Vega's story highlights the entrenched power relations within the region. The soft and hard power of the United States ultimately interrupts regional disputes and many regional interventions. Though separated by language, the men are united by the quest for a better life and by the transactions they hope to make, particularly those using women's bodies in the sex trade. In this small boat, history anchors Caribbean belonging, not to land, but to a diffident sea, a sea that repeats and reminds Caribbean people of the power the United States and previous colonizers wield in the region. This boat and these characters reiterate a lack of empathy.

Relation is fleeting and can be disrupted by shifting majorities, here linguistic but also racial, sexual, and economic. As Édouard Glissant observes:

> Experience of the abyss lies inside and outside the abyss. . . . [S]traight from the belly of the slave ship into the violent belly of the ocean depths they went. But their ordeal did not die: it quickened into this continuous/ discontinuous thing: the panic of the new land, the haunting of the former land, finally the alliance with the imposed land, suffered and redeemed. . . . Peoples who have been to the abyss do not brag of being chosen. They do not believe they are giving birth to any modern force. They live Relation and clear the way for it, to the extent that oblivion of the abyss comes to them and that, consequently, their memory intensifies. . . . For though this experience made you, original victim floating toward the sea's abysses, an exception, it became something shared and made us, the descendants, one people among others. Peoples do not live on exception. Relation is not made up of things that are foreign but of shared knowledge. This experience of the abyss can now be said to be the best element of exchange.[83]

In Vega's story, the boat is an abyss for the slave ship, the windjammer, and the migrant's sloop. As Glissant notes, the intense experience of the abyss is constitutive of exchange. And while he sees the abyss as a horrific place that fosters unity in the historical subject and "the descendants," Vega's story illustrates how micro-nationalisms are limited (in Anderson's words) and undermine the regional and submarine connections of the abyss. As various news accounts and multiple editorials in the *Nassau Guardian* on the "Haitian Problem" demonstrate, nationalism narrowly defined defies any larger sense of a Caribbean destiny and keeps the region locked in colonial patterns.[84] Immigration debates reveal the lack of empathy embedded in the violence of nationalism that is racialized and gendered. Vega's story, similar to the newspaper editorials, show the ways in which migrants are feminized and made vulnerable, as is Antenor. Additionally, because Antenor is not Cuban, he is further denigrated like most non-Cuban migrants. Cubanness is not a panacea in "Cloud Cover Caribbean," and everyone on the skiff is consigned to the hold.

Cauvin's painting conveys a story of desperation, of a woman fleeing something dire, preferring to take her chances on the open sea rather than remain static. Her left hand behind her and slightly above the water indicates motion as she propels herself through the water. With the support of the dead beneath her as well as her own efforts, this woman is clearly "running for her life." Though terrified, she is propelling her body forward, suggesting some measure of hope. The terror is stark in her open mouth and fixed skyward stare, but her push away from the boat indicates that she is not defeated and still believes in possibility. Her head is tilted upward, so that the base of her neck nearly touches her back, her motion toward the only opening of the canvas. Beneath the waves, her stride is wide, extended in a running split, with her right foot on the iron rung that closes the shackle nearest the dead person's head.

Bone Soldered by Coral

In May 2006, Jason deCaires Taylor established the world's first submarine aquatic park off the coast of Grenada. His twofold goal then, and continuing with his current post as founder and artistic director of the Museo Subacuático de Arte in Cancún, Mexico, was to create underwater sculpture gardens using specially made materials that attract coral growth, drawing "people away from the fragile natural

Figure 2. *Grace Reef,* Jason deCaires Taylor. Body cast of a Grenadian woman who now lives in England. Part of the world's first underwater park at Moliniere Bay, Grenada. (© 2013 Jason deCaires Taylor/Artists Rights Society [ARS], New York/DACS, London)

reefs," thus enabling the reefs to regenerate from natural disaster and human damage. He has several pieces in Grenada, including those that show the symbiotic relationship between people and their environment. Taylor's work features folkloric figures such as the siren-like La Diablesse, a beautiful woman in a long flowing dress that hides her cloven foot, as well as body casts of local residents. His piece *Grace Reef* is a "series of sixteen figures cast from the body of a Grenadian woman," while *Vicissitudes* is a ring composed of the figures of a woman and a young boy repeated twenty-six times, which Taylor hopes will "reflect the continuing evolution of the island and its people, revealing itself in dramatic and dynamic ways."[85]

While Taylor's environmental intervention should certainly be lauded, it is stunning that, other than "revealing the dramatic and dynamic ways" of the Grenadian people, no article nor the artist himself has connected these submerged pieces to slavery and the impact of the Middle Passage.[86] In fact, Taylor asserts that his vision

Figure 3. *Vicissitudes*, Jason deCaires Taylor. Moliniere Bay, Grenada. Also called *Perspectives* and misinterpreted as a ring of children rather than the two repeated figures of a woman and a boy. (© 2013 Jason deCaires Taylor/Artists Rights Society [ARS], New York/DACS, London)

is forward-looking and divested of history. "*Vicissitudes*, which is the most sort of famous one [sculpture] there, . . . I had no intention of it being about the Middle Passage or any relation to slavery whatsoever. In fact, it was a white female with a young local boy. It was about how the oceans or people's environments change [their] characteristics. [However,] people saw it as a piece on slavery."[87] Likewise, Taylor reports that a land-based copy of *Vicissitudes*, a ring of two repeated figures (that could be interpreted as young people) holding hands was defaced by Grenadians who were "angry about children being enslaved." It is interesting to note that though Taylor has Caribbean relatives and recognizes the historical tensions within the region, his reading of the piece is not historical; however, Grenadian people nevertheless continually attach historical significance to his work. In fact, in informal conversations, some Grenadians indicate that they see some of the pieces as manifestations of the Caribs who jumped to their deaths rather than surrender to the French at Sauteurs, better known as "Leapers Hill," in Grenada.[88]

Like the cruise ship industry, the underwater park plays with the idea of Caribbean bodies but empties them of the historical weight of the Middle Passage by limiting or erasing the visibility of the hearse element. To differing degrees, the cruise ship and the underwater park are public spaces and are seen, interpreted, and interacted with by diverse audiences, although it must be noted, that Taylor's sculptures are a tourist destination rather than a monument with which Grenadian people interact. As a site of tourism, the underwater park is about bodies seeking pleasure rather than commemorating the history of the nation.[89]

One website erroneously credits the following dedication to Taylor: "In honor of our African Ancestors who were thrown overboard the slave ships during the Middle Passage of the African Holocaust."[90] Taylor's removal from such intentional historical references indicates that people's appropriation of the image makes meaning of both Caribbean history and the erosion of the environment. The web link has been widely copied, recirculated, and represented as memorializing the Middle Passage in Caribbean waters. The authority of certain Internet sites has undermined Taylor's intention. "No! I had never made any reference to this and those are not my words. It is a certain interpretation on the piece that became viral over the Internet. Although it was not my intention from the outset, I am encouraged by how it has been interpreted differently within different communities and feel it is working as an art piece by questioning our history and stimulating debate."[91]

Taylor wanted the park to be a way for Grenadians to reflect on and ultimately protect their undersea resources, but Moliniere Bay, the piece's location, has become a highly trafficked tourist destination with sometimes more than two hundred visitors per day.[92] The site is managed largely by the Underwater Sculpture Park Action Group (USPAG), which consists of members from the Grenada Board of Tourism, the Molinere and Beausejour Marine Protected Area, and the Grenada Hotel and Tourism Association. The USPAG seeks to protect and repair corroded pieces and "preserve what has now become a national attraction" while generating sponsorship for new pieces. It also recognizes Taylor as a publicity juggernaut whose interviews in travel and lifestyle magazines, including *Vogue* and *OK!* and newspapers such as the *Daily Telegraph* have generated immeasurable financial gain.[93] Additionally, USPAG has a sponsorship component and invites companies such as Grenada Seafaris, Dive Grenada, and Flamboyant Hotel & Villas to sponsor pieces. In strategizing for the future, the USPAG will develop an artificial reef, which they "plan to decorate . . . with art and interesting features to create functional and visually unique pieces of Marine Art."[94] Taylor fears that his ecological intervention will quickly be polluted by mermaids and other sea creatures who will appeal to tourists, undermining his vision and the unintentional historical power (and, perhaps, hearse) his pieces have generated with Grenadians. His work has created a space of mutuality that foregrounds the tensions and contradictions of production and reception.

Indeed, Taylor's work allows people to rehearse with an often unspoken and difficult past. These pieces are lodged in Grenadian waters, seas that are the cemetery to so many peoples—Carib leapers, European pirates, African slaves—and they reflect the turbulence of memory and bearing witness. His work makes Caribbean inhabitants and visitors witness, perhaps unwittingly, to the past, present, and future simultaneously.

In *The Slave Ship* (2007), historian Marcus Rediker tells the story of an enslaved woman, renamed "Sarah" by Captain Jenkin Evans, who disembarks in Grenada. One of the captain's favorites, Sarah was held in high esteem because of her dancing and "Ever lively! Ever gay!" disposition. Smitten crewmembers admired her despite the fact that she was one of the captain's favorites "'to whom [Captain Evans] showed greater favours than the rest,' likely as small recompense for coerced sexual services."[95] Despite the freedom of movement and other tokens of goodwill bestowed on her, Sarah and her mother were accused of plotting a rebellion—a charge they both denied—despite the accounts of "fear or guilt [that] strongly marked in their countenances." Sarah was sold in Grenada "with almost three hundred others, in 1787."[96] Unlike Mintah's invocation to the gods through dancing to stop reproduction, Sarah's performance, perhaps another call for spiritual intercession, made her a favorite by ensnaring the crew, particularly the captain. Despite such favoritism, both fictional Mintah and factual Sarah cultivated insurrection. Mintah's fictional dance rehearses Sarah's historical cunning.

Sarah's story and Taylor's pieces, particularly those like *Grace Reef*, recall and restage those on the *Zong* and countless other ships that "live" at the bottom of the sea. As *Grace Reef* uses Grace's body to generate a space for coral to grow and rebuild, it brings Derek Walcott's poem "The Sea Is History" to the fore. Walcott imagines a conversation between at least two speakers: one asks, "Where are your monuments, your battles, martyrs? / Where is your tribal memory?" and the other replies, "Sirs, / in that grey vault. The sea. The sea / has locked them up. The sea is History."

The sea is a site of memory and rehearsal for many African diasporic people who engage with the Middle Passage and for the bodies lost in the Atlantic Ocean and the Caribbean Sea. It may not be Walcott's intent, but his poem presents the paradox between notions of remembrance valued by the colonizer and/or the colonial elite and notions of veneration practiced by the colonized, the popular, and the collective. Amid biblical allusions from the books of Genesis, Exodus, and Song of Solomon, as well as references to the European Enlightenment and the Renaissance, Walcott's poem is a conversation about what is valued, who gets to assign value, and how to subvert that value and recenter one's self in colonial dialogues. The poem deals with an inherited history, sacred and secular, and the juxtaposition of monuments within the story of the landscape, the place of violence on a biblical scale that is cleansed daily by the sea. The sea is a natural monument and a natural space of rehearsal.

Cauvin's painting visually voices the idea that we walk on the dead all the time, but she centers on a particular cemetery. As with Walcott's poem, in *Vers un destin insolite sur les flots bleus de la Mer des Antilles*, Cauvin illustrates that, in the Caribbean, the sea is a monument and an archive tangible and elusive.

The texts described in this chapter reveal the ability of women—real and fictional—to build and maintain their own archives, memorial sources, and rituals. Cauvin and D'Aguiar make affective and effective interventions to retell and restage silenced and erased histories. Cauvin's painting and the subsequent pieces—D'Aguiar's *Feeding the Ghosts*, Vega's "Cloud Cover Caribbean," and Taylor's *Vicissitudes*—show that art and literature offer alternative ways of creating mutual spaces by preserving and recovering memories. Past traumas are rehearsed through memorialization. Both creating a memorial and (re)visiting it constitute rehearsal because each engagement with the memorial or memorial site shifts perspective and leads to a deeper understanding of how the past, memories of the past, and the construction of the memories of the past create dynamic narratives that frame the present and make meaning in the future. The process of retrieving and rehearsing these archives generates deeper and richer understandings of the contradictions and particularities of the past while also pushing us toward a transformative future.

2 Their Bones Would Reject Yours

> Native citizens, men, women, girls, and children, let your gaze
> extend on all parts of this island: . . . Look there for your children,
> your suckling infants, what have they become? . . . I shudder to say
> it . . . the prey of these vultures.
>
> Instead of these dear victims, your alarmed gaze will see
> only their assassins, these tigers still dripping with their blood,
> whose terrible presence indicts your lack of feeling and your guilty
> slowness in avenging them. What are you waiting for before ap-
> peasing their spirits? Remember that you had wanted your remains
> to rest next to those of your fathers, after you defeated tyranny;
> will you descend into their tombs without having avenged them?
> No! Their bones would reject yours.
>
> —Jean-Jacques Dessalines, Haitian Declaration of Independence

HAITI AND ITS REVOLUTION HAVE BECOME for the world
a site of—to borrow the words of a Wilson Harris title—"infinite
rehearsal." Haiti's act of independence, signed on January 1, 1804,
begins with liberty—or death—but continues with General Jean-Jacques
Dessalines's exhortation to newly independent Haitians to neither forget nor forgive French treachery. In fact, in the declaration, Dessalines
persuades his generals (and, by extension, the nation) that not to avenge
the national family is a cosmic act of betrayal. He asks, "What are you
waiting for before appeasing their spirits?" And, like the Taino and Africans before him (who believed that bones themselves are animate),[1] Dessalines offers a most dire punishment—those who profane and squander
ancestral sacrifice, those who fail to avenge Haiti, will be condemned
to eternal unrest, their bones will be rejected: "Remember that you had
wanted your remains to rest next to those of your fathers, after you
defeated tyranny; will you descend into their tombs without having
avenged them? No! Their bones would reject yours."[2]
Ancestral bones, particularly the bones of the father, are the terra
firma of belonging, from the Taino to slain Haitians, and are invoked
here by Dessalines to inspire and cement all Haitians—men, women,
boys, and girls—to their newly liberated land. His invocation of rest-
less bones and ancestral rejection asserts that the task of Caribbean (or,
more specifically, Haitian) citizens is to defend liberty forever. Rejection

by the enslaved and founding ancestors whose blood and toil covered every corner of Hispaniola is the greatest castigation Dessalines can imagine. And indeed, actively remembering and revising the freedoms these bodies and bones fought for is an important aspect of democracy projects. While the previous chapter deals in the main with Middle Passage rehearsals and more contemporary ways in which black agency is still curtailed, this chapter focuses on revolution and freedom.

Although this reckoning with ancestors was initially about punishing Europeans, today Haiti reckons with its "native-born citizens," particularly men, who have brutalized liberty and traumatized generations of Haitians. Haiti's incomplete, unfinished process has mirrored the extremes of regional development and has maintained those extremes, even as it celebrated its bicentennial in the midst of its thirty-third coup. Nonetheless, the Revolution exists as a monument of black agency and continues to inspire new understandings of the discourses of power in the quest for Atlantic freedom. The leaders of this revolution were leaders with whom Caribbean countries have rehearsed: the rational, noble, and paternalistic men similar to Haitian general Toussaint L'Ouverture and Eric Williams of Trinidad; the dictators and kings, such as King Henri Christophe and Forbes Burnham of Guyana; and the hard-to-recover leaders reminiscent of Dessalines—most well meaning, but all seen in some capacity before—such as Emperor Faustin I of Haiti. And though these men are familiar, more constant are the external forces arising from governments and multinational companies seeking to contain Haitian possibility. Internally, Haiti's fight for freedom and power has produced contradictions, regressions, and frustrations that have been internalized by other Caribbean citizenries. Despite this, the Haitian Revolution remains a beacon of freedom in the Atlantic world, particularly in the Caribbean, where its audacity remains something to emulate. The writers highlighted in this study reclaimed a specific history of the black male hero and, at the same time, wrote themselves into it as legitimate patriarchs.

Because of this preoccupation with proving black worth, the Haitian Revolution becomes an ideal vehicle for romanticizing and rehearsing history in literature. Indeed, it is remembered as a time when strong, capable men took a stand for black people and changed the world—particularly the enslaved communities of the Americas. As C. L. R. James put it in referring to his history *The Black Jacobins*: "I was tired of reading and hearing about Africans being persecuted and oppressed in Africa, in the Middle Passage, in the USA and all over the Caribbean. I made up my mind that I would write a book in which Africans or people of African descent instead of constantly being the object of other peoples' exploitation and ferocity would themselves be taking action on a grand scale and shaping other people to their own needs."[3] Beyond its revolution, Haiti's current reputation is one of corruption, disease, poverty, and a myriad of inadequacies. Rehearsing the revolution is not and cannot erase Haiti's present, but it can serve to recognize its foundational space in any emancipatory project in the Americas. Replaying Haiti's story and the models of masculinity that C. L. R. James, Aimé Césaire, and Alejo Carpentier valued links the fragmentary history of the Caribbean across language. Herein exists a community of consensus from which several Caribbean stories can be drawn.

The Black Jacobins (1967), *The Tragedy of King Christophe* (1963), and *Kingdom of This World* (1949) are three literary representations of Haiti's revolution that build Caribbean consciousness through the method of rehearsal. These rehearsals, in turn, reflect prismatic shifts in meaning and interpretation. They result in nuanced understandings and critical engagement that can deepen with each iteration. This is in contrast to cyclic, repetitious readings of history, which yield more passive engagement with, and less dimensional understandings of, the past. In this light, feminist rehearsal deconstructs patriarchal masculinity to examine the aesthetic and sociohistorical moments of the Revolution and its representations. Here, the Haitian Revolution becomes one event that, through rehearsal, develops alternatives to and understanding of Caribbean citizenship.

The Haitian Revolution is a moment of asserting black people's humanity in all its complexity and contradictions. Rehearsing the revolution through these texts reveals differing interpretations, foci, and investments in and attachments to particular notions of History, that is, the "brand" of history, written largely to justify and maintain elite power. It also exposes the paradox of rehearsal as preparing for an ideal (the horizon, or the utopic performance) and cultivating different strategies of being and belonging, while existing in the status quo of colonial, neocolonial, independent, and globalized economic structures. These texts rehearse racialized masculinity in the Caribbean context and reveal the ways in which the male authors of these works, who themselves play significant roles in the articulation of "Caribbeanness" and "Caribbean maleness," remember the Revolution in the formative "post"-colonial twentieth century.

As part of anticolonial struggles, writers in the Caribbean and throughout the Americas looked to the Haitian Revolution as a moment in which the masses defeated insurmountable odds and liberated themselves. This transformative act signaled not so much a move from slave to subject as it did a demand for acknowledgment and a demonstration of black subjectivity, something not often experienced in the New World.[4] My examination reveals differing attachments to particular notions of history as well as to the tensions, instabilities, and transactions in each historical rupture. Such restaging and rehearsing of the Haitian Revolution may lead to shifts in perception of belonging by creating spaces of mutuality for Haitian and non-Haitian readers and by challenging both the ideas of male messianic leadership and Haiti as a diseased, perpetually impoverished site. Readers can safely encounter the past, engage with its contradictions, embody opposing points of view, and begin to revise their biases about the historical event and the current realities.

The primary subjects of this chapter are three creative works that engage with three of the most famous Caribbean men whose leadership styles continue to have an impact in the region: Toussaint L'Ouverture, leader of the Haitian Revolution; Henri Christophe, king of Haiti; and Ti Noël, a fictional character named for the Haitian Maroon leader. In each case, manhood is tied to individual singularity. These complicated black patriarchs are represented as founding fathers—stern and knowing—the ideal vessels of the nationalist project.[5] Thus, the texts themselves evoke a particular strain of Caribbean belonging, one in which the family romance is tied to reclaiming aggressive black manhood as father, fighter, mystic, and provider.

This chapter moves from understanding the context of the Revolution to exploring how ideas of belonging, through various transactions, are understood in and through these texts. I am particularly concerned with how the Revolution was used to document and share the drama and contradictions of the event, how these writers and cultural warriors used the Revolution to represent Haitian and Caribbean manhood in the eighteenth and nineteenth centuries, and how they constructed Caribbean masculinity in the twentieth century as part of their anticolonial struggle. Therefore this chapter rehearses the ways in which polygonal readings of the past lead Caribbean people to become citizens, not just by virtue of their birth, but by becoming agents through the many negotiations they make—negotiations that connect their bodies to the flesh and bones that created an initial path to freedom.

In 1936, Cyril Lionel Robert (C. L. R.) James—pan-Africanist, Trotsky-ite, scholar, and cultural worker—published *Minty Alley*, a novel about the working-class yard of Port-of-Spain, Trinidad. That same year saw his play, *Toussaint Louverture*, produced in London with legendary actor Paul Robeson in the starring role. James followed these works with his highly regarded history of the Haitian Revolution, *The Black Jacobins*, in 1938. In 1967, he revised and reworked his play, ultimately renaming it *The Black Jacobins*, and it premiered in Nigeria that same year. I examine this second version of the play here.[6] The dramatic version of *The Black Jacobins* renders Toussaint the man and the leader. It is a detailed, historical justification for the choices made by Toussaint and the various challenges of transforming a society of enslaved people to a society of free people, of struggling between being Haitian and being a black Frenchman. Toussaint opts for the latter, and it is his downfall, yet questions of identification remain. Are Caribbean people Adamic or tropical versions of their colonizers? This vexing construction is expanded across a range of experiences and contexts.

Poet, essayist, playwright, cofounder of the pan-Africanist Negritude Movement, and politician Aimé Césaire wrote the second play, *The Tragedy of King Christophe*, in 1963. At the play's premiere in August 1964, Césaire had already served as mayor of Fort-de-France, Martinique, for nineteen years and was known for his seminal *Notebook on a Return to My Native Land*, published in 1939 while he was still a student in France. His essay "Discourse on Colonialism" appeared in 1950 and preceded the plays *A Season in Congo* (1966) and *A Tempest* (1969),[7] among other works. Césaire's *King Christophe*, like James's *Black Jacobins*, discusses his main character as man and as king. Christophe is the great pater, and his faults are tragic only in as much as he is misunderstood. Césaire constructs him as a caudillo, a strong man who lived in uncertain and brutal times. Given those circumstances and the equally important need to make sure Haiti remained free, Christophe's choices are framed sympathetically.

Alejo Carpentier wrote the third text, the 1949 novel *Kingdom of This World*, and in addition to his work as a novelist, he is one of the definers of Marvelous Realism. Carpentier said he wrote the novel to recover from his disillusionment with a dying Europe.[8] Raised in Havana by

European émigrés, Carpentier was known for his novels *The Lost Steps* (1953) and *Explosion in the Cathedral* (1962) and for the history *Music in Cuba* (1946). He spent a lifetime telling Caribbean stories through a nonrealist framework, and *Kingdom of This World* is about various characters of the Revolution—Ti Noël, a slave; Makandal (also spelled Macandal), a revolutionary; and Pauline Bonaparte, Napoleon's sister and General Charles Leclerc's wife. Ti Noël is the character readers engage with most, but the historical and magio-spiritual excursions undertaken by both Makandal and Pauline Bonaparte give the novel a broad range of action rather than the solitary-leader dynamic of the two plays.

The contours of Caribbean citizenship considered by these innovators of Caribbean thought naturalize Caribbean patriarchy and, particularly in James's and Césaire's cases, a patriarchy built on race-based nationalism concerned with the liberation of blacks globally and the governing of blacks locally. These texts offer a way not only to rehearse the Revolution across regional languages but also to read both narratives in terms of gender—particularly black manhood—leadership, and belonging in the Caribbean.

Dessalines declared that sacrifice for the nation and for those who had already sacrificed was critical. Similarly, Benedict Anderson observes that the cultivation of fraternal feelings across a broad range of people is based on sacrifice. He connects the building of an imagined fraternity to religion, which "concerns itself with the links between the dead and the unborn." But, he contends, similar to religion, "few things [are] better suited to this end [understanding and answering existential questions] than an idea of nation."[9] Anderson connects these insights to the Tomb of the Unknown Soldier, which speaks to the willingness to sacrifice for unknowable masses, for the imagined fraternity. In other words, the nation provides the same emotional comfort and relation to larger questions of life as does religion. Furthermore, this sacrifice, particularly by someone unknown and unlabeled, connects "us"—here in an imagined and concrete fashion—and so creates a community through which the individuals become the "us."

To create that sense of connectivity, loyalty, and affection, France's National Assembly ratified the Declaration of the Rights of Man and of the Citizen on August 26, 1789, proclaiming, "Under a Supreme Being . . . the inalienable and sacred rights of man and the citizen [shall] constantly [be before] members of the Social Body . . . to continually remind them of their rights and duties."[10] The seventeen articles include an affirmation of the equality of men and the assertion that "political association is the preservation of the natural and imprescriptible rights of man. These rights are liberty, property, security, and resistance to oppression."[11] The idea that the social body needs constant interaction with and exercise of their rights and duties, signals the importance of repeated engagement with history, members of the community, and the members' rights and privileges. The document illuminates sacrifice and resistance to oppression as significant values of citizenship.

France's declaration enshrines personhood (limited to notions of racialized manhood) and solidifies a particular conception of law that justifies a person's right to be secure and to resist oppression.[12] This proclamation, influential to the Haitian revolutionaries, reinforced the notion of male privilege regarding rights and citizenship; the rights of man become the rights of the citizen. Indeed, despite the prominent role women played in the Haitian Revolution, the texts discussed here overwhelmingly represent the Caribbean citizen as a heroic man. The French declaration gives authority to men who are citizens, and Dessalines's declaration authorizes revenge as resistance to oppression.

Negotiating Virility

Haiti's emergence as a nation-state straddled the European Age of Enlightenment and the revolutionary foment of the eighteenth century. In this historical moment of creating a nation and rehabilitating a people, the early leaders of Haiti focused on recuperating blackness in an eighteenth- and nineteenth-century world that aligned and maligned it with all things negative and subhuman. Thinkers such as Carl Von Linné, Georges-Louis Leclerc, David Hume, Immanuel Kant, and Thomas Jefferson shaped an Enlightenment race discourse invested in the classification and justification of white supremacy, marked by philosophies linking "physicality and notions of race."[13] Black people, male and female, were branded (literally and figuratively) as degenerates beyond—or, more correctly, beneath—white civility.

Linné claimed that Europeans were "fair, sanguine, [and best of all] governed by laws; [while Native] Americans and Africans were not only ugly but governed by customs and caprice."[14] Leclerc's elaborate climatological ideas of race used the phrase "bile in the kidneys" to explain the origins and perpetuation of black skin (i.e., the hotter the climate, the darker the people) and linked it to Africans ranging from "very black [to] perfectly black [to] absolutely black."[15]

Hume and Kant furthered the pseudo-biological argument by attaching black skin to black inferiority and inhumanity. Hume concluded that all nonwhite races are inferior to even the most "barbarous" whites, like the Germans, who "still have something eminent about them, in their valour, form of government or some other particular."[16] Especially denigrated were "negroes . . . among whom none ever discovered any symptoms of ingenuity. In Jamaica, they talk of one negroe as a man of parts and learning; but it is likely he is admired for slender accomplishments, like a parrot who speaks a few words plainly."[17]

Kant's artistic fusion of weather theory, biology, and basic inferiority illustrates that

> [t]he Negroes of Africa have by nature no feeling that rises above the trifling. . . . Father Labat [a colonial priest] reports that a Negro carpenter, whom he reproached for haughty treatment toward his wives, answered: "You whites are indeed fools, for first you make great concessions to your wives, and afterward you complain when they drive you mad." And it might be that there were something in this which perhaps deserved to be considered; but in short, this fellow was quite black from head to foot, a clear proof that what he said was stupid.[18]

Though the carpenter's color is touted as "clear proof" that he is stupid, his opinion on wives deserves consideration. His treatment of women affords him limited, but eventually dismissed, access to the cult of imperial European masculinity. Ultimately, his color and Jamaicanness subordinate his masculinity. In this climate, capitalism is intertwined with the always-noble rhetoric of liberty, equality, and fraternity for citizens (who then could only be white men). Those invested with personhood are described as "rational, thinking and contributing," that is, human. According to this model, white women are incapable of rationality and deficient in their ability to make rational connections, while people of color all around the imperial world are less than both.

Caribbean masculinity is not a referent for *black* masculinity as Caribbean men are neither *just* nor only black; however, during the postcolonial period, black and colored elites were invested in proving their worth by equaling or surpassing their colonizers in terms of performing imperial codes of masculinity. Linden Lewis observes that masculinity is a "constellation of practices, behaviors, and ideologies . . . in which men seek the approval of other men and women" by exercising power and control.[19] Discussing the anglophone Caribbean, Belinda Edmonson argues that male writers of the early anticolonial struggles "interpolated meanings of manhood and cultural authority that have been passed onto them from British intellectual discourses of the nineteenth century."[20]

In essence, although Caribbean writers were writing counternarratives, they had to embody the "English vision of intellectual authority" and establish themselves as "gentlemen" worthy of self-government. I extend Edmonson's argument beyond Victorian England to include a broader articulation of imperial manhood populating all Caribbean colonies. Caribbean people, across language and history, were constructing their ideas of masculinity and femininity based on both colonial exemplars and African retentions.[21]

Belinda Edmondson and Curdella Forbes both persuasively claim that the nationalist project was entangled with West Indian manhood and that the authority to write and represent this history was intertwined with nationalist goals.[22] James, Césaire, and Carpentier were invested in particular representations of revolutionary Caribbean manhood for the sake of national and regional histories. Edmondson notes that "the primary proponents of anglophone West Indian nationalism had to 'own' something other than the land or commerce in order to produce the nation in its own image. That 'something,' as we shall see presently, was the 'purchase' of the manners, habits, and positioning of the English gentleman class through the acquisition of Victorian models of intellectual authority and knowledge."[23] Since black masculinity was lodged in the physical and not the intellectual, black people had to repurchase the commodified Caribbean.[24] Here the transactions of masculinity, nation, and emancipation reveal the interrelated and complex power dynamics embedded in nation formation through the narrative control of the writers studied here. These authors reclaimed a specific history of the black male hero and, at the same time, wrote themselves into being as legitimate heads of state and patriarchal figures.

The Haitian Revolution brought impossible-to-ignore configurations of a noble blackness embedded in the iron fist of manhood, a project shared by pan-Africanists James and Césaire, who continued this rehabilitation of blackness well into the twentieth century. In the francophone colonies, since 1848, the French pursued a policy that "allowed adult male ex-slaves to become simultaneously free *and* French,"[25] the most negative aspect of which was allowing the emergence of colonies of "mimic men," French imitators in blackface.

Such mimicry does not produce revolution; rather, it is hostile to alternatives since these colonial subjects are considered neither French nor civilized. Challenging the assimilationists' policy, Negritude and pan-Africanism sought, as Léopold Sédar Senghor put it, to "root oneself in oneself, and a self-confirmation; confirmation of being."[26]

Writing became the route to reclamation and deliberate intervention to counteract epistemic and physical violence on black bodies. As Nana Wilson-Tagoe argues, James's representation of Toussaint promotes James's own unexamined paradoxes: "James's account of . . . Toussaint's career glosses over the issues of freedom and appears to limit its responsibility only to the acquisition of culture, manner, and deportment. His historical perspective explains away Toussaint's failure too early and as a result deflates the crucial issues of the ex-slave's psychological relation to his freedom."[27] Writing became the avenue for representing historical muscularity in constructing the erudite leader as a Caribbean gentleman who could hold his own against any European and had both the capacity and the authority to lead nations in the same mode as European patriarchs. James and Césaire particularly wanted to prevail against the Enlightenment notion of the stupid black man.

Figures of the Haitian Revolution were born in Africa and the Caribbean, while planters fled with their slaves to Louisiana, Maryland, Trinidad and Tobago, Cuba, and other Caribbean colonies. Understanding the Revolution and its version of imperial masculinity is to learn simultaneously from a moment of freedom that arose against all odds, while reproducing the actual story of the Revolution. This history is particularly significant to building communities of consensus; demonstrating the concurrent nature of the past, learning from other emancipatory projects, and rehearing the negotiations embedded in those projects bring individuals to mutual understandings. The Haitian Revolution and all that it symbolizes are critical to Caribbean belonging because it synthesizes an audacious moment of Caribbeanness. It is the first event, to paraphrase James, in which Caribbean people see themselves as one people and so then build alliances across their individual interests to communally defeat the French and manipulate the Spanish. Rehearsing the Revolution reveals that sometimes these communities of consensus were temporary and their unrehearsed/unreflective infighting was detrimental to their cause.

Each of the three texts that are central to this chapter challenges multiple scripts of manhood at play: the paternalistic leader, the savage brute, and the effete mulatto. All of these versions are overlaid with representations of leaders as ultimate pan-Africanist freedom fighters. Historically, Alexandre Pétion, leader of Haiti's republic while Christophe was king, provided refuge and resources to the great liberator Simón Bolívar in exchange for the promise that he would liberate blacks in Spanish America.

Turning to the play *The Black Jacobins*, we see James's pan-Africanist and visionary Toussaint poised to liberate Haiti, the Americas, and the black world or, more precisely, to end slavery. James's Toussaint declares:

> In San Domingo we are an outpost of freed slaves. All around us in the Caribbean black men are slaves. Even in the independent United States, black men are slaves. In South America black men are slaves. Now I have sent millions of francs to the United States. You have heard about this. But it is not to build a fortune for myself so that if anything goes wrong I can escape and live like a rich man. No, Vincent. If this Constitution functions satisfactorily, I intend to take one thousand soldiers, go to Africa and free hundreds of thousands in the black slave trade there and bring them here, to be free and French.[28]

Historically and fictionally, Haiti and its leaders had served and continued to serve as an uneasy beacon of black freedom. Planters in the U.S. Gulf states and nearby British colonies greatly feared its example.[29] In this passage, Toussaint reveals his own rational humanism, his love of freedom, his investment in a functioning constitution, and his disinterest in riches. James's Toussaint is interested in black men in Africa and the Americas, and, once Haiti is safe, he will free those traded blacks and bring them to an enlightened Haiti, one that is free and, most important, French. Toussaint's naïveté, his belief that the imperial French model of manhood is the fraternity to pursue, is exposed. Toussaint and James, in their respective historical moments, represent the desires and noblesse oblige of a ruling class.

Equally important is James's delineation of leadership and the types of leaders produced by the structural issues that are part of the Caribbean condition. In his view, there are three paths to power. First is the path taken by the accommodationist, the benevolent, just, and eventually bamboozled Toussaint, who wants Haiti to be a French colony in blackface. French colonial policy was one of assimilation, which, following the Haitian Revolution, meant making African and black people culturally French. And so, Toussaint, to his detriment, believes he is French. Second is the path of Jean-Jacques Dessalines, the uncompromising and violent emperor of Haiti. And third is General Moïse L'Ouverture's vision, which advocated on behalf of the suffering masses.

In *The Black Jacobins*, Moïse speaks out against appeasement with the French and argues for full emancipation from France:

> Maybe you [Toussaint] wrote to him [Dessalines] and threatened him. But this brutality against the former slaves goes all over San Domingo. I will have

no part of it, I will speak against it and act wherever I see it or hear of it. The person responsible for it, Governor L'Ouverture, is you. . . . Is slavery abolished forever? Or is a French expedition coming to restore slavery? . . . I have told you to declare the island independent. Expel all those who do not want to accept it. Assure the ex-slaves that slavery is gone forever. . . . Break up those accursed big plantations. As long as they remain, freedom is a mockery. Distribute the lands carefully among the best cultivators in the country. Let everybody see that there is a new regime. That is what I have said and that is what I will stand or fall by.[30]

The psychological hold of the plantation haunts revolutionary leadership. Moïse represents the will of the people, the position conditioned by community rather than the isolation felt by the leaders. Moïse, Toussaint's nephew, embodies a model of democratic manhood that attempts to reconcile the physical and psychological hold of the plantation by redistributing wealth. However, in these new postcolonial governments, there is no room for disagreement (although it is allowed by Césaire's Pétion), and Moïse declares, "If to be against your policy is to be guilty of treason, then I am guilty, the most guilty man in San Domingo."[31]

Though Toussaint shares with Madame Bullet, his lover and former owner's wife, that he will send Moïse abroad instead of enforcing the sentence of capital punishment, events unfold quickly and that alternative ceases to be possible. Moïse calls Toussaint a dreamer who believes in an impossible fraternity. Responding to Toussaint's declaration that he will sign his death warrant later, Moïse taunts, "Yes, Toussaint, you shall sign it later. You will use your pen like a sword. But you will see, that until you use your sword like a man—until you cut yourself off from the symbols of colonialism and slavery and be truly independent, you will remain just an old man with a dream of impossible fraternity. Pitiful old Toussaint—and his dream."[32] Moïse realizes that if the Haitian Jacobins are to undo colonial violence, they must engage in a psychic and physical scorched earth policy to decolonize themselves. In other words, revolution—or the complete transformation of social relations—is impossible without violence.[33]

James is ultimately sympathetic to the moderate Toussaint, in part because of the intellectual implications of rationalizing brute force; the play's strongest moments of critique are in scenes that depict Toussaint's and Moïse's conflicting visions, especially those characterizing the former as a dreamer. Moïse sees Toussaint's approach as not only feeble, the virility of a pitiful old man, but a dream, not grounded in reality; Toussaint's basis for masculinity is a fantasy. Until he "uses his sword like a man," disconnecting himself from Father France, he will be an impotent and compromised leader of the nation, unable to suitably represent Haitian interests.

The 1801 Haitian constitution swears allegiance to France while maintaining self-governance; Toussaint's conflict remains because of his need for "the guidance of an elder brother,"[34] namely, France. Independence is a difficult concept for Toussaint, mainly because he is emotionally and culturally tied to France, while for Moïse, freedom is the ultimate claim of the person, the acting subject. Moïse as a representation of the dignity of the Haitian masses reveals the staggering gulf between ruled and rulers because the black masses advocated full emancipation while their leaders sought compromise.[35]

The idea of natural independence and personal autonomy remains at the crux of the emancipation struggle. The challenges of what the French Revolutionary principles—liberty, fraternity, and equality—mean, in light of kingship and other forms of manly leadership, haunt Haiti's revolutionary leaders. Toussaint claims that though Africans believe in a king, they are also republican.[36] Toussaint ultimately rejects the monarchist model, but the divine right of messianic leadership prevails.

In James's rehearsal, Toussaint (and later Christophe) is subject to paranoia and squeezes those around him, as exemplified by his convening of a kangaroo court that executes Moïse.[37] Such meditations on power highlight the ambiguous nature of the relationship between Toussaint and Moïse, with deeply embedded contradictions that implicate and inform constructions of self and constructions of the state. If the region follows Toussaint's model (as constructed by James), it will always be trapped in a cycle of dependency, with leaders unable to break their own psychological dependence on the former system. The alternative model articulated by Moïse is one of total independence, one that may not be possible given the region's internalized image of dependency and the realities of international commerce and politics.

Understandably, it was difficult, if not impossible, for Toussaint to imagine a country (or, for him, a colony) not linked to France. How would they survive? This issue of survival consumes Toussaint in the play as he repeatedly asks for teachers, priests, and advisers from France to build Haiti. Similarly, Caribbean leaders today find it hard to conceive of total self-sufficiency, in part because their small island nations cannot service the needs of their polarized and increasingly unequal populations, and in part because they are fully invested in and limited (mentally, politically, and economically) by the continued stranglehold of global corporate capitalism.

The American and British plot to topple Toussaint and install Pétion[38] foments policy that effectively seeks to put "blacks in their place," as Napoleon says.[39] Bonaparte's objection to black leadership is not that they could be seen as figureheads but that they would have economic control.[40] There are refrains of James's representation in the contemporary globalized world of U.S. policies that simultaneously tout and undermine truly democratic practice and eruptions of resistance to those procedures. Recently, international conglomerates operating in Haiti proposed minimum wage suppression and the humanitarian dumping of genetically modified grain seeds. Both these instances signal moments of rehearsal, particularly rehearsing Toussaint's survivalist concerns. In the first, the government accedes to international pressures to ensure a limited supply of work, but that work reinforces the state of poverty and calamity in Haiti. In the second instance, the farmers of the Peasant Movement of Papay burned argri-giant Monsanto's donation of seed. These farmers reject the Haitian government's survivalist tendency to accept "gifts" that would further exhaust the country's depleted soils.[41] The rejection of these seeds by peasant farmers is one democratic eruption against regressive political methods.[42]

Dessalines represents another path, one beyond subsistence and one that James and Césaire considered the most abhorrent. To James, Dessalines is a model of Caribbean despotism:

> Tomorrow, the Emperor will issue a proclamation. . . . We are going to kill every white man and woman on this island. They will never be able to restore slavery here because we are going to get rid of all of them. Not one is going to remain. You fools are not ready for that. . . . Man, woman and child, not one of them is going to be left alive. No more slavery here. The proclamation I shall issue tomorrow, signed by me—Dessalines, Emperor of Haiti. I have learnt to sign my name, Dessalines. I will learn to sign Emperor. All will be killed. All.[43]

Assuming Dessalines's violence is revolutionary in the sense that it overturns the norms of colonial society and physically frees Haiti, the psychological and oppressive script of tyranny remains, but in blackface.[44] This repetition is simultaneously a revolutionary rehearsal and a mimicking of colonial patterns. As Frantz Fanon argues, colonial violence, though overturned in the process of decolonization, does not end with the colonizer's removal. In fact, attempts to avoid enacting violence on colonial bodies often redirect violence toward other natives.[45] Dessalines's despotism is a rehearsal for despots to come, supported by external economic and political interests and egos. These scripts are enacted today at the global level through "friendly coups" and with support for dictators offered by countries such as the United States. The rehearsal continues because these sugar islands—independent and "self-determined"—are still conditioned by the outside forces with which they are forced to barter. The idea of "father of the nation" and "provider of the nation" is squashed because Caribbean masculinity, always in conversation and comparison with European masculinity, is found wanting.

James takes pains—in both his play and his earlier history—to place Dessalines in his historical frame. Yet doing so is not enough. James reluctantly concludes that, even though General Leclerc, Napoleon's brother-in-law, "ha[d] resolved to exterminate as many blacks as possible [and] General Rochambeau attempts to complete this extermination"[46] by tilling the soil with their blood, these events do not justify Dessalines's actions. Additionally, the British, securing their regional interests, made it plain that they could not do business with Haiti if French whites were allowed to survive, for they feared the attachment of newly freed people to their former masters. Despite these mitigations, Dessalines's act, for James, was unforgivable.[47] This "massacre of the whites is a tragedy for blacks and mulattoes" because it shows a lack of humanity and foresight, and primarily because "it was not policy, but revenge and revenge [no matter how historically contextualized] has no place in politics."[48]

For James, Dessalines's savagery is, in part, a direct contradiction to the mode of English manhood from which the author draws his authority. Dessalines, however, made a direct link between blackness and Haitianness, declaring that "Haitians, whatever their color . . . would be known as *blacks*, referred to 'only by the generic word *black*.'"[49] It is both Dessalines's acts of unrepentant violence for the liberation of black people and his claiming of blackness as integral to Haitian and Caribbean identity—gestures of self-determination and actualization—that transcend and mitigate his brutality. It is also part of the reason he is venerated in twentieth-century Haiti as a *loa*, "acquir[ing] unequaled power in the Haitian imagination."[50]

Despite this, historically it is the violence Dessalines unleashed through his policies and the abuses of the Haitian people by his ministers that led to his brutal end, accomplished by a conspiracy of blacks and mulattoes, rather than the slaughter "without guns of 3,000 whites."[51] On an October day in 1806 at Pont-Rouge (Red Bridge), after two and a half years in power, "one officer shot [him], another stabbed him three times, [yet another] filled him with bullets from two pistols. Then he was stripped naked, his fingers cut off."[52] The historical record reveals that once he was turned over to the masses, they "stoned and hacked [him] to pieces. His remains—variously described as 'scraps' and 'shapeless remains,' 'remnants,' or 'relics'—were thrown to the crowd."[53] Dessalines's brutalization and dismemberment dismantles his nation, mimicking his own brutality as he had mimicked that of the French. Dessalines represents annihilation—the erasure of the enemy—which, in his case, encompassed the French, fellow Haitians, and himself.

I contend that there remains a need to construct "positive and complicated" examples of Caribbean citizens *and* black manhood. *Positive* in the sense that black masculinity, like white masculinity, can exist not only as aggressive and brutal. This first generation of writers felt the pressure to create complex constructions of self-actualization that were also a response to inherited imperial constructions of masculinity.[54] In their plays, Césaire and James provide several Caribbean male leadership models, focusing on the most noble and understandable ones. Yet these examples highlight the contradictions of violence, nation, race hatred, and pride embodied by Dessalines. The emperor stands in stark contrast against the others while also being one of them.

As Edmondson asserts, in writing masculinity and authority, James is invested in Toussaint's literacy.[55] In fact, in both versions of *The Black Jacobins*, James emphasizes Toussaint's reading of historian and philosopher Abbé de Raynal and his knowledge of opera, juxtaposed with Dessalines's illiteracy. If Toussaint and James are, in a way, reflections of each other across time, then the playing out of imperial manhood as an educated masculinity is important to both of them and is particularly important in James's revolutionary representation. James negotiates through his lived experience as a black colonial in a tropical environment to find examples of black dignity that were not brutish but were instead refined and erudite, exemplified by men who enjoyed authority achieved via the pen, not the sword.[56]

Césaire's *The Tragedy of King Christophe* is as sympathetic a depiction of Henri Christophe, the self-proclaimed "King of Haiti," as James's play is of Toussaint. Christophe is a benevolent, overzealous, and slightly misguided father figure. Césaire renders "the tragedy" of Christophe by charting his megalomania—his quest for the patrimony of all black people—a noble, refined heritage that allows them to glory in their black skin. Ultimately, Christophe is unable to convince his court and his subjects of his vision; he is a messianic leader, shown in splendid isolation. Césaire employs a series of binaries to dramatic effect, beginning with the prologue. There, through a cockfight that pits the roosters Christophe and Pétion against each other, the primary characters fight for prominence from the outset. It is notable that this discussion of governance and manhood begins with two cocks, a phallic colloquialism. This opening gestures at the lewdness to come but also indicates that political power is lodged in aggressive masculinity. These binaries manifest in three areas: Christophe (north/monarchy) versus Pétion (south/republic); manhood conflated with humanity and respect versus weakness conflated with enslavement of a spiritual and mental kind; and form over substance.

In Césaire's work, Pétion is compared to a soft and indulgent mother while Christophe is a stern father.[57] Mothers in this play are sites of reproduction and mild reproach or are silent. Thus, comparing Pétion to a mother does not connote nurturing but underscores his ineffectiveness, especially vis-á-vis Christophe. Pétion's lack of manhood becomes more clearly drawn when Boyer, Pétion's successor, has already usurped him in his mistress's bed: "Well, I trust you've heard of Mademoïselle Jouste, Pétion's mistress. Young Boyer has shown himself a gifted jouster [and has] unsaddled Pétion"[58] (according to the historical record, Boyer marries Joutte Lachenais).[59] In the play, one unnamed cock dies in the cockfight, and, given all the references to infirmity, it is easy to believe that it was Pétion's cock; in reality, however, the dead cock is called "Christophe," foreshadowing that character's death at the end of the play.[60] Pétion pays France a massive indemnity that leads to international recognition of the Haitian state but is not fully paid until the twentieth century—another sign of his weakness because, Christophe says, a "man wouldn't do that [but] Pétion, the drag ass," did."[61] Though Césaire attributes this outcome to Pétion in the play, in reality the indemnity was paid in 1825 under Boyer's leadership. Haitian leaders in need of the opportunities recognition would bring signed away long-term resources for immediate gain. In the play, Christophe decries the fact that Haitian requests for technical assistance are met not with engineers or professors but with a master of ceremonies, since "form is what counts."[62] The resource question plagues Caribbean countries, as is seen with cycles of aid and humanitarian workers and as noted earlier in the discussion of the Peasant Movement of Papay's burning of Monsanto's donated seed.

In Césaire's portrayal, Christophe embodies republics—and Pétion's in particular—with weakness because "Napoleon has no respect for republics and Haiti has two."[63] Napoleon's imperial manhood model, and European models in general, continue to influence. And since

Napoleon respects only violent manifestations of strength—and textually, the gendered female Pétion is incapable of this—Christophe's
kingdom becomes a path to salvation. Vastey, one of the king's advisers, concurs:

> We too need a kingdom to gain worldwide respect. . . . The whole world is
> watching us, citizens, and the nations think that black men have no dignity.
> A king, a court, a kingdom, that's what we've got to show them if we want
> to be respected. . . . A black king! It's like a fairy tale, isn't it? This black
> kingdom, this court, a perfect replica in black of the finest courts the Old
> World has to offer.[64]

Black kingship and the desire for respect prefigures many a strong-arm
dictator in the Caribbean and the African diaspora. Black kings mimicking European forms of kingship echo Frantz Fanon's trope of black
skin/white masks, which can be restated as black kings/white crowns.
The internalization of brutish masculinity becomes a significant part of
being a "real man." The exercise of various muscularities is deployed
differently within black bodies. Christophe proclaims at his coronation,
after placing a crown upon his head and with his "hand on the Gospels,"
"I swear to preserve the integrity of the territory and the independence
of the kingdom; under no pretext to suffer the return to slavery or any
measure prejudicial to the freedom or the civil and political rights of the
Haitian people, to govern with a sole view to the interest, the happiness
and the glory of the great Haitian family of which I am head."[65] Christophe is not only head of the national family, but along those lines he
engenders; he fertilizes and impregnates the national body. Governance
and the familial model are correlated: "Papa Christophe is a precursor
to Papa Doc," and the model of the caudillo, as Jeannette Allsopp characterizes it, is rationalized. The strongman in the fairytale substitutes for
and subverts the dashing prince while maintaining the ideology of the
strong male savior.

James compares Toussaint and Moïse, while Césaire parallels Haiti's republic with its coexisting kingdom. Christophe's quest for control leads to his rejection of the presidency, which "is without flesh or
bones, the scraps of leftovers of power."[66] Monarchy in *The Tragedy of
King Christophe* is intertwined with manhood, while republicanism, the
domain of the "soft" Pétion, is about principles versus the person or the
personality.[67] Both factual and problematic, race discourse has mulattoes aligned with ostensible rule-of-law and Enlightenment notions of

citizenship, despite Pétion's eventual declaration of himself as "President for Life," while blacks are caricatures of the imperial and monarchist models.[68] Pétion, though positioned as a democrat who believes in the transparency of the nation and accountability of the government, is not heroic. Instead, Césaire's play celebrates strength and the valorizing of black manhood, which links humanity with monarchy. The "Black"/"Mulatto" dynamic is a comment on the politics of color in the region and the continued promotion of the pigmentocracy. The values of white supremacy that equate lighter skin color and European phenotypes with civilization and progress are briefly reversed in this text.

Ideas regarding manhood, monarchy, progress, and the rights of men versus the duties of black men are highlighted in Christophe's conversation with his wife. She is the first and only woman to have more than two lines in Césaire's play, and, as "good wife and mother," she warns Christophe to be wary of pushing the people too fast and too far. His angry response, enforced through proclamations such as Code Henri,[69] has resonance in the twentieth-century diaspora. "I ask too much of men? But not enough of black men, Madame. If there's one thing that riles me as much as slaveholder's talk, it's to hear our philanthropists proclaim, with the best of intentions of course, that all men are men and that there are neither whites nor blacks. That's thinking in an armchair, not in the world. All men have the same rights? Agreed. But some men have more duties than others."[70] Christophe's speech reiterates that belonging is and will be contextualized by race because rights and duties are distinguishing factors. Rights suggest entitlement and the conferment of privileges by virtue of just "being," whereas duties suggest action—work that proves and supports one's worth. Black citizenship and subjectivity are saddled with the need to prove "black worth." Césaire, as a pan-Africanist and proponent of Negritude, believes this credo. Implicit in this idea is black citizen as activist, always walking the historical path to justice. In the play, two of Christophe's courtesans engage in a drawing room discussion about the paths of history in which one character asks: "Do you mean that King Christophe employs the means of slavery to attain the ends of Freedom?" The female character asks this question as the group hears the story of Ooreka, from a novel that is all the rage in Paris. Ooreka laments her color, sees it as her tragic flaw, and eventually dies because of it. Responding with anger and frustration, Césaire's Vastey indicates that Christophe is forceful in forging a tireless and dignified people because he is fighting for "the day when no little black girl anywhere in the world will be ashamed of her skin, when no little black girl's color will stand in the way of her dreams."[71] These moments, associated with manhood, leadership, and the protective father who helps "little black girls" have pride, are entwined with Christophe's paternalism. In the wake of Martin Luther King's invocation of little black girls in his "I Have a Dream" speech, and the murder of four young black girls in their Alabama church, one could argue that this is a foreshadowing, if not rehearsal, of twentieth-century events.

Césaire (like Carpentier) was a member of the Society of King Christophe's Friends, an intellectual fraternity.[72] He constructs a generally praised version of the Haitian Revolution in his play and, of all the most-celebrated leaders, mentions only Christophe. When not fighting Pétion and Maroon leaders, King Christophe clashes with the people, declaring that "Haiti's enemies are internal . . . indolence, lethargy, lack of discipline."[73] The Code Henri of 1812 mandated fieldwork and other draconian measures (reminiscent of France's Code Noir), which Haitians viewed as a reimposition of slavery. In Christophe's mind, he was (re)building a nation and a people. His monumental building projects—first, his palace, Sans Souci, and, second, the fortress, the Citadelle La Ferrière—are national projects that Christophe justifies as a way of inspiring and educating his people. Césaire's vision is of Christophe bequeathing a tangible and recognizable patrimony of Haitian pride, success, and determination.[74] The Citadelle La Ferrière emerges as one way to inspire awe, and as Baron de Vastey, Chancellor of the Kingdom, remarks, "These two structures, erected by descendants of Africans, show that we have not lost the architectural taste and genius of our ancestors who covered Ethiopia, Egypt, Carthage, and Old Spain with their superb monuments."[75]

Sans Souci and the Citadelle La Ferrière were viewed by workers as embodying punishment and enslavement. Michel-Rolph Trouillot relates that Christophe built his palace near the place where he executed his eponymous enemy, Colonel Sans Souci. As Trouillot tells it, the archive valued by the European historian cannot recognize the significance of building a palace on the bones of one's enemy. Trouillot contends that Christophe was "engaged in a transformative ritual to absorb his old enemy."[76] The result is the transmitting messages (or reiterating the power and authority of the leader) to a population in the moment of the monuments' making.[77] The Sans Souci palace is a testament to the pride and determination of Haitians creating a new world. The paradox of these ruins, specifically the citadel, is that it is considered "the eighth wonder of the world, and is said to have cost the lives of some

20,000 workers during its construction."[78] Ironically, these pharaonic constructions serve as a transformative signal of the truly revolutionary capacity of Haiti. The inconsistency between contemporary testaments to Haitian/Christophe's audacity and monuments based on slave labor is biblical. Christophe's symbols signal both the possibility and the rationalization of authoritarian rule. His strategy was followed by subsequent Haitian leaders, including President Faustin Soulouque (1847–49), who became a self-crowned emperor, Faustin I (1849–59), and President Vilbrun Guillaume Sam, who governed as a dictator in 1915 and, similar to Christophe, "spread the rumor that he was immune to ordinary lead bullets and could be killed only by a silver one, and [like Dessalines] was finally hacked to pieces."[79] Christophe's abuses of his court and subjects are part of the universal tragic flaw of all despots before him and since. However, his installation of the Royal Dahomets, predecessors of the Tonton Macoutes, entrenches brutality and initiates his reign of terror. After his stroke, the citadel *becomes* Christophe, his *zemi*, and the keeper of his bones.[80]

Though Césaire has no "crowd" in his play as James does, the voices of the people are in some ways more evident in his text than in James's, with an overt debate on class signaled by Christophe's monumental enterprises. The peasants proclaim, "We threw the whites into the sea not to slave for other people, even if they are as black as we are,"[81] and Christophe counters with "Freedom cannot endure without labor."[82] Césaire layers the paradox with dissent from the top and the bottom: How to govern—monarchy or republic? The contradiction unfolds around intrarace class contentions, illustrating that black success built on black oppression will lead to another revolution.[83] Not only does this shaping within the play allow the playwright to have these conversations, but it shows the world closing in on Christophe, raising the stakes for this tragic hero as he is increasingly isolated.

Both *The Tragedy of King Christophe* and *The Black Jacobins* offer competing constructs articulated by Toussaint, Moïse, Dessalines, and Christophe. They reflect some of the leadership paths taken and juxtapose these options with contemporary realities, especially as seen in *The Black Jacobins* with the invocation of black power, language, and discourse. The two plays offer no closed or single solution; rather, they indicate that the solution will be ever evolving, even as core problems remain the same. Most of these texts portray Caribbean subjects as actors and agents fully invested in transforming the material and psychological conditions of their lives.

Women: Wives and Whores

In his novel *Kingdom of This World*, Carpentier depicts images of European decay in the exile community and in Pauline Bonaparte, the sister of Napoleon and wife of General Leclerc. In stark contrast to the portrayal of Christophe's death and burial, in which he is soldered with the blood of bulls and embedded in the mortar of the building, General Leclerc's end is pathetic.[84] It is painful but quick, his "body shaken by ominous chills. His eyes were yellow. . . . The death of Leclerc, cut down by yellow fever, brought Pauline to the verge of madness. Now the tropics seemed abominable, with the relentless buzzard waiting on the roof of the house in which someone was sweating out his agony."[85]

By the time of her husband's death, Pauline Bonaparte, the only female character to receive significant attention in the novel, is likened to blacks because of her "superstitious" Corsican blood. Pauline ostensibly embraces Vodou over Christianity, taking "an amulet to Papa Legba [*loa* of the crossroads], wrought by Soliman, her masseur and Henri's future valet, which was destined to open the paths to Rome for Pauline Bonaparte."[86] Lizabeth Paravisini-Gebert notes that Bonaparte "fills the vacuum left by [the omission of] Dessalines's military feats, [and, instead, readers are treated] to Pauline's sexual exploits."[87] Given Carpentier's interest in vilifying and exposing the debaucheries of a dying Europe against the essence of a generative and renewing America, his choice maintains a certain logic. The American continent, as represented in *The Kingdom of This World*, is not without its own violence, but Dessalines's actions, characterized primarily as "unreasoned," could not be part of the recuperative violence of Macandal (spelled with a "c" in Carpentier's text), whose struggle is linked not only to the *loas* but to the just cause of liberation.[88] Carpentier's inclusion of Pauline's story is another way of rehearsing the bodies that shaped the Revolution, particularly the bodies of white women. James includes the sympathetic white plantation owner and one of Toussaint's lovers, Madame Bullet, but most texts represent men. The chapter on Pauline serves as an interesting counterpart. Though her presence in the novel erases Dessalines, she typifies the world of pampered, elite women. She, of course, is the paragon of this auspicious group as the sister of the French emperor and wife of one of his generals. Pauline's place within the power structure gives her particular privileges. Her sexual relationships with her husband's subalterns and her use of Vodou place her at the crossroads of the imperial and national formations. Carpentier emphasizes the whiteness and softness of her body, even as he connects her superstitious Corsican nature to her impoverished upbringing.

Pauline's flesh is also a counter to the depiction of black bodies, which were routinely tortured in the eighteenth and nineteenth centuries. The narrative of Pauline's flesh becomes one of apparent ease, her childhood hardships erased by the repeated lubrications of her masseur. Pauline's natal class, history, and nationality intersect and inform her relationship to the Haitian revolutionary space for Carpentier. Carpentier begins part 2 of the novella with an epigraph from Laure Junot, Duchess d'Abrantès and Pauline's confidante. The duchess recounts that she told Pauline that "she would be queen out there; that she need not fear snakes, for there are no snakes in the Antilles; that the savages are not to be feared. At the end I rounded out my speech by telling her that she would be very pretty dressed as a Creole."[89] Sex was one way that black and creole (those born in the colony) bodies were policed, and Pauline masquerading as a hypersexualized creole provides an ambiguous space as sexual and imperial conquest.

These European voices reiterate both the fear and the uncertainty that Haiti generated, but also the ability to transform and perform creoleness, or, rather, their own interpretations of blackness. Pauline delights in wearing the madras turban of a creole, like her sister-in-law, Empress Josephine. However, her masking erases the black female bodies whose lives as creoles within the slave economy were sexualized, not as a performance, but as a complex series of negotiations.[90] D'Abrantès's eyewitness account is a clear counterpoint to Carpentier's and reflects not only the master narratives of the past but also the intimate stories that shape the past. Could the duchess's advice to Pauline be any more ironic? Haiti, while perhaps not a natural habitat of the snake, is the most symbolic snake site in the Caribbean. It is the territory of the Vodou god Damballah, creator of life, whose symbol is a serpentine cross, and of Vodou itself, a cosmology that eludes classification and confinement as it relates to her sexual exploits, another context in which Pauline becomes a worshipper of the "snake," that is, the phallus.

Of the two plays, James's gives the more significant voice to women.[91] He recognizes the centrality of women in the Haitian struggle and in larger representations of Caribbean belonging. In his text, centered on the heroic if ultimately tragic Toussaint, women are active participants in battles and bedrooms: the character of Marie-Jeanne is based on the historical figure of Marie-Claire Heureuse, wife of Dessalines, and Madame Bullet on the wife of Toussaint's owner. Throughout the play,

Marie-Jeanne has sexual liaisons with white men, first as the unwilling mistress of her master Monsieur Bullet, and then enticing French general Hédouville for the liberation cause. Hédouville claims to love her and wishes they had met under different circumstances; his desire for her masks the violence of colonial relationships by emphasizing ideas of romance and seduction.[92] But Marie-Jeanne rejects him and the notion of white male desire as a mitigating agent in slavery. She reminds him, "I am a mulatto woman. I am nobody, I was a slave."[93] The interaction exemplifies the core of this character: although doubly despised as woman and slave, Marie-Jeanne's identity is reclaimed through her participation in the Revolution. Her transformation from slave to person is also one from property to citizen. One could argue that she represents a revolution from within by claiming her body as her own, through both emancipation from slavery and her new sexual authority. Her body is no longer stock; it is a weapon of sorts. These women rehearse the history of women's revolutionary presence while gesturing to alternatives that emerge when women are part of the process of building communities.

More so than Madame Bullet, Marie-Jeanne is an agent. As Toussaint's devotee, she despises Dessalines until he asks her to teach him to read, making theirs one of the most intriguing relationships in the play even with its overtones of violence. He desires her, but she abhors him, and she sees being with him as another form of enslavement. To his offer of marriage and material wealth, she responds, "I prefer to be what I want to be. You don't own me. . . . Nobody owns me. Slavery is finished."[94] Marie-Jeanne is clear on the place of blacks and mulattoes in the French cosmos and (within the play) is able to coerce Pétion and the mulattoes to fight with Dessalines. She betrays Toussaint because she believes in her husband's philosophy of armed resistance and white annihilation:

> When I married you, you were rough and often brutal. But little by little I grew to understand you. . . . I fell in love with you, Dessalines. I trusted you completely. Here in San Domingo, people don't trust one another. For the first time in all my life, a man, my husband, meant something to me. In every battle in the bush, I was a person next to you, watching over you, ready to give my life for yours. Life meant nothing to me without you: Nothing. And just then, when I heard you plotting Toussaint's capture, I thought for a moment you had betrayed me, but I understand now.[95]

Marie-Jeanne calmly makes this declaration after Dessalines threatens to murder her if she does not follow his orders. In a life buffeted by circumstance, Marie-Jeanne reiterates that being with him has always been and continues to be her choice—one forged in revolutionary struggle. The transformations in their relationship reveal that though Dessalines tries to dominate her, Marie-Jeanne insists that it is her understanding of struggle that makes her an ally and his wife, not his threats or manipulations. She is emphatic that they are together because it is reasonable to her—she "understands him," and it is only because of her understanding of him and his mission, one she embraces, that she is by his side. Furthermore, throughout the scene, Dessalines's personal frailties are exposed. In his emotional need for her affection and approval, he remarks rawly that Marie-Jeanne married him at Toussaint's urging—as part of a civilizing project. His wife denies this and reiterates that it was her own understanding of Dessalines, the man, and the Revolution, that enticed her to marry him. The scene reveals the unexpected tenderness in their relationship. His forceful repetitions of his reputation as a barbarian and a savage lead to Marie-Jeanne asking him to sit at her feet as he did early in their marriage. "You have always been afraid of me. I must set that right."[96] Though James indicates in his directional notes that Dessalines sitting at her feet is a sign that he has won, this characterization of Dessalines as a man who fears, and fears a woman, no less, is polemically different from previous representations. This scene ruptures the unrelenting construction of his savage masculinity. Perhaps in part because she is literate, Marie-Jeanne intimidates him, which certainly comports with James's worldview that literacy is intimidating and an attribute of leaders. The scene ends with Marie-Jeanne reciting lines from *Iphigénie*, Racine's play about sacrifice for political ends. Dessalines and Marie-Jeanne find strength in their love and political project, with her literacy making her an equal to her husband in power.

Though Marie-Jeanne is an example of literacy and power, her historical counterpart died in poverty after living to the age of one hundred.[97] Born into a free and comfortable family in 1748, Heureuse was educated by Catholic clergy and eventually became Dessalines's mistress and mother to at least four of his children, including fraternal twins.[98] Their children and relationship were later legitimated, making Heureuse empress of Haiti until Dessalines is murdered and dismembered. Christophe shelters her until his suicide, leaving Heureuse and her surviving children to scratch out a living.[99]

The fictional Marie-Jeanne is a warrior woman whose sexuality had been used against her but which she ultimately reclaims in service to the new nation. Her citizenship, like those of other enslaved people, is embodied—marked on and in her body, literally internalized through the sex act. Marie-Jeanne's articulation of personhood and female subjectivity can be contrasted with the recuperation of black manhood in the eighteenth *and* twentieth centuries. The need for black people to have "a shining black prince"[100] is constant, and James's Toussaint is the noble and restrained hero for his time. However, James's investment in Toussaint's specialness has detrimental consequences; it prevents the development of a more complex character.

In Césaire's play, women are limited to one character, the supportive but knowing queen Marie-Louise, who is referred to only as "Madame Christophe" and counsels her husband against rashness, "as a good wife should." Women here are backdrops for the nation, their own personhood and citizenship relegated to marriage and procreation. The state, at its most patriarchal, needs a solid foundation and has determined that "women with permanent husbands" will be used as breeders for the new nation as they were for their former masters.[101] These representations of republican motherhood in Haiti emphasize women's roles, particularly as biological mothers, in producing the next generation. Such female representations obfuscate women's more complex roles in fighting for freedom. Yet Vodou is a site that enables all participants to have multifaceted political and spiritual involvement with a community dedicated to service in part because it challenges colonial state ideologies.

Vodou History

The emergence of the Haitian nation is spiritually, if not historically, tied to Vodou mythology and iconography. Joan Dayan characterizes her version of rehearsal as Vodou history, or the "superimpositions that reinforce each other."[102] Dayan's history as ritual is another reiteration of the structuring power of Vodou in art and scholarship. In Césaire's presentation of rehearsal, the Master of Ceremonies is an *ougan*-like figure, a Vodou priest, and then becomes commentator as the character Hugonin. These are the voices of both the people and history respectively; the former functions as Césaire's connection to the crowd and popular perspectives, while the latter oversees the cockfight and explains the action to the audience. Though neither character is listed in the character manifesto of Ralph Manheim's translation, they are important enough to be credited by Césaire and function as connections between the living (the audience) and their ancestors. Specifically, the Master of Ceremonies, by involving the crowd and the audience in the play, engages the living. Simultaneously, Hugonin participates in and comments on the death rituals scripted by Césaire. As Christophe shoots himself, Hugonin reveals that he is Baron Samedi, the figure charged with ushering the dead to the world of the ancestors.[103] The play ends with lavish funerary rites and the hope that Christophe's brand of strength, in Vastey's words, will find a home "upright against the mortar. Turned Southward. . . . Not lying down. Standing. Let him make his own way amid hardship, rock and the industry of human hands."[104]

Historically, Christophe denounced Vodou, but in the play, he invokes the power of thunder, as did "his Bambara ancestors . . . to speak, to make, to construct, to build, to be, to name, to bind, to remake."[105] In the end, Césaire's Christophe is staged with the African-based religion of the Haitian masses and invokes these gods in his final moments of strength during the Catholic Mass for the Feast of the Assumption, putting Christian gods in direct conflict with those born on Haitian soil.[106] As the new archbishop speaks, so too does Christophe, canonizing Toussaint and Dessalines. Seeing an apparition of Corneille Brelle, whom he had immured for speaking out "more than the nation required," Christophe collapses, believing someone has put *bakula baka* (an evil animal spirit) on him.[107] This leads to his paralyzing stroke, which he sees as a betrayal of nature: "Is there anything worse than surviving yourself?"[108]

Christophe's stroke signals his earthly end. His generals desert him, and the masses revolt.[109] Nonetheless, he rationalizes his display of strength as necessary for the times—"I regret nothing. I tried to put something into an inhospitable land"[110]—though this type of hubris and messianic, top-down strategy falls apart because the people are not invested in his vision. Césaire's rendering is not only sympathetic but also ennobling. As Fuyet and others claim, Césaire presents Christophe textually as an example worth emulating, yet, unlike Christophe, Césaire has had opportunities to refashion himself through rehearsal and rereading.

In Césaire's rendering, Christophe's tragic flaw is not that he was king or sought power but that he could not effectively communicate his vision to his subjects. Though Christophe's abuses—Brelle's entombment and the rise of the Royal Dahomets—are chronicled, when placed in the context of his larger mission of black empowerment, these cruelties are coded as understandable. Another manifestation of his communicative inability is his misunderstanding of the national religion, Vodou. When Césaire's character hears the drums, he exclaims, "Our persecutors are dogging our heels, and my people dance!"[111] Michel-Rolph Trouillot claims that Christophe is highly superstitious and a Vodou believer of sorts by the end of his life, embracing every device that might help him regain his strength and ward off death, yet Christophe is initially contemptuous of Vodou.[112] In the end, as Hugonin, the buffoon, morphs into Baron Samedi, "the head of the Gede family of raucous spirits of the dead,"[113] he explains that some "countries [are] given to commotion, to convulsions, and ours is one of them[;] that's its nature."[114]

Given Vodou's sense of duality and Dayan's contention that this Haitian religious practice is endowed with philosophical and intellectual power, there are several ways to read Baron Samedi's assertion. First, convulsions can be seen as an indication of rehearsal—the sudden, violent bodily eruptions are similar to those experienced by the Haitian nation. By the time of Christophe's death, the territory moved from rebellious colony to independent Haiti to a divided country with a kingdom and a republic. Each of these contractions or convulsions served as a rehearsal of the growing pains of nation building. Second, Vodou may be a commotion that disrupts linearity, relating to the idea of infinity. In other words, the rituals of Vodou are one way of linking to the infinite; these rituals offer a Legba-inspired gateway through which to enter the conversation. Vodou is about rehearsing ritual, and ritual itself is a type of rehearsal (and in the Vodou paradigm, a convulsion). Importantly, Vodou is a communal convulsion in which there is a mutual space of interconnection between the *loas*, the ancestors, and the living.

Vodou as a spiritual practice is the adhesive that cements Haitian society. Vodou congregants are in service to the spirits, or *loas*. It implies a reciprocal relationship between *loas* and practitioners and reflects various structures of belonging, particularly familial ones, with leaders of these congregations, or "societies," being the *ougan* (male) or the *manbo* (female).[115] The *ougans* are stern parental figures, possessing unquestioned authority and given "unconditional devotion. . . . It is to be hoped that [they are] not abusive parents, but the social world of Haiti is harsh, and family life is never easy."[116] Since Vodou is centered on the veneration of ancestors, it is fundamentally about familial association. Societies can be composed of several families in a neighborhood, congregating with a particular *ougan* or *manbo*, and forming *lakous*, or extended family compounds, especially in rural areas.[117] In the cities, a Vodou community comes together through initiation rather than through blood.[118] Vodou nations are no longer ethnic but a "means of classifying the variety of spirits by the kind of rites that are offered to them."[119] As Joseph

M. Murphy relates, the variety of African-derived rites in Haitian religious life is understood by believers through the concept of "nation."
The African origins of different spirits, dances, and drum rhythms are
remembered as those of different nations: "Each vodou community will
have arrived at its own constellation of nations to be invoked, . . . [the
most common being the] Rada, Petro (Petwo), Dahomey, Ginen, Congo,
Nago, Ibo and Wongol."[120]

Murphy claims that "the Haitian revolution is very much alive in
vodou ceremony and symbolism and it is this revolutionary spirit which
gives vodou its critical force and fearsome image."[121] Thus, within
Vodou, there are ritual constructions of the family, the nation, and resistance, and rehearsing these rituals stimulates the interplay between the
living and the dead. This energy accesses the past through spirit, dance,
songs, and the possession of bodies. The spirit and the body enter into
infinite rehearsal through these rituals; the disjointed body becomes a
gateway for a shifting consciousness.[122]

Vodou is the ultimate marker of Haitianness. It is a fusion of spiritual
and cultural practices from several African nations and is the ultimate
expression of enslaved people coalescing across language and experience. It was also one way enslaved people built communities of consensus. Carpentier represents those who fully embrace this religion, such
as Ti Noël, Boukman, and Macandal, as embodying what is truly generative and empowering about Haiti's example and contribution to the
Caribbean, the world, and especially Europe. Ti Noël, while exiled with
his masters and other planters who fled Haiti for Cuba, notes that Spanish churches have "a Voodoo warmth . . . a power of seduction in presence, symbols, attributes, and signs similar to those of the altars of the
houmforts consecrated to Damballah, the Snake god."[123]

Carpentier's unconventional vision, based on an emerging articulation of the Marvelous Realism, is not as overt in its linking of a black
Caribbean past with a pan-African present. His search for alternatives
to Europe meant a construction of Haiti through Vodou and its manifestation of Caribbeanness accomplished by highlighting the African
origins of his Caribbean characters. In many ways, while the other two
literary texts discussed here are indeed pan-Africanist, Carpentier's is the
most Caribbean—centered and most concerned with the cultural formations in the region. Carpentier's writing could be construed as reactionary
since he responds to the classification of postwar European decay. According to Barbara Webb, the novelist believed that "Haiti represented the 'magical crossroads' of the New World history and culture. . . . In Caribbean

discourse, Haiti is often portrayed as the site of a revelation of consciousness. . . . Carpentier saw Haiti as the antithesis and antidote to
European cultural domination."[124] Out of this revelation and his experience with surrealists in France, "Carpentier returned to the Americas to formulate his own concept of the marvelous," which, steeped in
a Caribbean past, is in keeping with Wilson Harris's representations of
the region.[125] Carpentier, like Harris, effectively chronicles the marvelous by confronting linear formations of space and time (see discussion of
Macandal's execution below). These writers scrutinize history as theme
and discipline by refashioning and rewriting Caribbean stories, defying
narrow notions of reality.

Carpentier obliquely refers to the revolutionaries most associated
with the liberation of Saint-Domingue and devotes much of his energy to
envisioning the worldview of magic-spiritual leaders—Macandal (from
Africa), Boukman, (a Jamaican), and Christophe (originally from Grenada or St. Kitts), king and builder of the ruins that Carpentier visited in
1943. Carpentier's Haitians, those who dynamically belong to the soil,
are, for the most part, Vodou acolytes despite the historical hostility to
the religion by Toussaint, Dessalines, and Christophe. He depicts this
religion, linked to the earth and the ancestors, in a mystical way. Vodou
is literally transformative: Macandal, Mama Loi, Boukman, and eventually Ti Noël are able to shape-shift. Their lycanthropic powers fuel the
fire of Carpentier's emphasis on magic and its traces to the highly problematic *Magic Island*. On the one hand, while Macandal and Boukman
are depicted in a way that veers toward the romantic, they are unswerv-
ingly loyal to the black liberation cause. On the other hand, Lizabeth
Paravisini-Gebert disagrees with any grand and noble reading of Carpentier's text. In her opinion, his novel never manages to move "beyond
its time."[126] Paravisini-Gebert's challenge focuses primarily on what she
terms Carpentier's exoticism and fetishism of Vodou and his emascula-
tion through omission of revolutionary leaders such as Toussaint and
Dessalines. Critics Jeannette Allsopp and J. Jebodhsingh counter, arguing that Carpentier recalibrates the vision of the Haitian Revolution by
shifting the gaze to the leaders most connected to the masses, namely,
Macandal and Boukman. Today, the Revolution has come to simultaneously signify hopelessness and audacity.

In rehearsal, choices are enacted: do it this way or try it that way. When
a method ceases to work, it is shifted, revised, sometimes just through
nuanced shifts in perception. Paravisini-Gebert quotes Joan Dayan's
call for "representations that remain open, incomplete, contestable, and

sometimes unsatisfactory in terms of 'literary' values: order, lyricism, eloquence, or beauty."[127] Accordingly, seeing the past through prismatic nuances leads to change and is ultimately the legacy of *Kingdom of This World*. As with the other texts on the Haitian Revolution, this novel uses these events to construct notions of Caribbean belonging juxtaposing Mandingo manhood, the hypersexual stereotype of black men, with limp European essence. Spiritual-political leaders, particularly Ti Noël's hero Macandal, are represented as virile, noble, African warrior—kings whose "precious seed distended hundreds of bellies with a mighty strain of heroes."[128] In this instance, as with Césaire's Christophe, Macandal is the nation's progenitor, implanting literal and figurative Haitianness. His African leadership style exists in opposition to European norms. As a king, Macandal leads his generals in battle, unlike the kings of Spain and France who "send their generals to fight in their stead."[129] The opening and closing chapters of Carpentier's novel juxtapose a waning, waxed, and debauched Europe with a throbbing, mysterious Africa in the Caribbean. Yet the throbbing harks back to the mystical, magic island, which is why Paravisini-Gebert's arguments are salient. Ti Noël awaits his master, M. Lenormand de Mézy, who visits the barber and observes that the wax heads in the barber's window are like the pickled calves heads in the neighboring butcher shop:

> [Ti Noël] . . . in a kind of mental counterpoint silently hummed a chanty . . . that even though the words were not in Creole, [heaped] ignominy on the King of England. . . . He had little esteem for the King of England, or the King of France, or of Spain, who ruled the other half of the Island, and whose wives, according to Macandal, tinted their cheeks with oxblood and buried fœtuses in a convent whose cellars were filled with skeletons that had been rejected by the true heaven which wanted nothing to do with those who died ignoring the true gods.[130]

These examples highlight Europe as waxen, waning, and headless—its future and its present entombed with fetuses in the cellars of virginal and/or celibate orders. Europe has its own pagan blood rites and rituals, and Ti Noël makes it clear that he has "little esteem" for kingship in a European mold. These kings who had no strength, who were associated with skeletons and the unborn dead, did not impress him because, like Christophe to come, they ignored the true gods.

Paravisini-Gebert convincingly claims that Carpentier creates an otherizing, mystical, sensational version of Haitian Vodou and likewise constructs the peasants of Haiti as passive subalterns of destiny. She effectively argues that Carpentier's use of the Haitian peasant and Vodou reinscribes Haiti—and by extension, Haitians—as fetishized and exotic:

> Carpentier stands in that slightly ambiguous terrain[,] . . . committed on the one hand to an alternative depiction of Haitian history that emphasizes the people's enduring faith in Vodou and the *loas*, yet not unwilling to fetishize aspects of that faith in his text in his quest for the magic-realist unveiling of that history required by the new literature he envisioned—a literature whose inspiration was to be found not in an autochthonous Caribbean tradition but in a more authentic version of literary Modernity than that proposed by European Surrealism.[131]

Paravisini-Gebert argues that while Carpentier links Dessalines to Vodou, he does so in a way that "underscores the connection between Dessalines's ferocity and . . . his adherence with a militant blackness," which she claims makes him the most radical figure of the Revolution. The veneration of Dessalines reached its apogee in the 1940s and, as Paravisini-Gebert argues, was widespread enough that Carpentier would have been made aware of it during his 1943 visit.[132]

Unlike in the Judeo-Christian example, in which death equals the end of possibility, African-connected heroes triumph over and are full of strength and vitality when they die. When the one-armed Macandal is captured and sentenced to be burned alive, black people gather to witness, but chaos breaks out and the crowd is distracted. In the fracas, soldiers throw Macandal into the fire, head first, but he is later believed to have escaped: "When the slaves were restored to order, the fire was burning normally. . . . There was no longer anything more to see. That afternoon the slaves returned to their plantations laughing all the way. Macandal had kept his word, remaining in the Kingdom of This World. Once more the whites had been outwitted by the Mighty Powers of the Other Shore."[133] Through metamorphosis, Macandal remains in this world and is able to propel the Revolution because he established himself as a shape-shifter. That aspect of his legend fuels resistance, and slaves can laugh in the face of seeming annihilation because a Vodou worldview allows them to envision more than one reality. Here, the "hearse" aspect of rehearsal does not simply carry a dead body; it carries possibilities. Macandal's "escape" from slavery and his outwitting of the imperial power structure reinforce black hope and the possibility of besting the slave system. Paravisini-Gebert characterizes Macandal's outmaneuvering as yet another example of Carpentier's otherizing of the Haitian masses because, "even in his depiction of Makandal's execution in the novel, which is intended to signal the extraordinary power of the slaves to maintain their faith in Makandal's survival despite the reality before them, Carpentier still inscribed the scene with their otherness. After all, the slaves may be deluded by faith into believing that Makandal survived. The planters and soldiers of the text—and most importantly, Carpentier and his readers—know he has not."[134]

Carpentier *does* implicate himself, the soldiers, and those who "know," in other words, readers, as a part of a dying society, their logic limited by the inability to imagine a revolution by slaves. This inability is similar to the distinction between science, or the knowable universe (man as god), and alchemy, an unknowable universe (man with God), in which linear characterizations are a death while a multiplicity of readings foster life. Carpentier, as the creator or writer of this representation, is implicated by his lack of faith and understanding of what the New World has produced. Suggestive of readers and these white characters, Carpentier-as-writer knows the facts, but these facts have led nowhere. Yet, implicated by his socialization and contextualization, he too may have found it difficult to embrace the uniqueness of this personality that he ultimately values. Carpentier illustrates that Vodou (and perhaps by extension Afro-Caribbean religions generally) is a way to reclaim the enslaved person's sense of self and humanity in the face of overwhelming obstacles. It claims a way of being in the world and is a more dimensional construct than one simply designed to evoke the magical. It is about believing that the facts are not automatically true or real.

The fact of death does not limit the power to lead and inspire. Boukman, leader at the Bois Caïman secret ceremony that began the Revolution, ends up with his head on a pike, but like Macandal before him, he lived on through transformation—in other words, being headless did not mitigate Boukman's influence on the revolutionary process. The people of Saint Dominigue fighting for their freedom believed in Boukman's spirit as their leader. Conversely, even the maligned and paralyzed Christophe actively chose "his own death, . . . would never know the corruption of his flesh, flesh fused with the very stuff of the fortress, inscribed in its architecture, integrated with its body, bristling with flying buttresses. Le Bonnet de l'Évêque, the whole mountain, had become the mausoleum of the first King of Haiti."[135] This death and the idea of Henri Christophe forever soldered to the bricks of the fortress—forever among the people—might inspire terror. As male-centered as the others, Carpentier's text more generally constructs Caribbean belonging and masculinity in opposition to European norms. His overarching emphasis on this dichotomy, though with male figures, is not the same salvation of black manhood seen in the works by James and Césaire. Nonetheless, these three representations of the Haitian Revolution are limited by testosterone-heavy constructions of masculinity. Apart from James's excellent and enlightened portrayal of Marie-Jeanne, especially in the absence of other models, there are no other counterpoints to the Revolution as an orgy.

It is clear in global constructions of black male savages why Dessalines remains a difficult figure to embrace. And though the Haitian masses embrace Dessalines in death, it is not until the advent of twentieth-century postcolonial struggles, especially those in Africa, that Caribbean writers confront—in their lifetimes, through their experience—issues of armed struggle and the notion of annihilating one's oppressor. Paravisini-Gebert's criticism of Carpentier is that he exoticizes Haiti and never takes the characters beyond the realm of fascination because he is locked into the idea of history as circular; he cannot move beyond embedded structures of power, therefore Carpentier characterizes Henri Christophe as the white master in blackface who will be followed by mulattoes "repeating" the same behavior.

This is one reading to which I would add that both James and Césaire were similarly unable in their representations to move beyond these conceptions. To Paravisini-Gebert's point that Dessalines is the only revolutionary to truly challenge the entrenched system and whom Carpentier replaces with a chapter on the excesses of Pauline Bonaparte, I would counter in two ways: first, the representation of Pauline as the alive-but-dead ultimate European zombie is exactly Carpentier's point; second, Dessalines as hero is something that James and Césaire have difficulty celebrating because they are both intimidated and overwhelmed by his savagery. Conceivably, if Carpentier had ingested Vodou, that is, had *be*come it rather than simply imbibed it, he would have embraced a worldview that allowed him to conceive and inscribe a more challenging text in that regard.

The transactions between fighting for power, maintaining power, and the power of memory are all critical parts of these texts. The negotiations between Toussaint, Christophe, Dessalines, and their generals were all aimed at doing what they believed best for forming the nation. Additionally, the representations of manhood that James, Césaire, and Carpentier propose are engaged in a series of exchanges with political and imperial European masculinity. The twentieth-century recuperation and validation of the leaders of the Haitian Revolution create a time line, a connection, and a justification of black (male) political power in the twentieth-century Caribbean. In both the event of the Revolution and the representation of it, Caribbean men negotiate belonging in the region—their home spaces—via the deployment of physical force, religious ritual, and their relationships with women. However, these same male identities are not formed in a vacuum; rather, they are created in relation to coercive pressures and other examples of male power from Europe and the United States, which produces and reproduces multiple meanings of power and masculinity. The three creative pieces discussed here reiterate the nature of symbolic power and how it relates to political power. Both historically and in these fictions, the leaders of the Haitian Revolution all deployed various symbols of power—castles, religion, constructions of the nation as family, and literacy—and used them to negotiate for power and legitimacy, both in Haiti and with the wider world, which sought to consign Haitian freedom to a space of degeneracy, savagery, and unmitigated evil. The need to establish both Haitian humanity and state legitimacy manifested through these texts. Similarly, in representing the revolutionary experience, James, Césaire, and Carpentier used symbolic power to create narratives of the past that would unite people across the region while also constructing a version of black manhood that was and is seldom allowed to exist in the Americas. Their constructions are not only rehearsals of historical figures as religious leaders, prophets, and soldiers, but each rehearsal emphasizes the multiple negotiations of these identities.

The negotiations that women make in these male-centered texts are marginally mentioned but equally relevant because they highlight the distortion of women and their representation in the nation-building process. In these texts, black women are either absent or, as in the case of *Kingdom of This World*, in which Pauline Bonaparte is the only representation of an avaricious elite white woman, as an imperial trophy and a sexual agent. In Césaire's play, women are encouragers; they nurture the nation into being by supporting male leaders or are vessels with limited voice whose intimate lives are regulated by the state.

James's text, however, manages to present complex representations of women. The construction of Marie-Jeanne makes legible the many transactions in which revolutionary women engaged. Marie-Jeanne has sex with French generals in order to procure information for the revolutionary forces, and she supports Dessalines once she realizes Toussaint plans to remain attached to France. These exchanges made in the context of the revolutionary moment highlight the nature of power and the use of power in a relational rather than hierarchical way. Furthermore, for the twentieth-century time line, Marie-Jeanne is the antecedent for the women who wielded political power in the decolonizing struggle, some of whom James knew by the time he rewrote the play in the late 1960s.

In essence, these writers answered the question posed in Haiti's Declaration of Independence: "What are you waiting for before appeasing their spirits?" These works are about appeasing the spirits, both the historical ones and those at the core of the postcolonial independence project. James, Césaire, and Carpentier understood the importance of resting with the ancestral bones. Their works celebrate and memorialize these bones and the history of men often consigned to the hearse of rigid boxes of interpretation, even as their depictions of women are generally flat. The tension between these depictions of men and women reveal the problematics of men involved in nationalist projects representing women. While the writers discussed here all felt it critical to recuperate black masculinity, they were less concerned about the role of women in the process of nation building. Such omissions mitigate some of the power and the possibilities of these nonetheless relevant texts.

3   Hope and Infinity

THE HAITIAN REVOLUTION IS ONE EXAMPLE of the belief in possibility and transformation against overwhelming odds. The triumph of enslaved people over Napoleon's forces, armies that had subjugated a wide swath of Europe, was hardly imaginable. The story is not just inspirational to Haitians and to the whole Caribbean, but it represents the nexus of black masculinity asserting itself beyond the colonial regime that oppressed and denied it.

In this chapter, I complicate the work of chapter 2 by situating the feminine within these masculinized constructions of national belonging. Here, feminist rehearsal places narratives of Haitian history by women at the center of the Haitian story. Implicitly, it is important to consider narratives presented in ways other than those privileging a male emphasis on particular forms of literary argument. Here, I incorporate the perspectives of Haitian women through two of Rose Marie Desruisseau's paintings from 1986, *Vodou Ceremony* and *The Ceremony of Bois Caïman*, and Edwidge Danticat's short story "A Wall of Fire Rising." These alternate representations of the Revolution do two things: value the revolutionary masses rather than the heroes who were central in chapter 2, and serve as a Haitian counterpoint to those three texts written by non-Haitians. Foregrounding twentieth- and twenty-first-century Haitian women's voices builds on Joan Dayan's construction of the Haitian heroine Défilée, or Défilée la Folle (Défilée the Madwoman), who gathered the pieces of Jean-Jacques Dessalines's mutilated body and buried them.[1]

I place Desruisseau's paintings and Danticat's story in dialogue with the representations of the Revolution by James, Césaire, and Carpentier for the purpose of rehearsing the Revolution from other vantage points. I hasten to add, however, that I am not arguing that non-Haitians should not present or re-present the Haitian experience. Instead, I want to focus here on twentieth-century representations of this seminal event by Haitian women.

This chapter extends my prolonged fascination with the possibilities of the Revolution as it relates to the Haitian and wider-Caribbean story. I am particularly interested in the feminist rehearsals of various Caribbean temporalities and the possibilities provided by cultural artifacts to help develop the creative capacity to understand and critically read these specific periods. The moment of the Haitian Revolution offers particularly fruitful opportunities, as Dayan has shown, to challenge the prevailing hegemonic narratives that generally consume representations of the event.

According to the following accounts, Défilée negotiated her belonging to the revolutionary Haitian nation in several ways. She was a patriot who mourned the death of her parents, brothers, sons, and perhaps a lover. In one account, she was a sex worker negotiating the space of grief and survival.[2] Rehearsing Défilée's story is important because she, while memorialized and celebrated as a national hero, reconstituted the Haitian nation by collecting the pieces of Dessalines's body. In these versions, Défilée's body is involved in multiple transactions—not only through sex work and as a market woman but also as the collector of Dessalines's flesh. Défilée's role as the nationalist adhesive is a romantic symbol indicating women's revolutionary function while, at the same time, emphasizing the limited revolutionary promise for women.

Défilée's apparent madness (discussed below) is brought on by a series of circumstances born of violence. Similarly, depictions of the Revolution by Haitian women occur within the context of women's daily realities. The conditions in the nation affect women's bodies in particular ways and have an impact on the negotiations they must make; Défilée's story, then, serves as a significant marker and reminder of women's experiences during national formation. While Défilée re-forms the nation, the figures in Desruisseau's paintings and the mother, Lili, in Danticat's story produce their own reformations, manifested through Vodou imagery and negotiations of the contemporary Haitian economic terrain. These representations are not grand schemes but intimate engagements of both revolutionary possibility and revolutionary fatigue.

Rehearsing Défilée's story—one intricately tied to the ways in which the Haitian nation imagines itself—reveals how women and their relationships to their own and other bodies framed belonging from Haiti's inception. The versions of Défilée's story begin with her more commonly known moniker, Défilée *la folle*, but she was born Dédée Bazile. Bazile's life is overshadowed by the gaps and absences that characterize the lives of the largely undocumented Haitian masses. Her shifting narrative occupies a great space in the Haitian imagination, and, as Dayan chronicles in *Haiti, History, and the Gods*, the myth of Défilée erases the reality of Dédée Bazile. The agreed-upon facts of her life are that she was raped at eighteen by her master, became a sutler for the Haitian army, and helped move Dessalines's remains for burial.[3]

There are some representations of Défilée as Dessalines's friend, and others as his maligned lover whom he discarded for his lighter-skinned wife, Claire Félicité Guillaume Bonheur, or, as she is more commonly known, Marie-Claire Heureuse. To these biographical details, Jana Evans Braziel adds that Dédée Bazile was born in Cap Haïtien to slave parents, gave birth to several children, and died during Pétion's presidency in 1816 when she was thought to be close to eighty years old.[4]

There are also varying stories about the reasons Dédée Bazile became known as *la folle*. Braziel recounts several narratives of Défilée's loss of sanity and also suggests that she may not have been mad at all. In one version, Défilée is crazy because Dessalines abandoned her for Heureuse. In another, her family's massacre by French soldiers is the reason for her madness. Dayan adds to these stories with several rehearsals of her own finding, the first from Ertha Pascal-Trouillot's work: "She had a wild passion for Dessalines that exacerbated the mental troubles caused by the slaughter of her parents by French soldiers. . . . She was not simply a market woman or meat vendor, who followed the Haitian Revolutionary Army as it marched, but, unstrung by the loss of her parents and her love for Dessalines, she supplied the soldiers with sex."[5]

In the second story, centenarian Joseph Jérémie recalls, "One night Défilée's two sons and three brothers, all of whom were enlisted in the army, did not return from a party in the Cahos mountains. There was an ambush and 600 'slaves' were massacred by General Rochambeau's officers. The news unhinged Dédée's mind, but she continued to follow Dessalines's army as a sutler."[6] Whereas Pascal-Trouillot alludes to the effects of Dédée's infatuation with Dessalines, her wild passion for him is transformed into the practice and pursuit of unhinged sexual labor, for Jeremie, Dédée follows Dessalines despite her madness, not as a result of it, and Jeremie is impressed by her inspiring effect on the soldiers and Dessalines's "fatherly love for his devotee."[7] Thus, from the earliest surviving accounts of Dédée Bazile, there is conflict and multiplicity. As Braziel elaborates, Défilée is a site of memory, and she explores Dédée/Défilée through her biography, her mythos, and her link to Dessalines as

La Marasa, "the contradictory and complementary forces of nature" in Vodou.[8] The idea of the body and legacy of Défilée as a site of memory— an archive per se—challenges our notion of "site" as a physical locale because Défilée's body has long turned to bone and disintegrated into dust. Nonetheless, she has become a national metaphoric monument, unlike Christophe, who is buried in Citadelle La Ferrière and is memorialized and represented as the Haitian nation.[9] But there are no physical memorials to Défilée, even in Haiti.

Dessalines rallied support by cursing reluctant fighters, telling them that the fallen and sacrificed ancestors would reject their bones. In turn, Défilée's attentiveness to Dessalines's remains seems part of not only funerary rites but the connection between material bodies and history. Défilée functions as a hearse in two ways: by physically carrying Dessalines's body and, by so doing, making his body visible to others as she walks through the streets. Furthermore, she also carries the violence of the state—initially French colonial forces and then revolutionary forces—on her body. She is marked. Dayan posits that this upends the notion of Défilée as crazy because she has become the wise diviner instead of the penitent, crazy devotee. If sane, Défilée as national foremother shapes both a ritual and a space of survival for Haitian women.

Dayan characterizes Défilée's story as one that embodies the Haitian nation, "crazed and lost, but then redeemed through the body of their savior."[10] Both Dayan and Myriam J. A. Chancy argue that people are more interested in the myth of Défilée than in the person Dédée. Such mythology obscures and erases the real woman, and the lives of Haitian women. Thus, this chapter emphasizes Dédée Bazile/Défilée as a visible and known representation of the many women who fought for Haitian freedom, who were traumatized, silenced, and made invisible by it. The emphasis on largely hagiographic representations of male revolutionaries by twentieth-century male writers creates a cultural void and erases women from our knowing. Whether as mythical Défilée or mundane Dédée, this story serves to create a mutual space for readers for reimaging Haitian potentiality.

As both Glissant and Chancy surmise, the lacunae in Dédée's story are part of an untold and rarely accessed archive. Chancy believes we need to remember that women were always part of armed struggles and revolutionary undercurrents: "The fictional is therefore a conduit for a historical narrative that is elsewhere denied existence."[11] Chancy argues that, in using the novel to realign the power structures of a given historical moment, "it becomes necessary to define the novelist literary tradition of Haitian women as one that transgresses nationalistic ideologies and reformulates nation and identity through the lens of personal and communal exile."[12]

Because fiction is one way of filling this archival gap, Défilée not only offers a counternarrative to the glories of national belonging, but her myth, madness, and rape are collectively an early inscription of the silenced traumas endured by women and men pursuing the most regressive nationalisms. Défilée and other women temper the glorification of foundational myths that sanitized and mitigate the brutality and violence of their belonging. And, as Dayan observes, women's "stories are something of an interlude in the business of *making history*. . . . More significant, at least in most standard histories, especially those written by foreigners, the mulatto women who fought with the black rebels, and even took part in the ceremony of Bois-Caïman, are not mentioned" (emphasis in the original).[13] These absences, and the rarity with which women are mentioned in historical narratives, mean actively engaging with history in order to undermine hegemonic constructions of national formation. Indeed, as Anne McClintock reminds us, nationalisms are always shaped by gender power, and women's contributions are reduced from being active fighters defending their homes to being producers of children, particularly of young men whose ideologies support the nation. By defining women as victims and weeping mothers, "their activism could be overlooked and their disempowerment ratified."[14] Indeed, Défilée as a madwoman roaming the streets fulfills both the victim and the weeping woman personification.

Therefore, using Défilée as a frame within which to read the revolutionary archives and these cultural representations reconstitutes the revolutionary time and the moments of visual and literary production. Rehearsing Défilée reiterates how national belonging, or citizenship, has been masculinized. Desruisseau's painting and Danticat's story allow alternatives to the hero worship of Haitian male revolutionaries. The previous chapter revealed the feminine as either passive or hypersexual according to anticolonial activists C. L. R. James, Aimé Césaire, and Alejo Carpentier in their masculinized construction of the Haitian Revolution. The feminine is often symbolic in nationalist accounts. Women's belonging either happens through male conduits (fathers, husbands, brothers, and sons), as the embodiment of republican womanhood (particularly motherhood), or as reviled sexual aggressors and deviants. Desruisseau and Danticat offer not only the everyday heroics of ordinary woman but also her experience as a contradiction to national narratives and male heroes; in so doing, they celebrate the extraordinary abilities women—and by extension the nation—need for daily survival.

Vodou Rising

In the words of art historian and curator Gérald Alexis, "one cannot deal with [Haitian] historical painting without mentioning Rose Marie Desruisseau. She devoted her entire life to a historical collection of colossal proportions."[15] Born in 1933 in Port-au-Prince, Desruisseau began painting at a young age. As a high school student in 1948, she took classes at the Centre d'Art with Lucien Price, one of the founders of the Foyer des Arts Plastiques (Home of the Visual Arts), who worked with abstraction as early as the 1940s and is considered the father of Haitian modern art.[16] Desruisseau's family was concerned about her reputation as a woman in a largely male artistic environment, and, under pressure from them, she put her art aside and worked in public administration for ten years.[17] By 1958, she had begun full-time studies at the Foyer des Arts Plastiques, eventually renamed the Academy of Fine Arts, where she found herself among the "painters and sculptors, poets and novelists, singers and theater people who frequented the Brochette gallery. [This] group of artists [had no formal mandate] and provided a haven, sheltered from the tourist market, which, since the late forties," had shaped what Haitian artists produced,[18] with its emphasis on the "primitive" artist.[19] Additionally, she sought out and worked with many of Haiti's most famous artists, including Pétion Savain, whose illustrated novel *Damballah's Shack* "mark[ed] the first deliberate use of Vaudou [sic] as a paradigm of 'the Haitian' in the visual arts";[20] Dieudonne Cédor; and Nehemy Jean. Jean was disgruntled with the Centre d'Art's emphasis on exploiting untrained "primitive" artists "as authentically Haitian" and so cofounded the Foyer des Arts Plastiques with Price in 1950, through which they sought to delimit the split between the primitives and the Haitian intelligentsia's focus on modernism by "translat[ing it] into something more relevant to the Haitian public."[21] In the 1960s, Desruisseau became a Vodou initiate, and her later work is infused with a modernist take on both historical and Vodou iconography, "which she considered the most important element of national culture."[22]

Desruisseau is known for representing historical, religious, and sensual themes in her work, often in unorthodox ways. Part of the generation of artists famous for incorporating Vodou as an aesthetic, a sensibility, a profound way of being, and a form of national identification, she was one of a handful of women at the forefront of midcentury visual art in

Haiti, "though she was at odds with the [largely tourist-driven] artistic traditions established during the thirties and forties."[23] The quality and range of subject matter, and eras of its creation, make Desruisseau's work significant to exploring questions of memory, belonging, and sexuality.

As part of nationalist projects of affirmation against colonial emotional, spiritual, and physical devaluation, visual art has played a meaningful role in Caribbean culture. In Haiti, the visual arts have a long history, though much of Haiti's colonial art was destroyed during the Revolution.[24] Nineteenth-century art was shaped by portrait and landscape painting that emphasized European styles. By midcentury, "obsequious copying" reinforced alienation from the country's realities, while also proliferating "amateur paintings with snow-covered mountains and still lifes with apples and pears . . . under the tropical sun."[25]

Formalized approaches in Haitian art began as early as Christophe's reign. He established the Academy of Arts in 1817, directed by the British painter Richard Evans.[26] Drawing was a mandatory part of the curriculum under Alexandre Pétion's government, Emperor Faustin I had an official court painter (Baron Colbert de Lochard), and the National School of Painting was founded in 1865, though it closed and reopened several times.[27] Additionally, L. G. Hoffman asserts that African American artist William Scott inspired his students, among them Pétion Savain, to start an art school.[28] This stop-and-start method of formal artistic training was largely imitative, but things changed in the 1930s when Haitians channeled their sentiments against U.S. occupation (1915–1934) into their art and the work of constructing a vision of themselves as a people through the culture of the masses.[29] Moreover, visitors from Cuba (Wilfredo Lam), Martinique (Aimé Césaire), and the United States (Aaron Douglas, Zora Neale Hurston, and Langston Hughes, among many others of the Harlem Renaissance) illustrate the circularity of ideas such as modernism within the Caribbean in the 1930s. By the 1940s, two Paris-based UNESCO exhibitions (in 1946 and 1947) internationalized Haitian art. These exhibitions, in conjunction with the May 1944 establishment of the joint U.S.-Haitian art school and gallery, the Centre d'Art, transformed the Haitian art scene.[30] In fact, the Centre d'Art's history is fraught with controversy: some credit it with formalizing Haitian art, while some, like contemporary artist André Juste, characterize it as "midwifed by the U.S. State Department's local proxy, the Haitian-American Institute, as part of a much broader strategy to buttress American hegemony in Latin America and the Caribbean."[31]

Nonetheless, twentieth-century Haitian painting intervenes in cultural, political, and social narratives of occupation and dictatorship and performs resistant—if sometimes co-opted—national identity by rehearsing history and commodification.[32]

Though historically under siege, Vodou is an important if contested part of Haitian identity. As the dictum goes, "Haiti is 90% Catholic, and 100% voodoo,"[33] which gestures toward the formulation of Vodou as a revolutionary spirituality, with an outlaw status, persecuted for more than 150 years, co-opted by the state, and marketed to tourists. Despite this riddled and complicated history, Vodou and its visual language serve as a "sign" of Haitianness whether one identifies as a practitioner or not. The Indigenist movement began as a "reevaluation to U.S. occupation"[34] and led to a valorization of Vodou and peasant culture. The mulatto elite and emerging black middle-class artists realized the treasure trove of stories, iconography, and performance embedded in Vodou and so exploited it in order to develop a national identity. Encouraged by Jean Price Mars's 1928 collection of essays *And Thus Spoke Uncle*, which decried European imitation and validated Vodou, these artists, across their many genres, signaled the beginnings of a Haitian cultural nationalism.[35] In addition, Vodou was and is positioned against Europeanness as a source of indigenous power in which Haitians see themselves positively as different from Europeans. Vodou-as-counterpoint is widely believed to be an empowering practice. But Sidney Mintz and Michel-Rolph Trouillot warn:

> Though we would firmly contend that Vodou was important in the emerging [revolutionary] struggle of the slaves against slavery and of the Haitian people against their French rulers, it seems to us simplistic to make of religious belief the linchpin of the resistance. It is probably more important to try to document the complex social organization of the colony . . . before speculating about the importance of religion in the formation of the slaves' resistance to slavery. We believe that the religious orientation of many or even most of the slaves played a part in their resistance to the horrors of slavery. But there were doubtless many individuals and some groups for whom Vodou was not important.[36]

And while this warning is valuable in understanding history, Vodou as central to Haitian identity was nonetheless believed, imbibed, internalized, and rehearsed by Haitian artists. Gérald Alexis believes that the lack of nineteenth-century visual patrimony has encouraged an emphasis on historical and historical-spiritual themes in contemporary works.

Indeed, the Centre d'Art "was mandated to develop an expression of Haitian painting rooted in folklore, and the national and natural history of Haiti."[37] These factors, along with a quest to solidify Haitian identity, thus meant that, whether for expediency or a quest for self, Vodou was centralized even while still illegal. Deployed by the mulatto and political elite, in what Mintz and Trouillot characterize as "cultural embezzlement,"[38] yet followed by the majority of Haitians in some form or fashion, Vodou thus inhabits and creates a complex locus for the negotiation of social, cultural, and sometimes political power among practitioners, drawn primarily from Haiti's peasantry; among artists, privileged with education and access to multiple audiences; and among the mulatto and political elite, who have manipulated its symbols in their efforts to consolidate political power.

Amid, and perhaps in part because of, the multiple demands placed upon it, Vodou remains a living religion born of the struggle of the Haitian people and based on serving the *loas,* or spirits, through rituals and ceremonies. Vodou is a practice not based on written dogma or a centralized church but, rather, is tied to the experiences of its practitioners and their deeply embedded relationships. The relationships among practitioners and between practitioners and the spirits are characterized through performance, be it dance or other ritual, and couched in deeply familial terms because Vodou is a communal rather than a solitary practice, one that mirrors the structures of family and mutual support. Vodou is about service, the performance of ritual practice, rather than a particular set of tenets. In other words, there is no scripture; instead Vodou emerges from the experiences of a community and that community's relationship with its ancestors, *loas*, and guiding spirits.

Desruisseau signals multiple rehearsals using a Vodou lexicon and historical themes with work she produced in the 1980s. Her images rehearse revolutionary ideas of several time periods, particularly in moments of transformation, that is, "convulsions" in Haitian history, some of which are discussed in chapter 2. Desruisseau's 1986 painting *Vodou Ceremony* is dominated by seven figures, divided by a shaft of candlelight into a group of five on the left and two on the right. Of the two right-hand figures, one is a man with closed eyes, shaking the *ason*—a rattle with a bell and netted beads used to call the Rada spirits; the other is of indistinguishable gender—he or she seems to have breasts but wears no headscarf—clad in black pants and red top, holding a knife above the flame. The figure opposite this character, with similar facial expressions, is clearly female, her own knife crossing that of her mirror image. Staged above her head are two similarly adorned women, though depicted in richer, deeper reds, each with a decidedly different expression: one looking askance in curiosity, the other with eyes calmly closed. Above these women are two bodiless heads, cast in shadow, receding into the soft indigo of the background.

The crossed knives intersect just above the yellow flame of the white candle, anchoring the viewer's eye and drawing attention to a bottle that hovers above them, the thumb of the right-hand background figure visible as the hand grasps it. The scene's backdrop consists of a red flag attached to a pole held in the hand of one of the figures on the left; it traverses the frame from left to right, flying like a pennant, its widest section illuminated by the column of radiant candlelight.

The central shaft of candlelight figuratively functions as the *pòto-mitan*,[39] the grounding pole of the Vodou temple: "The *pòto-mitan* is a vertical portal or gateway whose function is to create an open road between Ginen [the land of the dead] and the land of the living,"[40] simultaneously ascending and descending. Desruisseau's column of light also brings to mind the cornmeal-drawn *vèvès*, beacons that often surround the *pòto-mitan* and that call and then represent the *loa* in Vodou rituals: "a lighted candle . . . placed in the center of the *vèvè* reiterates the vertical lines of the *pòto-mitan* and offsets the intersection point between the place of the living, the place of the spirits and the dead."[41]

The painting depicts the intimate environment of an enclosed community, compressed by both the physical frame of the painting and their collective attention to the objects and performance before them. While there is no sense of what else exists beyond the frame, the space beyond the five humans is complemented by the two incorporeal heads—but are they human or spirits? This surrounding space is filled with *something* spiritual, iterated in the clarity of these two faces that recede from the plane through Desruisseau's fainter brushstrokes. This conveys ethereality, suggesting the merging of spiritual and physical spheres.

The light thrown by the candle dances among shades of bluish-white and deeper indigo. Among the seven figures, red, the color of Papa Ogun, the blacksmith and warrior *loa*, is the predominant color. These hues blend in some areas but are then bisected by a stark curvature suggesting the ring of light cast by the candle that follows the line of the left knife wielder's arm. The crossed knives are an entreaty of iron, another reference to Ogun and war, and the foreground figures who hold them, mouths agape as if singing or shouting a battle cry, thrust their torsos toward the light.

Where the crossed swords illustrate a call to arms, other of the painting's iconography tells a similar story. Both of the foreground figures wear the red armbands of the Cacos, an "irregular peasant-based militia, known in the south as *piquets*, and in the north as *cacos*, [who] mobilise[d] to challenge the authority of the central government" in the 1840s[42] and again in 1867.[43] The Cacos reemerged in the twentieth century to fight a guerrilla war against the 1915 U.S. invasion. Led by Charlemagne Péralte and Benoît Betraville, with more than two thousand irregulars, the Cacos Rebellion of 1918 was an insurgency supported across Haiti. Thus, Desruisseau's work, painted seventy years later, invokes multiple time lines by rehearsing the Revolution, Haiti's nineteenth-century rebellions, and the nation's twentieth-century resistance to occupation.

Desruisseau's use of circles rehearses the geometric design prominent in *vèvè* drawings, and her use of light calls to mind the work of Harlem Renaissance painter Aaron Douglas, who visited Haiti in the 1930s. Though Desruisseau was only five at that time, Douglas did meet Savain, her onetime mentor. Specifically, in *Vodou Ceremony*, the panels and circles of light are abstracted by decisive shifts in color and hue and challenge the naturalistic aspects of the image. The use of light and the manner in which Desruisseau imposes an abstract pattern onto the composition utilizes early twentieth-century modernist visual language (remarkably like Marc Chagall, who used abstraction to address the persecution of Jews during World War I). The flattening of space abstracts the images, especially those of the two possible spirits, one of whom is drawn with little color and shading, the other drawn only in black-and-white outline, while the contrasts between light and dark create a (constructed, if not false) sense of depth.

There is a tension here, a conversation between what is naturalistic, that is, the world of the living, and what is flat, the spirit world. Yet they coexist, just as Vodou does with the other Christian religions of Haiti. Desruisseau imbues *Vodou Ceremony* with the sense of emerging and retreating from the spiritual world, the living residing among and with the dead, and creates a liminal space between these worlds while never eliminating their interactive ability.

Desruisseau's depiction of the simultaneity of the dead and the living, of the past and the present, echoes the structure of Vodou ceremonies. Service to and for the *loa* often begins with an invocation of a universal god, Bondye. The *aprés Bondye* (after Bondye) begins with the pater noster followed by another, the Priyè Ginen, which recounts histories and

ruisseau's paintings of Haitian Revolution rehearsals show revo-
at its most collaborative and communal. The paintings emphasize
y the relational nature of Vodou practice but the fierce determina-
Haiti's men and women to transform their society and end slav-
eir determined faces and joyful dancing, coupled with weapons
g from sticks to knives, reveal a version of the Revolution at its
omestic yet most dramatic. Women in both pieces are armed and
and they are central actors in the frame. They are on the fore-
f the action because the systems of oppression—be they slavery
upation—affect their lives. These images rupture the romance of
itary messianic leader by painting broader tableaux of the actors
d.

ruisseau's *Vodou Ceremony* and *Ceremony at Bois Caïman* illus-
he transactions made between religion, representation, and con-
ary sensibilities. Carolyn Fick contends that "voodoo provided a
n for the political organization of the slaves, as well as an ideo-
force, both of which contributed directly to the success of what
e a virtual blitzkrieg attack on the plantations across the prov-
The paintings expose the negotiations made during this struggle
ysical, political, and spiritual emancipation. While these images,
larly *Vodou Ceremony*, are not quite images of the Crusades and
ights Templar, they clearly link the religious to the martial. Vodou
iritual practice is imagined as part of the struggle from the start.
tionary figures, including Boukman and Georges Biassou, were
be Vodou practitioners, if not *hougans*. As an initiate herself,
sseau depicted these rituals in historical tableaux, thus promoting
ks between Vodou and the formulation of the Haitian nation. By
ounding the feminine in these pieces as Vodou adepts and as fight-
esruisseau's representations do not cede ground to the overwhelm-
nale representations of the Revolution that emphasize the triumph
individual male. Additionally, the indistinct gender of some of
ures ruptures the ease of characterizing revolutionary action as
line or feminine. Instead, by rehearsing the Revolution in these
eces, Desruisseau recalibrates the gender hierarchy that has pre-
particularly in historic and artistic renderings of the Revolution.
sseau's characters, like Défilée, or perhaps Dédée, reconfigure the
in emotionally moving yet less singular terms. Défilée not only
l visibility for Dessalines's body and, in a sense, her own body,
is also memorialized in the Haitian national imagination, but the
aspects of her hearseness are embedded in Desruisseau's work.

stories of the community spoken and sung in call-and-response fashion. The Priyè Ginen is followed by the Priyè Afriken, which, in contrast to the Priyè Ginen, is sung in a combination of Kreyol and words from various African languages, referred to as *langaj*: "Some of the first Kreyol words that can be made out include the often-repeated phrase *zo-a li mache li mache, li manche* [the bones are walking, walking, walking], a reference to the ancestors, and the history continues."[44] At sunset, these prayers are followed by communal dancing, the invocation of the three families of *loa* (Rada, Petro, and Gede), and possible possession by the *loa*.[45]

These basic ceremonial components are present in Desruisseau's painting: the *pòto-mitan*, the singing, dancing, and the invocation of the spirits who hover above the ritual. The phrase "the bones are walking" reiterates the nature of bones, which is to shape and tell stories, to remind and memorialize, to incriminate (as Clea Koff would put it), and to connect. These walking bones likewise call to mind D'Aguiar's *Feeding the Ghosts* (as discussed in chapter 1), in which Mintah thinks of the slave children dumped into the sea and if and how their bones will find their way home. Referring to a little girl thrown overboard off the *Zong*, Mintah contemplates "[h]er small bones adding to a sea of bones."[46] Ritualizing the history, as Dayan suggests, is one way of rehearsing it. The systemic invocation is the constant reminder and physicality of ancestral suffering connected to that of the worshippers.

Vodou Ceremony has no recognized heroes, no stars; it is not a citadel built around and unto a single person. Instead, it celebrates and commemorates the presence of everyday men and women as active participants. This is belonging steeped in the masses, and it is this concept that Desruisseau celebrates. These nameless—even androgynous—people, draw together toward a single light, struggle side by side for a liberty with seemingly meager resources. In an interview, Desruisseau positioned herself within that struggle: "I feel like a miserable little woman confronted by these great moments of history . . . while nonetheless rewriting it [by] revealing the socio-cultural forces that were part of the Haitian struggles against slavery."[47] In this rewriting, the artist rehearses both the revolutionary aspects of quotidian struggles and the method by which the people, who were and are the source of revolutionary struggle, can rehearse them: Vodou. This rewriting is Dédée Bazile's struggle. Counter to other representations of the Haitian Revolution, Desruisseau places the mass of the people at the center when she imagines Haiti's past. Furthermore, she calls our attention to the realities of the community and its economic station—through their torn and tattered clothes and simple environment, and their political will to rise up and fight.

A second painting by Desruisseau, *Ceremony at Bois Caïman* (1986), is a representation of the famed 1791 religious ceremony that marked the beginning of the Revolution, narratives of which are largely mythical. The panel features rebelling slaves and two central figures: a dancing woman and a shirtless man in red pants with a red scarf tied about his head. They are presumably the *manbo* (priestess) Fatiman and the *hougan* (priest) Boukman. Encircled by a large crowd that extends deep into the woods and beyond the frame, Cécile Fatiman dances in a bright red dress, a knife held aloft in her right hand while a slaughtered black pig lies in the foreground. The multitude in the forest holds torches while lightning flashes in a background in shades of dark blue, representing the deep darkness of the night, the mystical nature of the endeavor, and the indigo plants enslaved workers produced for the plantation economy. The mouths of the figures are open, as in *Vodou Ceremony*, and the women and men in striped pants and vibrant headscarves, both genders bare-chested with breasts exposed, indicate Desruisseau's belief in the indistinguishable nature of all the participants—men and women, old and young, the healthy and the infirm—as part of Haiti's quest for freedom. The dress of enslaved people mark them as a unit, their troubles the same. Some hands are in the air, and some are dipped into the pig's blood contained in a bowl held by the *hougan*; they are taking the oath to live free or die.

Desruisseau's inclusion of women as essential participants in both paintings rejects the role of weeping maternal victim as described by McClintock. Female bodies are vital in both the ritual and the representation of it, both as leaders and as members of the extensive crowd;[48] leadership is shared between the sexes, and participation is equal. The use of androgynous figures reinforces the idea of rethinking and revising gender politics.[49] In both paintings, by using this visual language in the twentieth century, Desruisseau rehearses the idea that struggle—direct physical and spiritual resistance—is central to creating an independent and sustainable Haiti.

The originating moment for Desruisseau's rehearsal in *Ceremony at Bois-Caïman* is the fusion of legend and history in the story of this event. Dayan cautions that Haiti's enemies, who were invested in bloody and gothic renderings of Haiti's story, may have imagined this ceremony. However, she concedes that Haitians themselves have found the story

"necessary [and] continue to construct their identit[y] [accord]ing to the Revolution of 1791, but by seeking its orig[ins] possibly imagined by those who disdain it."[50] Laure[nt's] various accounts indicate that Boukman—driver, coa[chman,] along with Cécile Fatiman, healer and *manbo*, presic[ed over] of a blood oath of secrecy and revenge: "Boukman ap[pealed,] 'The god of the white man calls him to commit crim[e; our] good works of us. But this god who is so good or[ders us to] direct our hands; he will aid us. Throw away the [image of] the whites who thirsts for our tears and listen to th[e voice that] speaks in the hearts of all of us.'"[51] Boukman's pra[yer—if] imagined—conveys the idea that eradicating white [power] was as critical as overthrowing the political and ec[onomic] plantation. The prayer consecrates several transfor[mations:] psychological ties were as critical as severing phys[ical....] cal was disturbing the hierarchy of European just[ice....] the master to the enslaved, as was creating a dist[inct god] which "our god asks only good works of us." Ye[t....] and demands justice. "Our" god does not require [....] the face of oppression; in fact, this god will help u[s....] our hands"—possibly through spiritual leaders.

Other accounts suggest that the *manbo* was [....] nèt,[52] but both of Desruisseau's paintings featur[e....] fact, Desruisseau creates an environment simila[r to....] *Ceremony*, filled with physical and spiritual bod[ies....] the frame, giving a limitless sense of who is inv[olved....] While the second painting foregrounds leaders[....] those leaders are not alone; they are embedded [....] they are embedded in the canvas. Boukman and [....] had leadership roles because of their religious p[ositions....] space is taken up by a mass of people, each fac[ing....] in the revolutionary process. Desruisseau's wor[k....] rehearsing the past, the apparent simplistic ease [....] vidual heroes rather than remembering the thou[sands....] and sacrificed so equally. By foregrounding Vod[ou, reli]gious, and public ceremony valued by Haitians, [....] pate in the latter conversation. Desruisseau rem[....] and people forgotten, but she emphasizes the [....] leadership from an individual icon and distribut[es....] participants on their communal terrain.

As part of its ongoing history as a site of contention for the psyche of the Haitian people, Vodou in the contemporary moment is taking the blame for Haiti's problems.[54] The structural mismanagement and corruption of political and business interests, both foreign and domestic, are obfuscated and erased by "Vodou blaming." In the aftermath of the January 2010 earthquake that shattered Port-au-Prince and much of the country, U.S. televangelist Pat Robertson claimed that the event occurred due to Haiti's "pact with the Devil."[55] From its unabashed celebration in and of the nation in Desruisseau's work, to its current position of interest within diasporic spaces, Vodou remains a model of transgressive reciprocity that challenges dominant religious and political forms. As an epistemological device, Vodou rehearses and revisits the past through its rituals, which continue to undermine master narratives.[56] Desruisseau refers to this as Vodou's ingenuity in dealing with the real and surreal simultaneously,[57] in moving beyond accepted limits while building spaces of mutuality. In other words, Desruisseau's visual narrative of the Haitian Revolution undermines the story of the singular hero; instead, the significance of Vodou in Haitian national identity—embodied, communal, gender-equal, embattled, and battling back—is what her work communicates.

Fire Rising

As Desruisseau's paintings rehearse the role of women in the Revolution not only by acknowledging them but also by highlighting the importance of remembering them, so too does Edwidge Danticat's short story "A Wall of Fire Rising," which is part of her well-received first collection of linked short stories, *Krik? Krak!* Unlike the historical setting of the revolutionary texts discussed in this volume, "A Wall of Fire Rising" is set in the recent past. Danticat's protagonist, Lili, is the granddaughter of Défilé, the original progenitor in the long line of women featured throughout the collection, and an explicit reference to the historical figure Défilée. Lili, her husband Guy, and their son, Little Guy, eke out a living in a rural town. The story revolves around Guy's quest to find a job, any job, particularly one that provides the steadiness of the sugar mill, and Little Guy's role as Boukman in a school play, which offers a literal recitation of the rehearsal of history. These events are juxtaposed with Guy's desire to fly the hot air balloon belonging to Mr. Assad, the sugar mill owner. Guy flies the balloon and jumps out the basket to his death, leaving Lili and Little Guy, whose very name personifies the masses of Haitian people, to literally and figuratively pick up the pieces.

The story is not one of Danticat's most studied texts, and it does not chronicle the Revolution as such. Nevertheless, from a heroic angle, Boukman's lofty speech is a central contrast to the lives of the characters and the lost and corrupted promises of the Revolution. This is a story that challenges the romance of the Revolution; it is about the daily struggle of the Haitian masses, in a life of toil and pain, for the dream of the Revolution. In Danticat's story, a sympathetic European has written the play Little Guy performs, and, though not in the language of the Haitian masses, its affecting declarations make Lili and Guy "stand on the tips of their toes from great pride [because] they felt as though for a moment they had been given the rare pleasure of hearing the voice of one of the forefathers of Haitian independence in the forced baritone of their only child. The experience left them both with a strange feeling that they could not explain. It left the hair on the back of their necks standing on end. It left them feeling much more love than they ever knew that they could add to their feeling for their son."[58] Here, Lili and Guy's national pride is centered in the domestic space and placed on their son. It is through Little Guy's recitation that Lili and Guy are filled with pride for their nation's story. The contradiction of the heroic past as occurring in the barren present emphasizes the tensions of living and reliving this past. There is romance in the Revolution, but that romance is severely undermined by the realities of this family's life and those of other poor people in their community. It is Lili's role as guide to her son and her husband that most profoundly takes on the romance of the Revolution. Danticat's foregrounding of Lili's position is feminist rehearsal at its most consecrated, as she is the one who encourages Little Guy to find hope in great men despite their despairing circumstances.

Lili is explicit with Little Guy: "'Remember what you are,' Lili said, 'a great rebel leader. Remember it is the revolution.'"[59] It is this call to remember that continues to give the Revolution vibrancy in Haiti's present, as each generation rehearses its role in not only remembering but extending the revolutionary struggle. When Guy questions if indeed their son should "be all of that," Lili replies, "He is Boukman." The simplicity of her statement, "He is Boukman," reveals the deeply embedded internalization and "being" of Haiti's story of national formation. Boukman's quest for freedom embodied in Little Guy stands in sharp contrast to Lili and Guy, who are tied to the sugar mill because of their poverty. Yet the story, brought alive by their young son's performance, occupies their imaginations, and soon their reality, as they struggle to accommodate both. The story suggests remembering the reality: the emphasis on the repetition of words, "the same words" over and over, reiterates the Revolution's infusion into Haitian life. Thus, the story is kept alive among the poorest Haitians in hopeful yet frustrating dimensions.

Little Guy's sites of rehearsal take on significance as the domestic and sugarcane fields are spaces of learning and understanding the story. At home, he is learning his lines with Lili's help as she makes his character's motivation clear—it is freedom that motivates Boukman.[60] In the home, Lili facilitates Little's Guy's rehearsals and mastery of the text; in the fields, Little Guy performs the speech in front of the community and over his father's body. His performance is both a consolation and a commemoration of his father, his grandfather, and revolutionary forces and representations. But here, the nation is dying; a confluence of foreign and domestic interventions, which exacerbate the grievous conditions of the poor (illiteracy and hunger in particular), have been in rehearsal and dominated the Haitian stage since the moment of arrival in the New World.

One important distinction between the family in the story and the Haitian people is the family's ability to read. The characters simultaneously speak and read the Revolution, and the book's representation of Boukman is transmuted in Little Guy's various iterations, from his earliest mumblings—which still give his parents a chill of pride—to his final delivery of Boukman's speech: "There is so much sadness in the faces of my people. I have called on their gods, now I call on our gods. I call on our young. I call on our old. I call on our mighty and the weak. I call on everyone and anyone so that we shall all let out one piercing cry that we may either live freely or we should die."[61] These words, delivered *over* the prone body of his father and similar in tone and spirit to Dessalines's language in the Haitian declaration of independence, reiterate that the Haitian Revolution endures through its purpose to avenge black subjugation. Rehearsal highlights the bodies and bones of the ancestors and the workers still working for the promise of the Revolution. The death of the patriarch leads to a descending spiral in the community and in the lives of this family—Little Guy's migration and Lili's lonely life and death. The death of the patriarch rehearses abandonment of and by the state and the previous abandonments of earlier leaders. It rehearses the tragedy and pathos of revolutionary rhetoric for the everyday citizen, the domestic and unsung heroes who inherited the Revolution.

Little Guy has nightmares about forgetting his lines,[62] perhaps symbolizing the fear of forgetting the Revolution in the face of unending crises in Haiti. As he notes: "I need many repetitions." Likewise, the language of the speech rehearses the first revolutionary impulse, namely, Dessalines's articulation of freedom and full independence. In "A Wall of Fire Rising," independence is a fleeting idea as these characters are enslaved by poverty and their failure (particularly Guy's) to fulfill the promise of the Revolution, fulfill the promise of revolutionary manhood and, specifically, the convention of father-as-provider.

Lili claims Guy's bloody corpse, and his son recites the first set of lines he was assigned as Boukman: "A wall of fire is rising and in the ashes, I see the bones of my people. Not only those people whose dark hollow faces I see daily in the fields, but all those souls who have gone ahead to haunt my dreams. At night I relive once more the last caresses from the hand of a loving father, a valiant love, a beloved friend."[63]

During Little Guy's recitation, Lili decides to leave Guy's dead eyes open so he can look at the sky with hope and see infinity. The different spaces of Little Guy's rehearsal are ordinary—the home, the field by the sugar mill—and these were also Boukman's spaces. Besides the designated performance space of the school, the home and the field connect Little Guy to the caresses of his father and the bones of his people that Boukman, the character, employs as a generative and transformative force. Additionally, similar to the seemingly mandated, nightly communal watching of state-sponsored newscasts, Little Guy performs for a community of laborers who, like his father, are still linked to the sugar mill as slaves were linked to the same product before their uprising. Reciting his lines in these spaces indicates the multiple spaces of performance for the Haitian Revolution and its connection to a still-lived historical experience by Haitian people. Little Guy's performance of the play's lines is juxtaposed with the consequences of his father's dream and the hard realities his mother faces. Lili's rehearsals are tied most closely to the quotidian realities of finding food, encouraging her family, and ultimately dealing with the broken shards she's left.

Nightly the family and other dwellers in the town go to watch the state-sponsored news on a large television.[64] During one of these viewings, Guy's role as father, protector, and provider is challenged through a simple exchange with Little Guy. The child wants to recite his lines, his father admonishes him not to tire his lips, but the boy mumbles them anyway, which provokes an ear twisting. Danticat characterizes Lili as "tortured" by Guy's actions because, in admonishing her husband with a pained look, she, in his mind, undermines his power. This is relevant when compared to her earlier statement that she wasn't afraid of lizards in the grass because Guy is there "to protect me if anything happens."[65]

These two moments, if read symbolically, show the paradoxes of Guy's position and the tensions in their visions and parenting styles.[66] The forced television watching and Guy's violence against his son rehearse authoritarian leaders, "national fathers," who imposed state-centered versions of the remnants of the Revolution. However, the state's televised news account is undermined as the people, in community, tell their own "stories to one another beneath the big black screen. They made bonfires with dried sticks, corn husks, and paper, cursing the authorities under their breath."[67] The spirit of counternarrative and ritual storytelling propagated by Vodou emerges in non-Vodou spaces of collective contact. The need for many repetitions in order to retain the past once again signals the role of feminist rehearsal in creating mutual spaces.

Guy desperately tries to make his own story with Mr. Assad's hot air balloon. The final line of the speech, "I call on anyone and everyone so that we shall all let out one piercing cry that we may either live freely or we should die!" is significant, not only given the routineness and humbleness of Guy's existence—he is the Haitian everyman, whose role as provider is constantly undermined, born as he was "in the shadow of the sugar mill"[68]—but because Guy must find some other outlet for his masculinity, whether disciplining his son or fulfilling his dream of flying. Lili opposes Guy's desire to put Little Guy on the waiting list for a job at the sugar mill because "to be on any list like that might influence his destiny."[69] These issues of work, value, destiny, and how one belongs haunt Guy; he tells Lili, "Sometimes I know you want to believe in me. . . . I know you're wishing things for me. You want me to work at the mill. You want me to get a pretty house for us. I know you want these things too, but mostly you want me to feel like a man."[70] Guy's belief that Lili wants him to "feel like a man" and his inability to fulfill such a role exacerbate their problems and underscore the importance of masculinity and its link to work, material comfort, and inexpressible value. Similar to the works of James, Césaire, and Carpentier discussed in the previous chapter, Danticat's story portrays how manhood is important in this family's life. Guy's desire to enact provider masculinity and some measure of control over his life drives his actions.

Because he has no work, Guy, in his mind, has no place; he can find one only with the balloon flight, his attempt to secure his place in people's memories.[71] To Lili's constant disbelief and in response to her desire to keep him to their particular reality, Guy says: "Pretend that this is the time of miracles and we believed in them. I watched the owner for a long time, and I think I can fly that balloon. The first time I saw him do it, it looked like a miracle, but the more and more I saw it, the more ordinary it became."[72] Guy's desire to "just *be* something new" fuels his resolve to prove his masculinity.[73] The more Guy sees of the balloon, the less miraculous and impossible it seems. Rehearsing his flights makes flying the balloon possible.

By taking the balloon, Guy becomes a hero: the mill workers clap, cheer, and call out his name; women shout, "Go! Beautiful, go!"[74] Mr. Assad needs "a whole crew" to fly the balloon, while Guy maneuvers it alone, underscoring his individual and heroic manhood. As people revel in Guy's audacity, he jumps out: "Within seconds, Guy was in the air hurtling down towards the crowd. . . . He crashed not far from where Lili and the boy were standing, his blood immediately soaking the landing spot."[75] Guy's jump is both a condemnation of what the nation has become and a lament about what it could be. His fall from the balloon is, in essence, a return to the ancestors who preceded him and who may reject his bones. First, he tells Lili that he knows the answer to the question of how a man is remembered after he is gone: "I know because I remember my father, who was a very poor struggling man all his life. I remember him as a man that I would never want to be."[76]

"A Wall of Fire Rising" discloses a tension between being, imitating, and rehearsing the revolutionary forefathers and the reality of the ruptured romance in Haiti, in other words, the extreme hardships of making a living. Guy remembers his father, but he remembers him in order to reject him and to distance himself from the everyday and structural poverty that has been part of the Haitian landscape for so long. Guy's transactions—stealing, flying, and jumping out of the balloon—indicate that his quest is to be a man unlike his father. Guy wants to be a hero; he wants to be remembered, even if through tragedy. His inability to sustain his family and belong to his country as a poor man drives him to search for glory by making himself and his life visible. This visibility, expressed through the flight of his body, provides a sense of worth and personhood rather than the anonymity of a poor, struggling, and forgotten man who was his father. Moreover, Guy as a sacrifice, as one who spills his blood for the redemption of his community, illustrates the way in which internalizing the Revolution can be problematic. Ultimately, there is an intergenerational or even multigenerational failure of the male heroic narrative, which Guy's flight and death rehearse. Both Guy and his father struggle with their lives becoming rehearsals of invisibility. If memory is the marker of success, Guy's death intervenes in that. He joins the master masculinist heroic narrative through a grand gesture that kills him. Danticat seems to be commenting on the futility of individual heroism here. Guy has made a sacrifice of himself, but to what end? He has let the members of his community see themselves---and the possibility of their own freedom—in him, but he has no way back to them other than through death. Why does he jump when he does? Is he about to lose sight of them, become invisible again? Guy's failure is that of not taking communal action against Mr. Assad and the inequities lodged in the sugar mill plantation; Danticat is pointing to a revolutionary space somewhere between communal grumblings and individual heroism.

Lili's relationship with Guy challenges this history of submissive representations of Haitian women who are receptacles for male action. As Dayan argues, women in Haitian drama and mythology are "passive recipient[s] of history . . . [who] stay where [they are] told [and are] obedient to the wishes of those who make history."[77] Lili continually insists that Guy and Little Guy pay attention to their circumstances; she negotiates a world of poverty and possibility by trying to help Guy find work and feel valued, while simultaneously refusing to tie Little Guy to the sugar estate, the continuation of this subjection. Like the national hero Défilée, Lili gathers and pulls together the pieces of her life.

As Défilée reassembled Dessalines, Lili is left to reconstitute her life and that of her son. She is the antithesis of passive and nurturing motherhood; her actions are connected to tangible issues of survival. Angela Naimou, also deploying the trope of rehearsal in her reading of Danticat's story, discusses its conclusion as an encounter between the national romance and the postcolonial tragedy:

> Postcolonial tragedy does seem to overtake and subsume the mode of the anticolonial romance evoked by Boukman's lines. If, as anticolonial romance, the school play had an institutional function to commemorate the origins of the state as emancipatory, heroic, and authentically national, the suicide transforms the content and thus the meaning of Boukman's lines into a grievous lament at the loss of one's father in the fields of the sugar mill and a prayer calling for a collective liberation that cannot be commemorated because it has not yet come.[78]

Naimou's reading and her further elaboration of Guy as rehearsing Boukman's death are valid, and this moment draws particular attention to the pathos in Little Guy's speech. She argues, "What these rehearsals show is that every historical narrative has a history—a story of its production—and these narratives operate not only within spectacular contests for political and cultural power but also in the everyday social life that may be hidden in the shadows of such public contests."[79] Indeed, this story is a profound critique of the failure of political power. The authoritarian government does not offer solutions but rather uses guns to force communities to watch state-sanctioned newscasts. The economic power in Haiti belongs to a few elites, some of whom—presumably like Mr. Assad's family—immigrated to Haiti in the late nineteenth and early twentieth centuries. These Arab immigrants were able to take advantage of the nullification of Dessalines's law that foreigners could not own land in Haiti.[80] Mitigations in the wake of this law began in the late 1860s before it was ultimately removed by future U.S. president Franklin Roosevelt who, as "an assistant secretary of the Navy, ended the prohibition of land ownership by foreigners."[81]

With Guy's death, the sacrifices borne by the majority of Haitians are once again made visible: structural poverty leads to violence, including self-inflicted harm. And Lili will bear the brunt of Guy's actions—she will have to sacrifice further to provide for Little Guy—thus multiplying the sacrifices she made while her husband was alive. "Between the Pool and the Gardenias," another story in Danticat's collection, continues the narrative in which, years later, Little Guy is a migrant living in Miami. Unable to fulfill Haiti's promises to its citizens, Little Guy, an educated member of the Haitian masses, must leave to prosper elsewhere, while Lili kills herself in old age because she too has been depleted and defeated by what Haiti has made her. She becomes an ancestor whose own story, along with those of other female family members, is rehearsed by the protagonist Marie, the last woman in this family's line. As part of her morning prayers, Marie recites her matrilineage: "Mama had to introduce me to them, because they had all died before I was born. There was my great grandmother Eveline who was killed by Dominican soldiers at the Massacre River. My grandmother Défilé who died with a bald head in a prison because God had given her wings. My godmother Lili who killed herself in old age because her husband had jumped out of a flying balloon and her grown son left her to go to Miami."[82] Recounting the matrilineage also serves as a way of rehearsing the atrocities and bearing witness to the injustices done to these women.

The continued work, or now desire to work, on the sugar plantation supplanted the initial revolutionary impulse to destroy them. Like Défilée, Lili's everyday living resists any uncritical ideologies and reveals a romance gone wrong. Dayan argues that "it is unsettling to recognize that the hyperbolization necessary for myths to be mutually reinforcing not only erases these women but forestalls our turning to these real lives."[83] In essence, women seem to have a clear-eyed view of all this—and Lili's decision not to put Little Guy's name on the mill list and the multitude of other realistic accommodations that she makes, as a woman, in the presence of and in spite of all the heroic speeches, are her ways of simultaneously resisting and accommodating the Revolution. In effect, Lili refuses to rehearse tying Little Guy to the structures of economic, political, and social slavery as represented by the sugar mill. She is revising the rehearsal; she has learned, and her nuance is to not put his name on the list. In this rehearsal, the woman, even while she celebrates her son's speeches, always has her eye on reality and the daily exchanges she must enter into.

Lili's position starkly indicates that women belong to the domestic and national space simultaneously. Her family's dire circumstances—extreme poverty, hunger, minimal joy, and a repressive state—show the layering of both historical and contemporaneous experiences and the weight these structural realities carry. Lili negotiates as best she can within both an authoritarian state and a home space in which her husband feels emasculated. Here the tensions between "the state as emancipatory, heroic, and authentically national" (Naimou's words) remain an ideal lost to the fog of time, repression, and global exploitation.

In postcolonial and independent states such as Haiti, the goal of using literature to resist and displace Western ideologies must include confronting internal repression as well.[84] The women in these works present the ways in which revolutionary rhetoric has been internalized and sometimes conflicts with the social, political, and economic conditions of the Haitian majority. Rose Marie Desruisseau's depiction of the mass of people who were part of this revolution interrupts the way the Revolution is remembered as one of solely male heroic figures. Though Desruisseau includes heroic revolutionary figures in the second painting (and much of her other work), she does not forget the everyday people whose bodies were put on the line by this transaction, the bodies and people without whom these revolutionary heroes would have become as ineffective as Guy. The majority are thus heroically portrayed as fighting for their own emancipation and actively involved in transforming the colony of Saint-Domingue into the free nation of Haiti.

Similarly, Danticat's version of revolutionary consciousness produces a narrative representing people as "ordinary heroes." This type of heroism is something a little larger than the self who simply gets through the day. It manifests in Little Guy's recitation for his parents, for the community, and to commemorate his father's death. Another moment of the ordinary heroism of ordinary people is Lili holding things together and seeing a different future for Little Guy; it is even Guy's climb into the balloon basket. The idea of heroism is not abandoned but is instead tempered, as life in Haiti is tempered, and not a daily iteration of revolutionary romance. Again, this is Défilée's, or perhaps the more ordinary Dédée's, rehearsal—one that deals with the consequences of the hearse, the visible bodies affected by poverty, corruption, and history. This revolution is interrogated in terms of people who have been violated by this rhetoric and ravaged by the romance of the Haitian Revolution.

The contradictions and paradoxes of the Revolution veer between a glorious national memory of a bloody history and the national suicide of the contemporary moment with liberty or death fulfilled both actually and symbolically. In the simple depiction of this family, Guy jumps out of the balloon to his death, Lili later commits suicide, and finally their son goes to Miami, all leaving the national space. Marie remembers Lili as part of a genealogy of women who are both lost to the nation and ignored by it, which is much like Dayan's argument that Défilée was lost like the Haitian nation. The legacy of the Haitian Revolution seems to be one of mitigated hope and many rehearsals of structural poverty and political violence.

Desruisseau and Danticat interrupt and challenge the continued mythos creation. Though Desruisseau celebrates the Revolution and its heroes, she also emphasizes the mass participation, disrupting the idea of singular heroes. And when she does visualize the Bois Caïman ceremony, she inserts Cecile Fatiman and frames her as centrally as Boukman. Défilée is an ambivalent figure whose representations in historical chronicles and fictional narratives defy the violence of her life—the murder of her family and Dessalines—to embody both the hope and the horror of the Revolution.[85]

These texts collectively disrupt gender binaries and hierarchies by showing women's active participation in these national narratives. Unlike depictions of uncritical nationalism, these female characters occupy the shifting and unstable space of the national imaginary and help readers and viewers understand power and the dynamics of belonging. Desruisseau and Danticat rehearse women's disobedience in works that are counternarratives to solely heroic and mostly male representations of the Revolution. In them, representations of women speak eloquently about the impact of economic, social, and political violence and their imperfect survival strategies. While earlier texts are steeped in representations of heroic manhood, Guy's act is both heroic and a failure, and it is the woman, Lili, like Défilée, who is left to pick up the pieces. The paintings and short story are examples of women harvesting the exchanges and compromises that daily survival demands, performing heroically through the transactions implicit in their daily grinds.

4   Signs of Sycorax

THE PREVIOUS CHAPTER EXPLORED twentieth-century challenges to representations of the Haitian Revolution as solely a heroic romantic male enterprise. In this chapter, I explore contemporary manifestations of Caribbean women who rehearse *The Tempest*'s archetypal character Sycorax, Shakespeare's silenced female figure. Sycorax appears in an array of understudied texts of conquest: André Schwarz-Bart's novel *A Woman Named Solitude* (1973), Grace Nichols's poem "Ala" (1983), and the novels *Indigo* (1992) by Marina Warner and *The Salt Roads* (2003) by Nalo Hopkinson.

These authors' characters interrupt, challenge, and make way for the emergence of an oppositional consciousness against intimate and public power, as Sycorax did with Caliban, her son, and Prospero, the former Duke of Milan, who claimed her unidentified island. Schwarz-Bart's novel imagines the life of Solitude, a hero of Guadeloupean emancipation. Nichols's "Ala" is the African deity to whom the poem's enslaved women pray when one of their own is tortured to death for infanticide.[1] Warner's novel imagines Sycorax as an indigenous woman who raises an African child and is caught in the initial encounter between natives and Europeans. Hopkinson's text has three female protagonists who are Sycorax-like, from three time periods, each dealing with issues of sexuality, belief, and belonging in their respective eras. These texts rehearse Sycorax as rebel and mother and extend our expectations of nationalist mothering. Though victimized, these characters are not portraits of the weeping mother as injured and in need of the protection of the nationalist cause (per Anne McClintock); rather, they are integral to the cause and, because of circumstance, embrace nontraditional notions of how mothers fight for and within the nation. Additionally, they each nurture in quite different ways and sometimes, in rehearsing their care, particularly when manifested through absence, contradict the private and public power of motherhood.

Feminist rehearsal is both a guiding metaphor and a method for discussing significant moments—real and fictive—that highlight the gendered connections between culture and the implications of national belonging. This transformation of textual meaning through pauses, inflections, and movements produces multiple readings of Sycorax and the hegemonic and structural forces with which she is entangled. Each outcome or rehearsal furthers the understanding of a cultural artifact while producing the next rehearsal, thus becoming a type of praxis. Each rehearsal facilitates empathy, which means not only understanding another's story but being moved to make change, to wish to transform. These transformations develop communities of consensus that then seek accountability and transparency.

Rehearsing Sycorax means disrupting national or state-sanctioned gender discourses to expose the divergences in narratives of power and modes of domination in plantation states. Though dealing with a "limited archive," so to speak, it is imperative to reexamine evidence of characters called "Sycorax," but it is also necessary to use Sycorax and the discursive power she embodies as a model for reading women's stories that are replete with the contradictions of engaging with the plantation system.

The writers who have examined Sycorax in some way recognize her power and invoke her as a presence in challenging authoritarian male narratives that repeatedly evoke and invoke women as decorative but passive, and which erase the realities of sexual violence enacted on female bodies. The culture engendered by the violation of rape is one of impunity for male aggression and desires, which implicates women as teasers and instigators of the violence perpetrated against them. Rape culture and heteronomative desire make impenetrable the structural violence of plantation economies.

Sycoraxian Solitude

I examine the interplay between Schwarz-Bart's *A Woman Named Solitude* and Jacky Poulier's statue because Poulier's work, located in a roundabout on the Boulevard of Heroes in Abymes, Guadeloupe, is inspired by Schwarz-Bart's conception. *Solitude* commemorates the historical woman who escaped slavery, became a Maroon, and fought Napoleon Bonaparte's 1802 reimposition of slavery in Guadeloupe.

Figure 4. *Solitude 4,* Jacky Poulier.
Situated in a roundabout on the Boule-
vard des Héros, Abymes, Guadeloupe.
(Photograph by the author)

With arms on her hips, pregnant belly extended, and head held high,
Solitude towers above a traffic junction as Guadeloupeans go about their
daily lives. Solitude's rebellion, part of the legend of collective acts of
Caribbean resistance, occurs at the same time as the Haitian Revolution
(1791–1804) and on the heels of France's own revolution (1789–1799);
she is but one manifestation of a Caribbean woman who negotiated her
desire for freedom within the degradations of slavery. While Poulier's
representation celebrates Solitude as mother, she was more vessel than
nurturer in this context: French colonial forces executed her a day after
she gave birth. As various sources indicate, she was a child of Middle
Passage rape traumatized by the slave system, against which she eventually rebelled.

The statue, six and a half feet tall, stands on a three-foot-tall platform. A sarong tied beneath the figure's heavy belly emphasizes her
fecundity, and the arm on her hip postures defiance; a red flag—
reminiscent of Desruisseau's *Vodou Ceremony*—ripples behind her.

Passersby are unable to see her face or look her in the eye; they can observe only the outline of her strong jaw. She must be looked up to. Solitude—and all she signifies—dominates. This rehearsal of Solitude commemorates and acknowledges the historical Solitude, even as it consigns her to the distance of the past and the public's receding memory. Solitude as a historical figure is lost to myth, leaving her legend as sacrificial nurturer, much like Défilée, to be recounted and celebrated.[2] Thus, the Solitude who is commemorated along the busy avenue is the overused representation of republican motherhood: the pregnant mother tied to her nation, ripe for uniting its disparate forces.

Solitude's representation as the essential and sacrificial mother functions in multiple ways. First, she is a historical and imaginary site of belonging, a woman who challenged French colonialism and rebelled against European imperialism. That "she was captured, after leading a Maroon Battalion against Napoleon's troops and sentenced to death,"[3] invites us to consider Solitude as iconic mother, nationalist martyr, one who does not threaten Guadeloupean patriarchy, her citizenship tied as it is to the exclusivity of a woman's maternal role.[4] Though her maternity is obvious, she is not the weeping mother, another pietà; her victimization is transformed by Poulier's representation. In a sense, she goes beyond Défilée: Solitude was not the gatherer of revolutionary ideas, she was a creator of them, an instigator.

Furthermore, this version of Solitude is also a fiction. Historian René Bellaneuse argues that there was a mistranslation of Louis Auguste Lacour's account of Solitude's story in his four-volume *History of Guadeloupe*. Lacour is the authority "contemporary historians cite when allud[ing] to Solitude in their work," according to Bellaneuse, and most interpreters read Lacour's word *suppliciée* as "death." However, it can likewise mean "mutilated" or "tortured," not "executed." Additionally, Lacour's documents refer to "Solistude," a synonym for solitude in French, a woman who was imprisoned and died at the age of sixty, concurrent with Solitude's time line.[5]

What might it mean if the sacrificial mother of the nation, though tortured and imprisoned, was not sacrificed in the way most Guadeloupeans imagine? Reimagining Solitude as prisoner rather than martyr revisions her story in a domestic way. Like Lili in Danticat's "A Wall of Fire Rising," Solitude—and most women (and men)—live and struggle within the circumstances that frame their lives. Solitude as Solistude upends the idea of an easily categorized, definitive ending for this heroine by complicating readings of the past to avoid overly essentialist images and imaginings of historical events and monuments. By archiving her story, the statue reimagines belonging in a manner that challenges the fallacy that the nation and nation building is a solely male enterprise.

Schwarz-Bart's construction of Solitude complicates the stereotype of the unrelenting black superwoman or the idea of black women's mythic endurance, which characterize them as enduring all manner of violence without succumbing to psychological trauma. Oppression creates a fraught ideological terrain in which black people are magnetized by heroic, often mythic, and towering icons of resistance. Though *A Woman Named Solitude* sometimes veers into the territory of another stereotype (i.e., the distressed and tragic mulatto), Schwarz-Bart's reimagining and re/presentation of Solitude as a woman damaged at every turn by slavery, dehumanized, and mentally unstable is compelling. This version of Solitude's story begins in Africa with Bayangumay, her mother, who, raped during the Middle Passage, eventually abandons her daughter by becoming a Maroon.[6] Bayangumay, called Man Bobette on the du Parc plantation, is unable to forge a nurturning relationship with Rosalie, as Solitude was called as a child. In plotting her escape, Man Bobette confronted the processes of the plantation that corroded all relationships by beating Rosalie nightly, intoning that "this flesh thinks only of betraying."[7] In plantation societies, skin color is "one's country," through which loyalty and belonging are determined. Rosalie is valued and given some protections by the plantation machine as a mixed-race woman with European features, who even as a child is cossetted and pampered to be sexually exploited. Rosalie resists by throwing herself in mud, running from the offerings of the big house to her mother at every turn, yet this does not suffice in terms of bridging racial allegiance between mother and daughter. The discourse of the flesh here is one of division based on complexion as Man Bobette cannot trust Rosalie's flesh because of a sexual and market economy that values people based on gradations and closeness to whiteness. Though Solitude rejects this, as imagined in Schwarz-Bart's novel, she is ostracized and distrusted for the privileges gifted by the plantocracy. The intricate relationship of abuse, love, and plantation politics unravels and reveals the psychological and physical traumas for slave mothers and daughters.

Solitude's moments of strength are conditional and contextual. She fights as she flees; she is constantly moving from one unstable space to the next. In the end, Solitude names herself, chooses her aloneness, and claims her own space, which, in turn, leads to her death.

While Poulier's rehearsal of Solitude is one of towering maternal strength, and Schwarz-Bart's is full of vulnerabilities, these rehearsals of Solitude transition between her legend and her relation to the daily lives of contemporary Guadeloupeans. Solitude's status as a child of rape, mulatto, Maroon, and marginal mother all speak to her role in amplifying the black female experience during slavery. As Poulier's monument, situated as it is in the midst of daily life, connects Solitude to the contemporary world, so too are black women's experiences both historicized and dramatically connected, past to present.

In both readings, Solitude's temporalities highlight power distortions and the structural implications of enslavement: rape, abandonment, family separation, mental trauma, and resistance. The violence in the lives of enslaved women in the home and public sphere is part of her life from conception to execution. She relives the hearse aspects of the imprisonment and mutilation of black female bodies. In her historical time, Solitude negotiates with the slave system and her own psyche before eventually challenging her victimization and naming herself. "No one knew when the strange name came to be hers, when it settled on her face like an emblematic mask. No slave sale certificate made note of it. It only appeared toward the very end, upon the writ condemning her to death."[8] In the most common version of her story, Solitude became visible to herself and acknowledged her sense of self with a new name, which is recognized by others only via her death certificate. Solitude's transformation as imagined by Schwarz-Bart is not a linear one; there are stops, starts, and relapse in her journey to subjectivity. Solitude's metamorphosis emerges from her lived experiences of torture and violation within the slave system. Her cycle of change includes these occurrences and the stories told about them. As the novel attests, it is in repeating Solitude's story that we can affix new meanings to the experiences of enslaved women and their descendants. Thus understanding her experience within a historical framework—rehearsing the history and creating a tangible link between the past and the present—that makes transformation possible.

In Poulier's representation, the towering figure embedded in the quotidian minutiae of Guadeloupean urban life highlights the present-past (or past-present). The transactions of Schwarz-Bart's and Poulier's belonging make way for concrete memorialization in the hustle and bustle of tropical France. The sea is history for these islands because it connects the colony and the metropole. Without the sea, there is neither colony nor metropole; the sea is what creates both ends of the spectrum. The complicated and perhaps coercive relationship between France and her administrative units construct these colonial and structural ties on a daily basis. Guadeloupe fights a diurnal battle of dependence or independence with France in the shadow of Solitude's sacrifice. What we know of Solitude's story is one of psychological loss and a triumphal death that is simultaneously mythic and domestic and that lingers within and above the landscape.

Transactions and Sycorax

In this landscape, "doing" these multiple social locations, Caribbean people cannot forget the plantation machine in their assessment of gendered relations. The plantation machine, according to Antonio Benítez-Rojo, is composed of ancillary "machines" such as military, religious, and bureaucratic institutions that came together to create the singular device that structures Caribbean history and current reality: the plantation.[9] Plantation inheritances from economic structuring of largely monocrop industries to gendered interactions remain with the region; it is important to rethink them. Moreover, Christine Barrow clarifies the deep structural impacts of this machine as the penetration of European ideologies into everything from work to respectability: "The Caribbean has always been a site of pure capitalism—the plantation; slavery was gender-blind; female-headed households . . . began with slavery and are reinforced with male economic migration in the early 1900s;[10] domestication [among other ideologies] . . . was promoted by the church, school and law;[11] and the impact of Eurocentric value complexes of respectability and domestication have affected gender equality after slavery."[12] The extensive and invasive tentacles of this machine meant and mean that negotiation takes place at the "individual level of the workplace or the home and also at the cultural, public, and collective level—the level of debate."[13] Gender negotiation is an inherent but often naturalized and unacknowledged part of the public sphere for Caribbean women.

Women disassociate from society when unable to read themselves and their experiences, which means that they lose vital political awareness.

Caribbean feminism, both scholarly and lived, seeks "to produce alternative histories"[14] and reconstruct knowledge by retrieving experience.[15]
Retrieving Sycorax's experience provides a model of how literature and
history can come together to mitigate gender stereotypes and colonial
and patriarchal silencing. The primary function of rehearsing Sycorax is
to reclaim women's stories, to enlarge and understand their roles in the
family and in their communities. This complex vision of the past allows
women to more critically examine their current positions and to desta-
bilize rigid public and private dichotomies.[16] This process of recognition, especially in so canonical a text as a play by Shakespeare, makes
historical and literary emancipation possible because it allows readers to
reread, reframe, and reimagine the world. These understandings generated in rehearsal create a consensus among the shared histories of plantation violence.

Sycorax Genealogies

In *The Tempest*, visible violence begins when Prospero, former Duke
of Milan and a book-trained magician, orchestrates a shipwreck for
the purpose of transporting the two men who conspired against him—
his brother, Antonio, and Alonso, King of Naples—to a mysterious
island he now claims as his own. Prospero tells his daughter, Miranda,
his version of the facts in order to justify his revenge. He conscripts
the services of Ariel, a magical spirit, and Caliban, the island's native
and Sycorax's son. The shipwreck divides the survivors, and they
experience different adventures engineered by Prospero, one of which
includes the romance between Miranda and Prince Ferdinand. All ends
well for Prospero, his daughter, and Ariel—he reunites with his enemies and returns to Italy, Miranda and Ferdinand marry, and Ariel is
set free. Caliban, distracted from his attempted overthrow of Prospero
by beautiful clothes, ultimately repents of his desire for freedom and
urge to rebel.

Like other women in the play, with the exception of Miranda,
Sycorax is barely mentioned; she does not have a single line. We know
that she was banished from Algeria, pregnant with her child Caliban,
but we do not know the particulars of that banishment nor why she
so quickly becomes Prospero's nemesis. Despite her vocal absence,
her presence haunts the action. Her offense and the reason for her
subsequent banishment are unknown, but she is a rebel woman who
casts spells of magic that rival Prospero's. While he is in a continual
space of justification, rationalizing his power against the remnants of

Sycorax's authority, he reminds Ariel, and later Caliban, that it was his "art . . . that made gape the pine and let thee [Ariel] out" of the tree that Sycorax imprisoned him in. Though Prospero tries to erase Sycorax and enslaves her child, he is destabilized and made insecure by her trace, most visible through Caliban. Sycorax marks Caliban through land and language, and he inherits his claim to the island through her:

> This island's mine, by Sycorax my mother,
> Which thou takest from me. When thou camest first,
> Thou strokest me and madest much of me, wouldst give me
> Water with berries in't, and teach me how
> To name the bigger light . . . and then I loved thee
> And show'd thee all the qualities o' the isle
> . . . Cursed be I that did so! All the charms
> Of Sycorax, toads, beetles, bats, light on you!
> For I am all the subjects that you have,
> Which first was mine own king: and here you sty me
> In this hard rock, whiles you do keep from me
> The rest o' the island.[17]

Caliban teaches Prospero the island as Sycorax had taught him. Caliban's speech is Sycorax's language, giving him another way of being, another way of constructing himself, and shaping his reality. In essence, Sycorax's language offers Caliban the power of a latent oppositional consciousness and an alternate construct with which to relate to the island. Hoping to subvert Sycorax's power and eradicate her, Prospero renames the landscape, but Sycorax is buried on the island. That her body is entombed on the island enacts the hearse—it makes the body visible for accountability—in a new way. Her body is not seen, but *knowing* it is there both frustrates Prospero and emboldens Caliban. Furthermore, as her child, Caliban is a visible manifestation of her trace. The power struggle between Prospero and Caliban is embodied through language, land, and Miranda; it has also become a foundational trope in postcolonial discourse.

For novelist, critic, and philosopher George Lamming, the Caribbean relationship with colonial overlords (i.e., the colonial relationship) is best characterized by the Caliban/Prospero paradigm. When reclaiming this text as fiction in the Americas—in Aimé Césaire's *A Tempest* or José Enrique Rodó's *Ariel*—focus has been placed on Caliban and Ariel, the masculine inheritors of the island. However, when charting Caribbean women's experience in narratives of imperialism that invoke *The Tempest*, the stories begin with them as Caliban's women—his wives or sisters. Feminist scholars have increasingly begun to pay attention to Sycorax and Miranda.

To understand the relational connection between Sycorax and Prospero, scholars have reimagined Sycorax as a character, a trope, and one way of understanding women's relationship to the colonial and postcolonial state. One of the first to reexamine the character was Edward Kamau Brathwaite, who has been calling attention to the "lost" Sycorax since the early 1980s, discussing her language as mother's milk,[18] and even developing a "script"/typeset that challenges spatial arrangement on the page through the inclusion of pictures, hieroglyphs, and icons for conveying regional stories. Abena Busia's 1989 intervention "Silencing Sycorax" focuses on the mute Sycorax in an African context and interrogates Sycorax's subalternity, while Michelle Cliff's "Caliban's Daughter: The Tempest and the Teapot" of 1991 presents Sycorax as a wild and unpredictable precolonial Caribbean female identity.

Cliff argues that there are many rehearsals of Sycorax in the modern literature: the Jamaican national heroine Nanny; Antoinette Cosway/Bertha Rochester in *Wide Sargasso Sea* (1966); and, Miss Mattie, Clare Savage's grandmother in *Abeng* and *No Telephone to Heaven* (1984). These older female characters are drawn beyond the feminine expectations within the gender system that serves to organize society; they are fighters who take up arms in defense of their communities.[19] Cliff asserts that Sycorax is a vital trope in decolonizing the Caribbean mind because colonial culture and education deny colonized people's history, hide their unbelonging, and render them "unable to locate" themselves in colonial narratives and, eventually, even in their own landscapes.[20] Because Sycorax has no lines in the original play, it can be difficult to locate her, but it is in examining her nuance and using feminist rehearsal to open new lines of inquiry that we can more effectively see her impact. In addition to Sycorax's function in the decolonizing process, she also offers a way to read, see, and acknowledge same-gender-loving relationships and the women who have the power and desire to shift, transform, and perform nonnormative sexualities:

> In literature, the proposition of one woman loving another woman has too often been used as a heavy-handed emblem of western decadence, the seduction of the tropics by Europe, the colonization of the dark woman by the white one. But [Dionne] Brand [in her "Hard Against the Soul" series]

locates herself on an island in the Caribbean . . . where to imagine oneself in another woman, to connect psychically and physically with another female, can be an act of empowerment, a step toward describing oneself in a new language (or, perhaps, an old language), being *self*ish (in my girlhood the thing I was never supposed to be).[21]

The desire and practice of being *self*ish convey both the quest for personal autonomy and a rejection of literary inheritances.

In addition to Cliff's and Brathwaite's early interventions, other Caribbean scholars—notably Myriam J. A. Chancy and Brinda Mehta—have called for reexamining and reclaiming Sycorax on several fronts. Chancy challenges Lamming's masculinist reading of exile in the play and highlights his missed opportunity to explore Sycorax's power by exploring Caliban's "doomed" quest to dismantle the master's house with the master's language.[22] Chancy believes Caliban is doomed because he tries to outwit Prospero on his terms rather than tapping into the deep reservoirs left to him by his mother: "In [Sycorax] and her memory resides a potential for the transformation of Caliban, in his desperate attempt to master his master through an imposed language, [he] is doomed."[23] I agree with Chancy's observation: invoking Sycorax is not so much about deploying Shakespeare's character; rather it is

[b]y resurrecting, not Sycorax the character, but what she stands for—the lost heritage of the Black woman—by returning her spirit to the living so that it may assume new life, that we can begin to see how the condition of exile can be transformative. If it is not rendered as a nostalgic search for access to the very power that has produced exile, but turned into a politicized search for that which will free [people of African descent people] from the physical and psychological chains of imperialism, colonialism, and more recently, neocolonialism, that search becomes powerfully transformative.[24]

Though certainly there are several ways in which to utilize and rehearse Sycorax, it is clear that the psychological and the physical are significant interventions. I deploy the character and all that she symbolizes so that I may rehearse the psychic and physical implications of colonialism upon women's bodies. Let me be explicit: rehearing Sycorax creates alternatives and means exposing and exploring the intertwined dimensions and transactions women make. Moreover, Sycorax's story critiques embedded structures of power while implicating her own deployment of power: how did Shakespeare's Algerian Sycorax expropriate the island? Sycorax as stateswoman and/or colonial aggressor who exercised power before Prospero's arrival retrieves another aspect of women as rebels and mothers of the nation.

Mehta argues for recuperating Sycorax as a maternal figure and describes this philosophy as "Sycorax Historicity." She implores readers to embed themselves in the stories that examine and highlight Sycorax as a *mambo* (i.e., a Vodou priestess and healer), a serpent, and a purveyor of culinary epistemologies. Mehta uses matrilineage, the emphasis on women's culture (food preparation and healing), and women's interpretation of broader culture (Carnival dancing and curative practices) to find Sycorax's latent body. Her analysis provides a method for reading Sycorax in these multiple spaces and lauds re-creating history from a female point of view as an important component of developing subjectivity. It is "reclaiming the lost vocabulary of Sycorax's multiple tongues, a precolonial linguistic authority," that provides an alternative feminist positionality and historiography.[25] Mehta's "The Voice of Sycorax: Diasporic Maternal Thought," rich with the manifold and "polyvalent" languages of Sycorax, unapologetically celebrates the maternal: "Through a woman the transition of spiritual beings is made. This point is crucial in that it explains why diviners are women and why men must become transvestites to be diviners."[26] In Mehta's configuration, the connection between women, divining knowledge, and healing does not essentialize a woman's capacity for mothering and nurturing a community; it demonstrates how, in ancient traditions, women have healed themselves by their spiritual access to "underground" knowledge.[27] For the fluctuations of the state feeding on itself, Mehta offers a maternal solution.

Indeed, the cannibalistic state is where May Joseph situates Sycorax in her 1999 essay "The Scream of Sycorax." Her piece uses Sycorax to discuss performing citizenship and the alchemy and exchange of the cannibalized state. Joseph argues, "The systematic omission of Sycorax in these texts opens a series of meditations on the gendered nature of the struggle for postcolonial statehood across national contexts."[28] Joseph claims that Sycorax's maternal body effectively moves her beyond the historical, social, and sexual confinement of women's general experience: "Sycorax challenges her assumed animality, which is linked to her pregnant, maternal body. She exceeds the anthropological and historical anecdotes of cannibalism available by revealing their discursive limits."[29] Furthermore, Joseph implicates the networks of capital that consume Caribbean bodies, particularly those capable of reproduction: "Sycorax's pregnant body produces the free though maleficent labor of 'a freckled whelp hag-born—not honor'd with a human shape' whom

Prospero will keep in service. She emerges cannibalized by the systems of capital through which the pregnant black body is consumed as free labor."[30] Devouring Sycorax in this way suggests not only the double reproducing of enslaved women but also the republican motherhood assigned to women by the independent state. Fundamentally, Joseph points to the constrained nature of belonging imposed on Sycorax.

Joseph's argument, similar Mehta's, demonstrates that Sycorax is both an epistemological challenge to Prospero's Enlightenment modernity and an avatar for the cannibalized consumer:

> Performing Sycorax is one way to disrupt the cannibalistic postcolonial state. . . . Sycorax's alchemy is too terrible to be remembered except as a shadow of the archetypal scenes of national and colonial encounters. Her alchemy is always narrativized as a struggle between men, between nations: Prospero and Caliban, . . . Europe and Africa, . . . Britain and India. Sycorax corporealizes [an] allegorized masculinity that takes for granted the presence of women as backdrop in the performance of statehood.[31]

Joseph emphasizes negotiations within the intersections of identity and the power Sycorax might deploy with her scream. The emphasis on the cannibalistic state makes transparent the economic logic that consumes the political and social uncertainty of postcolonial states. Indeed, Sycorax provides a space in which to explore the oppositional: she is exiled, an immigrant, a stateswoman, mother to a native, a healer, and a historical destabilizing memory. Sycorax forces us to look beyond the easy narrative and repeatedly engage with her nuances.

Sycorax as a mother, mother figure, and part of mother discourse is foundational for the reason that women's belonging has often been linked to their function as republican mothers—producers of new citizens. Mehta's project of recuperating the language and tasks of mothers and the domestic sphere in general, while laudable to a certain degree, is disconcerting. Sycorax as mother tongue and the latent tongue to a new consciousness gateway cannot be denied. At the same time, it is critical to explore how celebratory motherhood and republican motherhood erase and deny the real fissures of belonging among women, between men and women, and between women and the state.

Celebratory motherhood demonstrates how women's belonging is tied to reproduction, both biologically and through adoption. Sycorax as mother and nurturer in these various manifestations raises complicated questions about notions of "mother" and, by reducing these figures to their maternal function, continues the logic of the plantation. Benedict

Anderson links national fraternity to death and the willingness to sacrifice one's life as a soldier.[32] Though women are generally not imagined as soldiers, they have sacrificed for the larger community with their lives, in the violence they endure, in the children they bore and nurtured, and with the concessions they make in the domestic sphere, much as Lili does in "A Wall of Fire Rising." And as Grace Nichols's poem "Ala" demonstrates, these sacrifices for freedom were rehearsed during and beyond slavery.

Rehearsing Ala

As people equal under the whip but voiceless in political participation, enslaved women occupied multilevel positions in which their bodies became sites of contestation. Though owned by someone else, they found ways to reclaim their bodies for themselves. Grace Nichols's poem "Ala" rehearses work, space, and reclamation. "Ala" is the story of Uzo, an enslaved woman who refuses to create another laborer—perhaps another Caliban—for the plantation system, rupturing the discourse of the good mother along the way. Uzo is

> the rebel woman
> who with a pin
> stick the soft mould
> of her own child's head
> sending the little-new-born
> soul winging its way back
> to Africa—free.[33]

Ala is the Dahomean earth deity whom the women call on to reclaim Uzo's soul because her body will remain in the Caribbean. For her crime of infanticide, Uzo is held

> face up
> . . . her naked body
> to the ground
> arms and legs spread-eagle
> each tie with rope to stake
> then they coat her in sweet
> molasses and call us out
> to see.[34]

Here, as Nichols explains in the video *I Is a Long Memoried Woman* (1992), the commodity that Uzo produced, molasses, is used to coat her body and attract the "red and pitiless ants" to pick away her flesh.[35] Her body is tortured both by what she produced (molasses) and by what she refused to produce (a child).

Like Sycorax, Uzo is a rebel and a mother. She rebels against the power structure by refusing her condition as a plantation breeder. The rejection of her role in reproducing the plantation places Uzo in direct conflict with the power system. Her punishment is not banishment or exile, but torture, physical death, and use as a deterrent threat. Similarly, Sycorax is Prospero's example with which he repeatedly threatens Ariel. While Uzo does not leave a child to mark, she does mark the landscape and the other "rebel women." Her defiance buoys other women, and her tortured molasses-coated body, feasted upon by ants, marks the land. Sycorax's experience is marked by psychological violence—exile from Algerian society. The violence of Uzo's experience is psychological and physical. The damage to the collective unconscious wrought by enslavement leads to Uzo's physical acts against the system, her body, and her child. Uzo's violence is prismatic, at times, heroic, and at others, pathetic. Her actions cannot be read in a one-dimensional way.

This poem exemplifies several rehearsals: first, retrieval of women's experiences, which demonstrate female networks and rebellion and coping strategies; second, the body as a site of work and torture, not just discourse; and third, the body as a gateway to another form of consciousness.[36] Like the flesh that cannot be "discoursed away,"[37] Uzo's body is central to understanding the experience of black women. Here her body does not perform being eaten by ants; it *is* eaten by ants. The visible process of Uzo becoming a corpse, the slow gnawing on her flesh, presents as gruesome a hearse as is imaginable. The reality of her agonizing death fuels something in the women who watch: they become stronger, and her persecuted body, made visible in the space of her labor, entwines victimization, visibility, and work for the women who watch and sing. The convergence of motherhood, work, and a female support network reflects the realities of enslaved women's experiences. Uzo's desire not to create another slave is understood by this community of women. They witness her further degradation and torture by the slave system and "sing, weep, work" and pray for her. The weeping here is not for the passive victim-mother of the nation; it is grief for Uzo and perhaps themselves. In weeping, singing, and praying for Uzo, the women demonstrate their defiance of a system that constructs Uzo as a "bad" mother. In good-mother discourse, Uzo is a failure. Her child, any possibility for the future, is destroyed. Uzo is completely outside the space of domestication. She is a savage. Her transgression and punishment take place under the blinding sun, literally outside the house.

"Ala" is a piece on mothers—Uzo as a mother, other rebel women as mothers, and Ala as a mother/earth deity. The women call on a goddess from the motherland, and the female body metaphorically becomes the land. Nichols's creation of this historical (enslaved) mother remembers the past and relates to women today, illustrating that choosing motherhood for African-descendant women in the Americas has not been and is not a simple choice. Motherhood in the context of plantation and globalized economies always falls outside the simplistic idea of nurturer-mother. Uzo is tied to the Caribbean landscape; her remains, like Sycorax, will be put to rest in this space.

The body in this context is functioning as a site of contending forces: one of subversion and rebellion for Uzo, and one of reclamation and empowerment for Nichols. Denise deCaires Narain notes that "postcolonial writers have used literary texts to catalogue the violence done to the black body under colonial regimes and to celebrate the power of the black body to survive such violence."[38] Uzo's body, similar to most black female bodies, is simultaneously de-gendered and re-gendered; the plantation profit system situates her body outside the domestic sphere, yet her body is reinserted into the domestic sphere for childbearing. This reinsertion is doubled since reproduction is for profit. The enslaved woman's reproduction then traverses the public and private divide. In this instance, the gendering and racializing of the black body is tied to the disruption of the public and private spaces and betrays the unstable gender ground that the enslaved woman occupied.

Finally, in terms of raising consciousness, creating empathy, and establishing communities of consensus, "Ala" offers several possibilities: Uzo's story is one way of rehearsing Sycorax's latency, her unseen power. First, as an embodiment of Sycorax's latent consciousness, the women return to a spiritual and intangible antecedent, Ala. Resembling Sycorax, they had to call on pre-Columbian spirits and ways of knowing and coping. Second, this poem and the larger collection from which it springs are about performing history, memory, and belonging. These transactions connect Caribbean people across borders by making visible the historical and continued experience of plantation economies. Additionally, Uzo's story presents the negotiations women make at work and as mothers outside formal political structures, which marginalize their real concerns and characterize them solely as nurturers of the nation.

Indigo Witch

Like Uzo, Sycorax in the novel *Indigo* works the land and is ritually connected to nurturing it; she also mothers children who are biologically not her own. Similarly, in *The Salt Roads*, Mer, the most Sycorax-like figure, ritually engages with the land while cultivating many characters on the plantation.

Indigo is a dye used as currency around the world because it "creates the bluest of blues [and] has been one of the world's most valued pigments."[39] Considered "the Devil's Dye," indigo is closely associated with ritual, healing, and cosmetics. The sorceresses of Dogon wear indigo wrappers as a means of telling their stories, and "because of the distance that had to be traveled to obtain the dyestuff, the strange and difficult alchemy necessary for its production, its power to bewitch, and its transcendent beauty, the value and demand for indigo became ungovernable."[40] Indigo serves as a way to tell stories, a valuable commodity and in dyeing it Warner's Sycorax becomes Shakespeare's "blue-eyed hag."[41]

In her rehearsal of Sycorax, Marina Warner's protagonist dyes indigo and possesses the skills of a healer and wise woman. Told using the two time lines of the seventeenth and twentieth centuries, Sycorax is an indigenous woman who is an outcast from her tribe. She lives on her own in a majestic saman tree, with her familiar, Paca, a cavy, her notions and potions, and her adopted children, Dulé, renamed Caliban, and Ariel, an orphan from another indigenous community, living nearby. The seventeenth-century period replays the European conquest on the islands of Liamuiga and Oualie, renamed Enfant-Béate. Christopher "Kit" Everard, the first British colonizer—and Prospero figure—subdues the island in the 1619 Battle of Blight Sloop, killing and capturing the Amerindians, Africans, buccaneers, and other outcasts who had plotted to eject him and his men. Everard showed violence before this battle when he and crew tried to destroy Sycorax's tree and nearly burned her alive. The second time line, twentieth-century England, replays the ashes of the Empire and Britain's diminished role in the world. It features Miranda, a descendant of Christopher Everard, and several traces of Prospero through the characters of Miranda's father, another Kit Everard, and grandfather, Sir Anthony Everard.

The Salt Roads features three interconnected story lines: eighteenth-century Haiti—Mer's story; nineteenth-century France—Jeanne's story; and fourteenth-century Egypt—Meritet's (or Thais's) story. La Sirèn, goddess of the deep sea, connects the three stories: she who is born as she simultaneously lives multiple aspects of herself by possessing each of the protagonists in an effort to exercise and comprehend her power in the world. As she declares: "If you have a body, you can act."[42] La Sirèn wants Mer to do two things: open the "salt roads" in the minds of her people as way of connecting with the gods and stop Makandal, a man who aspires to become a *loa*, from poisoning whites.

The second story line features the historical figure Jeanne Duval, a mixed-race prostitute, lover, and muse of the French poet Charles Baudelaire. The third story is that of Thais, a young ancient Egyptian girl sold into prostitution, and her quest for home with her friend and coworker, Judah. All the story lines historicize gay, lesbian, and bisexual characters, giving visibility to these lives and experiences.

Ritual is the gateway to an oppositional consciousness and connection to alternative ways of being. In *Indigo*, Sycorax is eventually worshipped as a *loa*, and her grave, the saman tree, functions as a *pòto-mitan*, the Vodou grounding pole, connecting past, present, dead, and unborn.[43] The saman tree is likewise a metaphorical *pòto-mitan* as it connects the physical and spiritual worlds, yet it can also be read as the hearse of Sycorax's entombment. In *The Salt Roads*, Mer (French for "sea") connects the worlds of the living and the gods through ritual: "The sea in the mind of my Ginen. The sea roads, the salt roads and the sweet ones, too; the rivers. Can't follow them to their sources any more. I land in the same foul, stagnant swamp every time. You must fix it, Mer."[44] La Sirèn is concerned about the salt roads losing their connectivity because, without them, she cannot be part of the story stream and interact with her devotees. The *æther* in which La Sirèn lives ruptures time and space and allows her to experience multiple lives concurrently. The young-and-old La Sirèn can be sucked into "the blockage," a foul-smelling place full of horror and corruption: "When I start to be dragged down into human time as I have been before, start to feel the weight of bones and flesh again, it makes me . . . bitter. . . . I scream anger into the careless ocean of æther, but there's no reply."[45] She asks what is wrong with her flowing world of stories; without them, this "guerilla warfare,"[46] our vessels with which to rehearse alternatives in form and content, are inaccessible. The *æther* is a space of alchemy and mutuality for the goddess, which in turn becomes a space of mutuality for a community when its members gather in ritual service to the gods. Rehearsing stories alchemizes communal spaces, re-creating a violated logic and way of understanding place and time. La Sirèn and Sycorax interrupt the idea of time as linear because they conceived "differently of time and space they occupied, and see it as a churn or a bowl, in which substances and essences were tumbled and mixed, always returning, now emerging into personal form, now submerged into the mass in the continuous present tense of existence, as in one of the vats in which Sycorax brewed indigo."[47] Rehearsal telescopes the past into the present, changing temporalities and generating diverse responses to contemporary conditions. Reconceiving time beyond linearity shifts perceptions and the conditions in which exchanges are constructed.

Mer's religious practice helps her maintain an oppositional consciousness, but religion has been an important component in the matrix of control—in these texts, both the religion of the colonizer and the spiritual practices of the colonized can liberate or subjugate. Official religion (i.e., the religion of the colonizer) undergirds male power and is used to keep women in the background although they perform much of the work that maintains the institution. Conversely, religion has been integral to black and Caribbean liberation struggles as a means of revising the world.[48] African-based religions, and/or religious practice within European-derived churches, have been flexible—eluding erasure through camouflage, interplay, and incorporation of syncretic layers and in rituals; however, the elasticity of these spaces means that they are constantly shifting. Colliding religious universes, one unofficial and the other state-sanctioned, have investments in the cult of true womanhood, which is constructed on the religious doctrine that "good" women are submissive, pious, and sexually pure.[49] The cult of true (white) womanhood informs the continued reduction of Sycoraxian representations as "merely maternal" and as a way of ideologically and actually representing women as outside the founding histories of the nation.

These principles, or "cardinal virtues," circumvented women's participation in the public sphere—the world external to the home.[50] They determined acceptable feminine and masculine behavior and shaped ensuing gender relations. Though this model was the jurisdiction of middle- and upper-class women, it was an aspirational marker and continues to inform ideal behaviors for men and women. In the Caribbean, such domestication is characterized as "good woman" and "good mumma" discourse as exemplified by the lifestyle of a married upper-class European woman: "With limited education in the classics, housewife (but with servants), subservient to her husband and confined in her public life to social work, became a model for 'the good woman.' The loud, working-class, unmarried African woman became the opposite. Migrant Indian women, . . . at their point of entrance into the society, were reconstructed into otherness, often in opposition to the negative values associated with working-class African women in the society."[51] Though this characterization of the good woman is beyond the boundaries of most Caribbean women's experiences, it remains vital—tenaciously clinging to cultural norms, especially as celebrity culture and the valorization of wealthy people's lives are ubiquitous across popular platforms.

This image of the good woman, enshrined in the nineteenth century, has a historical, ideological, and material presence. Hemispheric American history is a story of plantation economies that subverted patriarchal views on sexual division of labor for profit. From the point of conquest, Europeans put indigenous men and women "to work on ranches, and in mines and fields as virtual slaves."[52] Indentured European women, enslaved African women, and, later, indentured Indian, Chinese, and Javanese women followed these Amerindian women. Indentured and free white women, however, were granted particular protections by virtue of race, class, and sex, while enslaved African women, constructed outside the norms and values of African and European womanhood, were subjected to a different set of gender negotiations.[53] Thus, from the beginning of the transatlantic slave trade and New World plantation economies, gender has operated as an ever-changing and unfixed system.[54]

At the core of physical resistances are those of the psychological domain that must exist even if at the most embryonic level. Women and men do resist "good woman" domestication while they simultaneously hold it as an ideal. These contradictions characterize women as often authoritative in the home but not in the public sphere,[55] which has meant coding women's power as "cunning," relational, and "circumstantial, not apparent to wider society and [without] great impact at the level of national decision-making."[56] This type of subversive authority offers ways of understanding power as multidirectional, process-oriented, and textured.

The issues faced by mothers in both *Indigo* and *The Salt Roads* recall Mehta's and Joseph's discussion of Sycoraxian maternity. Reminiscent of the *Zong* incident, in which 132 captured Africans were thrown overboard, in *Indigo*, twenty Africans wash up on the Liamuiga beach, apparently having been cast overboard since, in the absence of other flotsam, they were found with "bones pok[ing] through the ribbons of their battered flesh."[57] Though the villagers bury these pungent African bodies in a shallow pit, Sycorax hears them: "Another cried, 'I could not see you, my darling, in the dark! Call to me so that I may know where you are.' The reply came, if it was a reply, 'the bed we lie in is a grave.' 'Yes, the vessel that brought us became our hearse."[58] As she hears the voices of the dead and dying, Sycorax remembers seeing a pregnant woman, the distension of her body distinct from the swelling of other brine-laden corpses. Sycorax delivers the infant, whom she names Dulé, meaning "grief." By cutting into the maternal cavity, Sycorax ushers in new temporal and spatial dynamics that cause conflict: "His delivery set Sycorax apart; her husband proclaimed her magical powers marked her as an official wise woman. At the same time, he took the opportunity to announce his own remarriage [and returned her to her family]."[59] The ship as hearse makes the body of Dulé's biological mother visible, which in turn enables Sycorax to save his life. Furthermore, Sycorax's attentiveness to these bodies, her ability to see life (and other alternatives) among the dead, leads to her ostracism. Sycorax is punished for being able to rehearse. Dulé's birth creates multiple origin stories, with some villagers believing that Sycorax is his mother and that he was born of "her concoctions."[60] Ultimately, because of an increasingly discordant time in this place, Sycorax and Dulé leave the village, and the patriarchs of Sycorax's community believe they have trumped her "magic."[61]

At this point, Warner's reimagining of Shakespeare's character is "simultaneously the native woman and modern subject of the new nation. Her audible screams unleash the unspoken economies of the alchemy of exchange."[62] The arrival of the beached Africans "was the beginning of a new world for her and her people, the start of a new time, and as yet Sycorax did not know it."[63] The alchemy of temporal exchange means that Sycorax is simultaneously a historical trace of the native and the African, a fictional archetype, and a modern woman. Sycorax's existence across these planes is concealed and distorted by linear history. However, it is through rehearsal that the power and reverberations of the multiplicity emerge to create nuance and spaces of mutuality.

In *The Salt Roads*, another baby boy, this one stillborn, ushers in the tale of the most Sycorax-like character in the novel: Mer. An enslaved healer, Mer is considered an elder while still in her thirties because she has survived the plantation longer than most. In her role as elder, Mer feels a responsibility for those on the plantation and will not leave, even when she has the opportunity to find her own freedom. Mer's husband and child are dead, and she is alone save for Tipingee, her lover since their Middle Passage voyage. Like Sycorax and her tribe, Mer is out of time and place as she tries to retain the rituals and ways of her African culture. The mixed-race Georgine, despondent over her stillborn child, born to her and a French carpenter's son, decides to bury him near the river where her foster mother, Calliope, drowned. The prayers and songs performed by these women at this unorthodox cemetery birth La Sirèn.[64]

Compared to La Sirèn's unorthodox beginning or rebirth, Prospero is the more entrenched manifestation of patriarchal parenting. He, the embodiment of the law of the (European) father and Miranda's pater, is concerned with her potential defilement and debasement at the hands of black Caliban. Miranda is inside this space, held hostage by Prospero's managing of her education, socialization, and sexual and reproductive life. Hilary Beckles characterizes white women as the moral center of the white community and the household authorities who "found it impossible to 'live' at an ideological distance. [Thus,] no distinct culture of the white woman as mediator of slavery emerged; rather her subscription to slavery and colonialism led to an ideological assimilation that produced . . . political sameness and symmetry."[65] Elite women maintained the "law of the father" and were compelled to maintain the slave system. Some working-class white women were displaced by slave labor, yet others profited from it.[66] Miranda, in all her guises, is another justifier for the father. She reinforces Prospero's truth, despite their problematic relationship centered around his denial and erasure of her mother.[67] The essence of Miranda's citizenship and selfhood is based on the us/them conflict or, more precisely, the dynamics of free white woman in contrast to enslaved black woman. Miranda, though under Prospero's thumb, exercises his deferred power over poorer white women and black women—free or enslaved.

Just as there are several types of Sycoraxian characters, there are also multiple Mirandas, and Xanthe, the second child and daughter of Sir Anthony Everard, is one of them. She is removed from the fray in *Indigo*: cherished, golden, but detached until the moment of her death by drowning, the same end that befell her father's first wife. In fact, Miranda characterizes Xanthe as a "monster" with a taste for conquest,[68] and Xanthe's guiding principle is to frustrate her doting father:

> "Sy's [Xanthe's asexual husband] right about Poppa. Everybody loves him, because he seems so mild and calm, but that's just his way of keeping you in his power. All that rot about his *sangay* [preternatural insight and power], it's sheer mystification, there's nothing behind it. I'm grown-up now, I'm not his little woman anymore. You know, Poppa would have liked to marry me himself if he could, that's what Sy says, and he's spot on, I'm telling you. Under lock and key, lock and key, in the tower forever."[69]

Xanthe's casual observation of her father's psychological incest reveals not only her hostility to his authority but also the dynamics of historical mirroring and devouring: her name, X*anthe*, reflects a digestion of her father, whose nickname is "Ant." Xanthe's casual mention of an incestuous relationship with her father marks the patriarchal colonial project as one that desires and exploits native, black, and brown bodies, while simultaneously policing and demarcating white women's bodies for white men exclusively. Xanthe is her father's double while also being an aspect of Prospero's daughter. The girl child forever encased in the tower whose purity is rationale for all types of violence. It is Xanthe more than the twentieth-century Miranda who is tied to neocolonial conquest; she is an imperial justifier through her role as hotelier. She and Sy own and manage lucrative gambling and hotel interests on both islands of Enfant-Béate, characterized much like a foreign invasion.[70]

Unlike Xanthe, who is not consumed by postcolonial guilt, Warner's Miranda is an anxious character, longing for peace, justice, and a better place. She listens to family nursemaid Serafine's stories and values them above the inherited glories of her family's past. Serafine, based on Jean Rhys's Christophine in *Wide Sargasso Sea*—herself a twentieth-century Sycoraxian character—left her daughter behind so that she could serve the Everard family in England.[71] However, it is Miranda who becomes, in a sense, Serafine's child—she ingests her stories and names her daughter "Serafine." Miranda procreates with black actor George Felix, a twentieth-century Caliban—a role he has played and understands as one of being a Maroon. While Chantal Zabus has characterized the ending of the book as Warner's capitulation to political correctness, it could easily be read as Warner's attempt to retell and reckon with her own family's legacy of colonialism, with the triumph of miscegenation and the mixed-race colonial. Warner is not the only author to do this. Elizabeth Nunez's *Prospero's Daughter* (2006) attests to this relationship between Virginia (Miranda) and Carlos (Caliban). Both authors craft stories in which the Miranda and Caliban characters triumph over Prospero's power and people these isles with little Calibans.[72] While Shakespeare imagined that only rape could unite Miranda and Caliban, these reimaginings propose more complex interracial relations. In fact, the interracial relationships in *Indigo* are consensual—Miranda and George, and Ariel and Kit—though the latter are not durable, and somewhat coercive.

As new world Mirandas embrace racial mixing, Shakespeare's Prospero speaks of Sycorax only to curse and devalue her—she is a hag, a whore, and a criminal.[73] Caliban learns this language in order to curse

Prospero, but linguistic acquisition places Caliban in a psychological conundrum with a language that devalues him and his antecedents. The only positive power the language offers him is in privileging his position as a male; ergo, Caliban internalizes systems of racial and gender oppression. However, critics such as Roberto Fernández Retamar point out that the language of the colonizer is "now *our* language."[74] What "our" languages encompass, as well as their various registries, is a constantly debated psychological and epistemological issue in the Caribbean region. Nonetheless, in representing Sycorax in this way, Prospero, not unlike black men who inherit gender, political, and economic power, "puts her in her place to safeguard his manhood threatened by the authority of the female upstart."[75]

In *The Salt Roads*, at La Sirèn's bidding, Mer tries to intervene in the plotting that culminates in an earlier ceremony at Bois Caïman (though not the purported 1791 ceremony featuring Boukman Dutty and Cecile Fatiman). This ceremony features competing deities who mount Mer and Makandal—she ridden by La Sirèn, and he possessed by Ogu, the warrior *loa* of blacksmithing and "more recently the crafty political leader."[76] The fight between Mer and Makandal mirrors the domestic fight that is part of the lore of the two gods and reflective of the issues of rebellion brewing in Haiti. Ogu wins. In an effort to stop La Sirèn and Mer, her horse, from warning the whites, they silence her: "Ogu in Makandal's body used his good hand to draw my tongue out from my mouth. Then, smiling, he used the arm that was not there and sliced the spirit machete across my tongue. Pain exploded like light in my head. I tried to scream, but with no air in my chest it came out a gurgle."[77] Mer's flesh is tortured, not by white plantation masters, but by a black man seeking his power on the plantation. Makandal/Ogu's cut with the spirit machete merges the violences of the domestic, public/revolutionary, and spiritual spheres. The commingling of these forces and their ferocity robs Mer of her ability to scream and verbally decry the cannibalistic forces embodied in Makandal.

Prospero's construction of Sycorax reminds us that black "women occupy a position whereby they are the inferior half of a series of converging dichotomies, and this placement has been central to our subordination."[78] Sycorax is simultaneously the Jezebel, "the whore or sexually aggressive woman,"[79] a loose woman because Caliban's father is absent and unknown (to us), and the emasculating black matriarch, the very reason for black poverty and underdevelopment. The black matriarch is characterized as a "bad" mother.[80] She "fails to fulfill [her] traditional womanly duties," violating spherical boundaries and republican belonging through a simplistic nurturing motherhood. She is outside the domestic space, to the detriment of her family. We know Sycorax to be "bad," because she was banished, a violator in Algerian society, and she certainly challenges any construct in which Prospero has the authority. As a violator of Algerian space, Sycorax does not belong and is forced out. In the Caribbean, in making a way, perhaps within an indigenous community, the dynamics of belonging shift. She is an initial outsider who shares or appropriates the land from the native people; to some degree she may be no better than Prospero. While in fact we do not know how she appropriated the island, Caliban uses her to assert his claim to it. This new space defines Sycorax as worker more than as mother, and she has little to lose in challenging the sociopolitical order she has inherited.

Resistance always connotes engagement with often hierarchical constructions of power and has played a crucial role in Caribbean development, manifesting itself in many forms throughout the region and in every sector of society. From the beginning, "indigenous women have a tradition of resistance before European arrival in 1492. Taino women, captured by the Kalinago, resisted by holding on to their language and culture."[81] Additionally, indigenous women fought Europeans and greeted Columbus's second voyage "with a shower of arrows."[82] But some cooperated with colonizing forces. Warner's Ariel, rendered female and within a mother-daughter dynamic that shares some similarities with Prospero and Miranda's relationship, becomes mute after the Battle of Blight's Sloop and runs with her son, Roukoube, fathered by the seventeenth-century Kit Everard, to another island. Ariel also rehearses the role of Warner's indigenous connections. She recounts that her ancestor, Sir Thomas Warner, governor of St. Christopher's (St. Kitts) and Nevis had an "Indian wife," Madam Ouvernard, with whom he had children. In addition to these children, there are several documents referring to Governor Warner's wife as "Barbe" (for "barbarian," Marina Warner suspects), a native woman who foiled an indigenous ambush of the English "because she held them in affection and esteem—she was Warner's mistress."[83] May Joseph imagines Sycorax's scream as integral to her resistance; her sonic intervention shatters Prospero's logic and language. While Sycorax has a voice in the novel, Ariel is mute for a time, silenced after her child's birth: "Ariel herself made almost no sound, she choked on speech, for nobody could return an answer. . . . [S]he had no more words, indeed it seemed to her she no longer owned a voice, but only a hollow drum for a head on which others beat their summons."[84]

Ultimately, colonial violence and Ariel's failed attempt to seduce and kill her son's father push her to Oualie, the smaller of the two islands that form the state of Enfant-Béate.

Ariel's muteness is reminiscent of the voiceless Sycorax of *The Tempest*, and, as a native and a mother, Ariel replays Sycorax's role in the original Shakespeare play. Kit and his English wife, Rebecca, appropriate the land, while Ariel and her mixed child retreat as the colony is taken into the English imperial fold. As Zabus argues, *Indigo* is a series of fairy-tale rehearsals, including that of Pocahontas, what with Ariel's "eroticolonial encounters and collaborations with Kit."[85] Ariel's resistances are not black and white but contained and negotiated throughout her colonial encounter. She transitions from lover to enemy over the course of a year and during that time occupies the space of collaborator for a period. Warner calls this space the "hyphen" or space of native female collaboration: "women, through their bodies, became the hyphen between the forest/*morne* and the *habitation*/house/plantation, either by force or by choice. Madam Ouvernard . . . is neither Maroon nor docile house slave; she figures as the connection between the two societies, a connection that has been effaced from memory just as her own name has been lost under 'Barbe,' under her married title."[86]

Correspondingly, African resistance predates arrival in the Americas, and "resistance began in West Africa and continued during the [M]iddle [P]assage. Anti-slavery mentalities, therefore, preceded the plantation. It connected African women to their creole progeny delivered on the plantations by enchained wombs, collectively, these women set their hearts and minds against slavery."[87] Other forms of resistance to the plantation system included maroonage, malingering, property destruction (of tools, of self via self-mutilation and infanticide), and work slowdowns.[88] A particularly female form of resistance was "back chat." Lucille Mathurin Mair chronicles that "it was a notorious fact that female slaves more often deserved punishment than male[s], for they used to great effect 'that powerful instrument of attack and defense, their tongue.'"[89] Retrieving all these forms of resistance has been important in the Caribbean quest for self-determination across gender largely because they illustrate non-violent and violent modes of resistance.

Recognizing Sycorax and her relationship to this paradigm of colonialism, resistance, and emancipation is necessary to constructing communities of consensus that value women's contributions. Sycorax, like all enslaved African women, was brought to the island against her will; she was pregnant, then abandoned, perhaps with only Ariel as a helpmate.[90]

Shakespeare explains that she "litters" Caliban on the island, mixing womb and blood with earth. The land ingests her placenta, creating a connection that is hard to sever. Caliban's birth signals that Sycorax has birthed a nation and a discourse. From this beginning, Sycorax has to find a way where, ostensibly, there is no way. She has to make life and meaning in a space where her sex and gender performance are diminished by her need to create a home for herself and her son.

Sex and Sycorax

Hopkinson's uneven novel locates religious practice, particularly African-influenced spiritualities, as vehicles of a history of sexual difference that has not been politically visible: "We are all here, all the powers of the Ginen lives for all the centuries that they have been in existence, and we all fight. We change when change is needed. We are a little different in each place that the Ginen have come to rest and anyone of is [*sic*] already many powers."[91] Through all the echoes and streaming possibilities, the goddess La Sirèn realizes that "my own face gazes back at me from those infinite reflections, and it is all in their faces. They are me."[92] Hopkinson takes the "they are me" further, relating the mutual experiences of resistance to an emancipatory project that is simultaneously historical, national, racial, and sexual. She links Queen Nzingha's fight for freedom in Angola, to Bois Caïman in Haiti, to the Underground Railroad and the Stonewall Rebellion in the United States:

> One summer New York night, a group of men who love men and women who love women hang about the front of a nightclub, harassed and kicked out by the police. Inside, the police arrest five women with men's bodies and one mannish woman. As they try to leave with their prisoners, a Puerto Rican woman with a man's body throws her high-heeled pump; the first missile of resistance. A tall, black drag queen breaks his bonds and flees free. Another six-foot black vision in sequins and glitter throws himself into the attack led by queers, faggots, transvestites, and street youth, into the victory they will call Stonewall. Black Madonna, Sylvia Rivera, and Marsha P. Johnson all teach us Ezilis more about beauty, defiance, and resistance.[93]

In addition to locating gay, lesbian, and bisexual lives throughout history, Hopkinson's most compelling narratives locate these identities on black bodies in the West—France and Haiti, specifically.[94]

Rehearsing Sycorax subverts the binary of public and private. As was true for enslaved women who were part of the public but not the political sphere, Sycorax has been mentioned, alluded to, and recognized as

Caliban's mother but not regarded as a political agent. The imperial codes for ideal manhood and womanhood have meant that a silent Sycorax is an ideal Sycorax. She is a person unworthy of consideration, but to acknowledge her intrusion in colonial and postcolonial societies is to realize that Caliban has a history. A politicized Sycorax challenges not only Prospero but also Caliban, who is a popular figure by virtue of the valuable theoretical work of male Caribbean and Latin American writers and intellectuals. In identifying with Sycorax, Caliban arrests the universalizing tendencies of master and mistress narratives. Throughout the Americas, gender discourse, and broader society, have been historically characterized by "the overarching [and, often, overbearing] rule of the father,"[95] though contemporary discourse emphasizes continuums of gender and sexual identities. As Omise'eke Natasha Tinsley emphasizes, in the Caribbean there is a fluidity of sexual identities as well as behaviors; often what may be considered "gay" or "homosexual" in the United States does not translate as such in the region. Indeed, while there are clearly same-gender erotic relationships, the term "gay" has not been used to characterize those relationships until recently.

Sycorax, as Shakespeare disembodies her, politicizes the text for black women and for working women and men who have not had to consider her presence. Similarly, in *The Salt Roads*, the lives of same-gender loving people have not had to be considered in the Caribbean nation-building project, but in Hopkinson's novel, these lives become visible in their ordinariness and their sexual expression. In an early love scene, Jeanne Duval and her coworker-cum-lover, Lisette, have sex: "'Mm.' I burrowed my head in closer and tunneled my tongue into her gully hole. Lisette giggled, then sighed, my girl and opened her knees wider. The salty liquor of her spread in my mouth. . . . She collapsed back onto the bed and released my head. She was sobbing; gasping for breath. I wriggled up beside her and held her until she was still again. I licked my lips, sucking salt."[96] While heterosexual sex is ubiquitous, lesbian love is rarely given this type of graphic presence in Caribbean literature. Though characters may be in same-gender loving relationships, as in Ana-Maurine Lara's *Erzulie's Skirt*, their sex lives are circumspect—limited to pecks on the cheeks and petting. Lara's characters are endangered, which may explain the erasure of their physical pleasures. This is not the case in Hopkinson's text; in all three story lines, despite the dangers encountered, her characters have vivid sexual experiences. These homoerotic representations may be surprising because they are so rare. In making the bodies and flesh visible in lesbian sex, *The Salt Roads* rehearses both the power to challenge the norm that Sycorax represents and the process of making these bodies legible and legitimate. As in various manifestations of heteronormative patriarchy, there is an investment in regulating desire and policing appropriate masculinity and femininity and appropriate sexual/erotic/intimate relationships. Though gender regulations may differ from sexual regulations, they are part of the same overarching desire to control society and limit expression. And while it is difficult to separate the two because assumptions of heteronormativity designate what and with whom men and women are sexually appropriate, when gender norms are violated, the assumption is that sexual norms are likewise breached, hence the assumption that strong women are lesbian or asexual. Furthermore, Belinda Wallace argues that "these relationships are equally supportive socially, emotionally, culturally, and sexually, and reflect multiple levels of trust and support, not just desire."[97] Wallace, like Mimi Sheller, Faith Smith, and others, recognizes that sexual identity has become intertwined with national identity. Emerging Caribbean nationalism "institutionalized the second class status of women through a public/private sphere divide and women's access to rights through men," while criminalizing homosexuality. This modeling of "developed world patriarchy" affects the ways in which sexual identities are marginalized and not included in the national identity. Ultimately, "citizenship has been constructed on the denial of the experiences of the black and Indian masses . . . and also on the denial of the experiences of women and homosexuals."[98] The characters in *The Salt Roads* interrupt belonging to heteronormative patriarchies by making same-gender loving and bisexual relationships visible and normative. Additionally, the Sycorax-like characters in *The Salt Roads* embody much of what Michelle Cliff sees as Sycoraxian. They are rebels and mothers, who, unlike previous generations of same-gender-loving Caribbean people, are able to "locate themselves" in Caribbean narratives.[99] This embedding of non-(hetero)-normative sexualities in cultural production provides a way of rehearsing these identities and extending the definition of who can belong to Caribbean nations.

With emancipation, the white and free-colored population, along with newly freed slaves and newly indentured East Indians, subscribed to the domestication of women. Attempting to transcend the boundaries of the slave system meant adopting the Eurocentric values that were part of the plantation system. Social mobility in the post-slavery period meant the representation of black women in the "good mumma" mold, rather than the actuality.[100] Although "female slaves . . . reverted to a subordinate position within the black family after they were freed," it is argued that this "position was aspired to but unattainable under enslavement."[101]

Women's ability to control their lives and bodies continues to contradict male-centric ideologies.[102] As these texts demonstrate, women find their political voices within the boundaries of specified social units, and, though Caribbean women may be perceived as matriarchs, their authority does not effectively transcend the domestic space since those who head households are among the poorest and most destitute. Sycorax determines Prospero's justification narrative that is born of his illegitimate access to power.[103] She exercised enough influence in Algiers to be transported rather than executed. Once on the island, she sets the agenda vis-à-vis Ariel, Caliban, and Prospero, thus highlighting the ways in which women's power is conditioned by relationships and interactions. Theirs is not seen as an active power, a phallic power, nor as one inherently imbued as an agent of change. Retrieving Sycorax's voice and experience from the ruptures of *The Tempest*, allows us to explore—through colonial, postcolonial, and nationalist discourse—issues vital to women's experiences of the plantation, the colony, and the (in)dependent state. Examining Caribbean women's lives means interrogating their experiences in community.

As such, issues that have been central to understanding Caribbean women and their communities have included ideas of proper feminine behavior, sex and sexuality, and work in public and private spaces. Whether defined as inside or outside these boundaries, these notions have influenced women's responses to themselves and their families. Good mumma discourse has influenced whether Sycorax, Solitude, Uzo, Mer, Jeanne, and Miranda can be "good" mothers, or even mothers at all. These deeply held constructions of masculinity, femininity, and sexuality, intersected by nationalist desires and mediated through institutions of power, can delimit and marginalize women as agents. The psychological contradiction of not being the ideal woman—but wanting to be—has influenced the negotiations that inform the communities these characters make.

Rehearsing in the Caribbean builds on women's historical experience of self-sufficiency and community. These projects not only promote a woman-valued historical consciousness but also explore contemporary experiences and contradictions, as well as encourage action. It is important to recover and lay bare the stories of women by making the public voice a political voice. The excitement of recognition enables people to see their common interests, which, in turn, allows women to weep and pray for Uzo and thus embrace and build on a shared experience. Moreover, it is this recognition of experience recovered by rehearsing Sycorax that can ultimately enable Caribbean people to access the latent oppositional consciousness, thus transforming the personal and the local, where women's stories usually reside, to the national and the regional.

5   Rehearsing Indigeneity

PAULINE MELVILLE'S FIRST NOVEL, *The Ventriloquist's Tale*, offers a model for rehearsing the ramifications of gender, globalization, and transnationalism as they relate to the rights of indigenous peoples. Set in the South American—though culturally and historically Caribbean—country of Guyana, *The Ventriloquist's Tale* focuses on the lives of the biracial (half Amerindian, half European) McKinnon family, their interactions with one another, the state, and the larger global order.[1] Rehearsing these stories helps us consider notions of the "native" and the relation between colonial history and the formation of independent nation-states. The novel uses three parallel love stories to juxtapose Amerindian, European, and Coastlander (a mix of African, Asian, and European) worldviews: Chofoye "Chofy" McKinnon and Rosa Mendelson, a Wapisiana man and his British lover; Danny and Beatrice McKinnon, engaged in an incestuous brother-sister relationship, which results in a child, Sonny; and patriotic love of community or nation as expressed by Tenga McKinnon, Chofy's cousin.[2]

Through the lens of feminist rehearsal, *The Ventriloquist's Tale* invites the reader to do several rehearsals of Amerindian identity and belonging by reading these characters through an oppositional gaze. For example, reading Chofy through the gaze or perspectives of the Coastlanders and his family provides multiple scenarios. Extending this idea, it is important to examine the ways in which perspectives shift if the Wapisiana idea of nation is read, not only from colonial or Coastlander perspectives, but also from a precolonial (hinterland) perspective. Melville's text offers the opportunity to do these multiple readings, and if conscious of these as rehearsal opportunities and giving them equal weight, our interpretation of the novel and the Guyanese nation could be different.

Economic hardship forces Chofy, the protagonist, from Guyana's savannahs to the coastal capital, Georgetown. His journey between these landscapes highlights contemporary conflicts within Amerindian communities, and between those communities and the settlers who surround them. Chofy, along with his Aunt Wifreda, who needs a cataract operation, leaves his wife, Marietta, and their eight-year-old son, Bla-Bla, in the savannahs when he relocates to Georgetown. The bodies and bones in this novel reveal how the flesh of native peoples has been and continues to be part of genocidal encounters, and how the visible hearse aspect of their bodies troubles postcolonial nations. Examining the novel for indigenous understandings of belonging calls attention to the varied and complex implications of reproducing dying and dysfunctional notions of the nation within familial, national, and physical borders in terms of spatial and sexual relations.

In Melville's novel, Chofy, unlike his cousin Tenga, goes out to the primary Guyanese landscapes, the coastal areas of the capital. Georgetown supports 80 percent of the Guyanese population and is one part of a physical, historical, and psychological divide between hinterland and coast. The name "Guyana" is an Amerindian word for "land of many waters," and the country has been characterized as aquatic, with four major rivers—Essequibo, Demerara, Berbice, and Courantyne—dividing it. In many regards, Guyana's geography has been its destiny, maintaining separation between aboriginal peoples and colonizers and, later, between enslaved and indentured workers. Georgetown has been the site of "development," while the rest of the territory has remained "pristine." It is to Georgetown that Chofy goes to recoup financial losses caused by bat bites to his cattle and to send remittances to the Rupununi. In this solitary and uneasy landscape, Chofy is stifled.[3]

Georgetown, the "city built of space," with elastic buildings, is a grid of contradictions, full of stuffy offices and narrow streets. Stabroek Market, once a slave market, is a maze of stalls unlike the open savannahs. Georgetown is a place of miscegenation, heat, humidity, and rot. In a sense, the city is representative of a "larger world," one closer to the West. Though claimed by Spain, the Dutch gained a foothold in the territory by the 1620s and established two settlements, Berbice and Demerara. The 1763 slave uprising led to a flight of Dutch colonists, and by the mid-1700s, the Dutch had invited British immigrants to settle in the area. International conflict, including the Napoleonic wars, meant the colony changed imperial hands several times, but by 1803, the British held the area.

Georgetown, built on the foundations of Dutch slave markets, is an uneasy ode to European engineering. Like other colonial cities, it connected the colony, and now the independent nation-state, to Western values, ethics, and knowledge. Guiana, as it was called during the colonial period, suffered from parsimonious absentee planters whose estates were run by managers and the extraordinary influence of the transnational corporation Bookers Brothers, McConnell & Company, known simply as Bookers.[4] This firm owned factories and plantations in Europe and across the colonial world from India to Barbados, Nigeria to Guyana. Known primarily for its sugar holdings—it owned 75 percent of the market in Guyana—Bookers diversified into cattle, consumer goods, shipping lines, heavy machinery, and a host of other interests and ran a neo-state that paralleled official governing structures.[5] As Gordon Lewis characterizes it: "Bookers became, in itself, an almost separate sovereign kingdom, undertaking and controlling an extensive set of essentially public services which the political state, for want of organizational skills and capital revenue, was unable itself to provide for its citizens. This produced a society . . . in which solid blocks of [the] population received without charge social services frequently better than those provided by the local government authorities."[6] In essence, Bookers enlarged Georgetown's foundations as a marketplace, with the entire geography controlled, contained, and managed by the company. The company's ability to provide services normally provided by the state while remaining a profitable enterprise maps the inability of both colonial and postcolonial states to fully function.

Chofy enters Georgetown, an environment of symbolic political, social, and economic mismanagement and itself a symbolic parallel of the colonial era and the novel's present. In the historical scenario, the plantation was king, and, as Brackette F. Williams contends, members of Guyanese society were judged and valued according to their relationship to labor on these estates. Thus, "Amerindians were relegated to the interior and then defined as noncontributors to whom (apart from humanitarian sentiments) nothing was owed."[7] Amerindian economic worthlessness, combined with the characterization of them as helpless children and backward relics, meant that they functioned as a mythological backdrop rather than as participants of belonging in colonial and postcolonial Guyana.

Thus, given Melville's sensibilities (i.e., her desire to upend long-held beliefs and her use of humor and irony throughout the text), it is no accident that while Chofy is in the city, he works in a library arranging and restocking validated bits of European knowledge.[8] Libraries, like museums, have been spaces in which Amerindians have generally been the objects of study, reproducing European constructions of the primitive native, their culture, their bones reassembled in museum spaces for the consumption of people outside their communities. Chofy, as an arranger of his ancestors' spines and bones in this environment, inverts the idea of who owns and catalogs knowledge.

But like Chofy's stay in the city, a hermetic place in which he finds love with a Jewish, British, literary Marxist researcher, Rosa Mendelson, Georgetown also offers a contradictory reading as a site of Western connection. Georgetown rehearses Western technologies in inhospitable spaces. While it is spatially the most technologically and structurally Western space in Guyana, it is also "contaminated" by the mixtures of Western colonialism, mixtures that, the novel suggests, foster the "tingalinga tingalinga"[9] culture and history of the steel pan, a drum invented in 1930s Trinidad and Tobago. Because of limited road and rail infrastructure, Georgetown is an enclosed space, isolated from the rest of the country. The contradiction of Georgetown is that, while Western, it too is alienated from the West. It is stuck in a colonial mode of imitation and reaching for something it can never be, in both spatial and temporal terms. The structural dependencies in the city from its time as "Bookers' Guiana" govern relationships.[10] Georgetown is a spatial manifestation of cannibalism and contradiction. The precision of Dutch technology and engineering is undermined by an unforgiving climate with a terrain that is reclaiming itself. This below-sea-level landscape devours many man-made encroachments, especially if they are not vigilantly managed. Georgetown is not well drained and so succumbs to the natural intrusion of the environment: the sea, which, with the appetite of water, devours the land.

Even as space is subdued with the taming of the landscape in order to make a city, Georgetown is a space that reiterates Amerindian unbelonging and alienation. Instead, salvation is linked, somewhat romantically, to the open vistas and "brown clumps of grass" of the savannahs.[11] Georgetown, for Amerindians, is a place where they are teased, tormented, and on the fringes of society, only considered part of the national story as a romantic and symbolic backdrop, ossified as the naked savage of the initial point of contact. As Chofy walks the streets of the city, he is teased by black residents and told to return to the bush: "'Look at de moon-face buck man [pejorative for indigenous person].' One of the others threw a chewed mango seed at him. 'Get back to the bush, buck man.' Chofy ignored them, seething inwardly. He put on a blank expression and continued walking."[12] In this moment, as with Lili's experience in Edwidge Danticat's "A Wall of Fire Rising," one becomes conscious of the need for various rehearsals of Amerindian identity so that the society can become conscious of different dimensions of the Amerindian experience. Those in the city continue to see no connection to the "moon-face buck man," like Chofy's Uncle Danny, who finds the idea of his sister Beatrice dating an Afro-Guyanese man threatening.

Everything in colonial history indicates that Georgetown, as Melville constructs it, cannot be ideal for Amerindians. Chofy's sojourn in the city illustrates that Georgetown's possibilities of love (Rosa) and inversion of knowledge (his job in the library) can only be temporary. Rehearsing the native reveals that even endogamous tribal communities have been penetrated by external influences. The idea of the noble untouched native is a fiction. Rehearsing the native rethinks the idea that indigenous people are simultaneously premodern and invisible. In Guyana and a few other Caribbean spaces, native peoples are more than symbolic throwbacks to colonial invasion.

After Chofy begins an affair with Rosa, he argues the positives of mixing with other communities. Disagreeing with Tenga, he says, "We [Amerindians] have to mix; otherwise we have no future. We must get educated. We can't go backwards. Guyana has to develop."[13] Chofy means education in a formal, European sense. In this instance, integration seems to be the obvious and correct progressive answer. Chofy and his family are products of mixing fostered by colonization and globalization. Retreat for them is, if nothing else, genetically impossible, and they rupture the idea of the savannahs as a pure and uncontaminated space. Amerindian communities rehearse colonialism too—first in what we recognize as the initial colonial encounter and then again with twentieth-century postcolonial nations. Indigenous people are changed at the genetic and cellular levels through intermixing. Furthermore, as Chofy's conversation with Tenga indicates, they are likewise changed at the social level. The languages spoken in the border communities are not only native languages, but they are more often Spanish and Portuguese with the language of indigenous conversation highlighting the sociocultural contaminations that are already present.[14]

Paula Burnett posits that Chofy "is one of the Wapisiana who inhabit a zone of exchange between the constantly hybridizing cultural communities of the coastal strip and the unmodified traditional cultures of the interior."[15] In part, Burnett's argument suggests that Chofy's singularity, his entrance into the zone, is made possible by his racial mixture, a heritage not all Amerindians can claim. Therefore his genetic identity—the building block of his flesh—enables him to enter this buffer zone where he is invited to negotiate two cultures. While this exchange zone is one way of characterizing transnational belonging, I disagree with Burnett's point that Amerindian culture is unmodified. While Tenga would hope so, the fact is that interior cultures have changed precisely because people like Chofy exist.[16] There is no "original" culture to return to if the contemporary is rejected. The interplay between so-called original cultures and contemporary ones is constant and, as Shona N. Jackson's research shows, is manifested through the adoption of Spanish and Portuguese as native languages.

Chofy's buffer zone embodies and rehearses his delinking from his Wapisiana home—which he territorially considers part of the Guyanese nation-state—and from his wife, Marietta, to pursue Rosa; he also breaks from Wapisiana notions of education, as indicated by his belief that the Amerindian "must get educated." Chofy's disassociation from a pure Wapisiana home and identity is, like the rest of the novel, mitigated by his return to the savannahs because of his son's death—a return that prizes cultural identifications over political ones.

Initially Melville's vilification of the city heightens the restorative properties of the savannah, yet this rehearsal too is undermined. Though Chofy eventually leaves Georgetown and Rosa, his return to the Rupununi is not celebratory; it is with a heavy heart. Bla-Bla's death is caused by the mistranslation of Chofy's name.[17] The Hawk Oil engineers were told that "Chofoye" means "explosion." As they prepare to detonate explosives and shout "Chofoye" as a warning, Bla-Bla runs toward the call, thinking his father has returned, and is obliterated.[18] Bla-Bla's death is a rehearsal of the many native deaths that began with the coming of Europeans, but in this case it is the idea of the native's return to the savannahs that brings death. Hearing Chofy's name, Bla-Bla *believes* that his father has returned from the city, but in reality, it is Bla-Bla's demise that brings Chofy back to the Rupununi: "The expression on Bla-Bla's face was a sneer of accusation. It seemed to accuse him of many things: of abandoning his family, deserting his son, of not being able to keep the land safe for his children. With shock, he felt that he had lost not only a child but a whole continent."[19] The visibility of Bla-Bla's body—the hearse—haunts the Wapisiana community and serves as a reminder of the consequences of engagement with outsiders. His body accuses Chofy with its sneer, and his dead bones implicate his father's actions. Chofy's return and Bla-Bla's death are weighted with blame: "Tenga blames Chofy for deserting his own people . . . [and he was] silenced by the guilt."[20] For Chofy, the landscape is poisoned not only by the multinational Hawk Oil's extraction of fossil fuel but also by a history of extraction of mineral wealth from indigenous lands.

Eventually, however, the savannahs facilitate his recovery: "The great, unchanging open spaces gave him time and a frame in which to think. Despite the grief and guilt, in the savannahs his son's death seemed contained within a certain order of things and not just an extra, random confusion, as everything was in the city. From a distance, the affair with Rosa began to seem like a sort of bewitchment, something unreal."[21] The contradiction of Chofy's choice continues when collocated with other concrete events; Bla-Bla's death and the return of Aunt Wifreda's sight both belie Chofy's dream of multiracial fulfillment. Aunt Wifreda's myopia, brought on after learning of Danny and Beatrice's incestuous relationship, becomes full-blown blindness with Rosa's inquiries about the British writer Evelyn Waugh's visit to the savannahs. As April Shemak argues in discussing the role of the native informant, "Wifreda serves as a link between Chofy's story and Danny and Beatrice's story, and she also represents a reluctant native informant. In fact, her blindness is brought on when Chofy brings Rosa to interview her about having met Evelyn Waugh, when he visited the Rupununi in the 1930s. Wifreda refuses the role of the native informant, telling Rosa, 'That was a long time ago. I can't recall too much.'"[22] Rosa had been told, "Nothing keeps in the tropics,"[23] and the warning is made real via the dissolution of Rosa and Chofy's romance and the return of Wifreda's sight. The predisposition to rot and tropical impermanence reproduces the savannahs as a space of integral change, but this is masked by reclaimant yet fragile grasslands. These territories—Amerindian and Coastlander—seem capable of only temporary encounters, suggesting that the space is always in rehearsal, always shifting, though its basic architecture remains the same.

By apposing city and savannah (though she seems more authorially predisposed to the savannah), Melville questions which models of belonging are best suited for the Wapisiana. In this context, the native, paradoxically, reminds us of other forgotten or denied Caribbean identities. In Guyana, a state plagued by ethnic, economic, and environmental duress and political stalemates, the need for solutions to ethnically charged divisions are important and might be found through feminist rehearsal. As the Coastlanders and the wider Caribbean communities with which they are aligned consider notions of homeland and the effect of transnationalism, studying the experiences of oft-forgotten Amerindian groups allows for a deeper understanding of Caribbean realities than does studying the space exclusively from the perspective of its colonial inheritance. In this arena, transnationalism for indigenous people has meant that alien nation-states have been built on *their* territories. While they have always belonged to a particular nation with its own practice, colonization has meant that their nations now exist within other states. Their transnational practice does not necessarily involve migration and travel in the traditional sense (i.e., outside their national borders) but rather consists of negotiation between their nations and the states that have cut across their communities in order to establish themselves.

Amerindians, who construct themselves horizontally across the borders of Venezuela, Guyana, and Brazil, rupture Guyana's vertical territorial space and complicate any notion of national communities operating as a psychosocial homeland for the postcolonial Caribbean. Due to the treaties signed by various colonial powers, "Amerindians enjoy certain entitlements linked to their status as first inhabitants of the Latin American countries. Amerindians are free to cross the borders between the different ex-colonies in South-America," indicating the lasting transnational nature of the indigenous experience.[24] Amerindian sovereignty, beyond the purview of states, is entrenched in smaller notions of community explicitly linked to ethnicity and tradition.

In order to understand the complexity of belonging, we have to rehearse the ramifications of colonial history and the structures of the independent state. One of the central consequences of the colonial project has been the multiracial and multiethnic nature of the "adventure." In the region, this has generated consternation, celebration, and questioning of the nature of mixing and hybridity. Mixing for the Wapisiana people in the novel illustrates the larger problems of the postcolonial state: unity. This explicitly points to the lack of mutual spaces where enemies, or contending factions, can congregate around their shared biases to understand disparate positions. Other than Georgetown, there are few places in Melville's text that bring members of the nation in contact with one another. Chofy does interact with his East Indian landlords and the black Coastlanders who were a threat to the indigenous community in his uncle Danny's mind, but the day-to-day tensions between Afro- and Indo-Guyanese are not explored. Rather, Melville elides these tensions in favor of a rare examination of Amerindian realities and perspectives on black and Indian Coastlanders.

Children of the Forest?

Characterized as "children of the forest," psychologically and physically tied to the hinterland, and erased from national view, the Wapisiana struggle with two aspects of belonging—endogamy and exogamy. Tenga, Chofy's ideological foil, articulates a position on not mixing: "We Amerindian people are fools, you know. We've been colonized twice. First by the Europeans and then the coastlanders. I don't know which is worse. Big companies come to mine gold or cut timber. Scholars come and worm their way into our communities, studying us and grabbing our knowledge for their own benefit. Aid agencies come and interfere with us. Tourists stare at us. Politicians crawl round us at election times. . . . Amerindians have no chance in this country."[25] Tenga's response is to leave the corrupters and colonizers of the European and Coastlander varieties alone. On the question of surviving in the margins, characters retreat to focus internally and relegate the external world to the periphery. Here the notion of community is ethnically, linguistically, and historically shaped by precolonial traditions; to rehearse communities of consensus is to replay Amerindian myths and histories for pan-indigenous organizing rather than for collaborating with Coastlanders.

According to Melville's fictional portrayal, Tenga's retreat from the "states"—Guyana, most clearly—is one endogamous response. It asserts the power of retreating from state margins since Guyana cannot or does not address Amerindian concerns. While Amerindians were historically characterized as an interior police force deputized with returning escaped slaves to plantations, their reality is more complex. With the Dutch and English colonizers, they did indeed serve in a security role, but, as Williams reports, it is a "myth" that indigenous people were "primarily . . . a security force or that, when no longer useful, they willingly withdrew to the wilderness and returned to a preferred, so-called carefree, indolent existence."[26] In fact, the rates of miscegenation between Europeans and native people resulted in many mixed-race children who were educated in Europe and went on to own plantations.[27] Though incorporated into the economic elite in some cases, Amerindians were defined by the English as "lazy, indolent 'children of the forest' by ignoring their involvement in and contributions to the colonial economy."[28]

In reality, outside the world of the novel, Amerindians prioritized their own interests by forming a coalition with ranchers in which the two groups were part of "the aborted January 1969 Rupununi Uprising," which Prime Minister Forbes Burnham characterized as an "insurrection [which] was planned, organized and carried out by the ranchers of the Rupununi—the savannah aristocrats. . . . And which was drawn mainly, but not exclusively from the Hart and *Melville* families"[29] (emphasis added). The Melvilles in the above quote are the historical models for the McKinnons in the novel. The author Melville's personal history and Amerindian agency are intertwined, and her representations, like the contentious history between native groups, Europeans, and postcolonial governments, challenge discourses of native passivity and absence. These border issues indicate the levels of autonomy, which then and now influence the shaping of Guyanese economic and sociopolitical realities.[30] Similar to Marina Warner (as discussed in chapter 4), Pauline Melville is coming to terms with the legacies of her own story as native and colonizer. Melville manages to document a moment, capture a time, but also create an alternative vision of the natives whom Burnham categorized as "secondary participants." While Burnham places blame on the ranchers, what is revealed is that Amerindians led the insurrection while also negotiating with Burnham's administration for land title and other recognition of rights; these negotiations resulted in land grant titles for native people for "those areas occupied by [them] at the time of independence,"[31] rather than the 50 percent of Guyana's landmass, which approximately fifty thousand Amerindians were claiming as their ancestral lands.[32] Claims to ancestrally held lands serve as the crux of the debate on belonging for native populations and the inheritors of the colonial apparatus. Indeed, as Eric Cheyfitz argues, notions of "property" and owning space define belonging[33] and, I would add, organizing.

Issues of purity and contamination emerge in the sometimes binary relationship between Tenga and Chofy, cousins who have different notions of racial, cultural, and intellectual integration within the Guyanese state. Melville interrogates the meaning and usefulness of interaction with the outside world, a world that characterizes indigenous people not on their own terms but for and in the interests of those occupying their lands. The tense relationship between Professor Michael Wormoal and the researcher Rosa Mendelson exposes who owns and controls knowledge about the Amerindians. Wormoal contends that he "probably know[s] more about the Amerindian peoples than they know about themselves" and laments that "Indian culture is disintegrating these days—contaminated mainly by contact with other races."[34] He blithely appreciates his new form of plunder: "Knowledge is [my] way of owning them—I admit it. We fight over the intellectual territory. But it's better than stealing their land isn't it."[35] The professor's need to know, catalog, and categorize delineates Europeanness against nativeness and concretely illustrates Tenga's point on double colonization and complete exploitation.

Similarly, Rosa, though a literary scholar, asserts her ownership of Chofy. "She felt an inexplicable rush of possessiveness" when Wormoal expresses an interest in meeting him.[36] Her liberal politics suggest openness, but her colonization of Chofy and his knowledge is similar to Wormoal's ownership of indigenous stories. Like Tenga and Chofy, Rosa and Wormoal discuss the value of mixing. The professor favors racial and ethnic retreat, characterizing it as "all the rage": "People want to be with their own kind. Everyone nowadays is retreating into their own homogenous group. Black with black. Serb with Serb. Muslim with Muslim."[37] Rosa, appalled by Wormoal's "purity of nation" thesis,[38] maintains her position as an internationalist and advocate of racial mixing. Wormoal's statements betray his lack of empathy (or even the idea of empathy) for sameness for one's in-group.

Reacting against the interference of outsiders, Tenga wants to reassert a precolonial space where intellectual and actual resources are out of foreign reach. He proclaims, "I am not Guyanese, I am Wapisiana."[39] For him, this means ignoring the Guyanese state and its borders; he wants to rehearse a pre-Columbian space. The Wapisiana nation—which predates the contemporary states of Venezuela, Brazil, Suriname, and Guyana—spills across these borders, undermining them all. The border as a site of flux and contemporary contestation is reinforced. The deterritorialized border is transparent, porous, and problematic. The precolonial Wapisiana nation claims the rights to its sovereignty across this vast territory. The Wapisiana rehearse nation in familial terms—their communities, less imagined and more genealogical.

However, the Wapisiana do not acknowledge the state; they do not seek its validation in any respect.[40] They have delinked, and, as symbolized by Tenga, ignore outsiders and construct (and represent) themselves and their nation on their own terms. The difference between the Wapisiana people and the Guyanese state is that the people have never had pretensions to participation in the international economic order. Thus, the Amerindian ability to imagine and practice indigenous communities and nation building continues to challenge postcolonial states. As globalization challenges the legal limits and sovereignty of European-ordered and -endorsed states, the Wapisiana nation reasserts its right to nationhood across borders and beyond legal administrative structures of the West. The Wapisiana and other Amerindian communities in the Guianas never relinquished their land rights to colonizers, such as the British, by "conquest, cession, treaty or papal bull, yet [the British] asserted sovereignty over them, enshrining a policy of assimilation over Amerindian objections."[41]

Melville's Tenga, though the primary proponent of an endogamous lifestyle, lives in a non-Wapisiana Amerindian village near the capital and is theoretically (or imaginatively), rather than physically, aligned with the open vistas of the savannah. The high, wide grasslands of the savannah appear harmless but harbor hidden dangers, which nurture shadows, and which are exacerbated by their remoteness. Given the overall physical environment of the country, each space can maintain the illusion of exclusivity.

Due largely to colonialism and globalization, Tenga's Amerindian world is one of conflict. He lives with other Amerindians on land occupied by the Coastlanders and multinationals whose worldviews, to his mind, are genocidal. With Chofy—his potential enemy and most like his mirror-self—Tenga shares landscape, biology, and traditions, but Tenga's preferences are based on his understanding of how Wapisiana history and culture have been corrupted:

> Look at this shop. Before it opened, people used to fish and share everything with the other families here. Now they take the fish to sell in Georgetown for money to buy things in the shop. And did you see the well outside? Some people came and asked us what we wanted. We didn't know. We just said a well. They built it for us. But people missed going down to the creek to fetch water and talking to each other. It destroyed the social life of the village. And the well water tastes different—horrible—like iron. Then somebody shat in the well or children threw rubbish in it and half the village got poisoned.[42]

These external development initiatives, while not exactly imposed, "destroyed the social life of the village." For Tenga, development and technology are at odds with his way of life, yet he has no plan for rectifying this problem; his beliefs on returning to an imagined Wapisiana purity are still conflicted: "'You say we should mix,' said Tenga bitterly. 'What to do? We're destroyed if we mix; and we're destroyed if we don't.'"[43] The novel does not explicitly answer these questions, and Melville confesses that she too is ambivalent about the possibilities.[44] In this case, rehearsing indigeneity means examining how marginal communities belong and the ways in which miscegenation is considered extinction or survival. In the novel, Amerindians are on Georgetown's periphery but are central in the savannahs, denoting that their belonging shifts by degrees depending on location and that their identities potentially shift from *space* to *place*.

Like his Guyanese enemies, from Chofy to the Coastlanders, Tenga grapples with the idea of mixing. Though he values the ideal of Wapisiana purity and wants Wapisiana unity, he recognizes the impossibility of achieving it. However, he sees both—interethnic mixing and its opposite—as resulting in crisis. Similarly, in Guyana, Trinidad, and other Caribbean nations with significant "ethnic" populations, prejudices and racist attitudes about "other" groups are evident. While governments push the "national" identity ("We are all Surinamese [Cuban, etc.]"), the material realities based on a history of colonial governments pitting groups against one another have resulted in access inequities and bred resentments that continue to foster, at a minimum, injustice.

Because mixing or not mixing yields the same result, Tenga is maintaining the status quo; taking an active stance one way or another is too great a commitment for him. According to this Wapisiana citizen, full integration of Amerindians into Guyanese society means a loss of culture—a poisoning of cultural wells. Limited integration, that which is currently in place in the book, is a slow poisoning of indigenous people. Tenga's reference to the rum shop, which he names "Jonestown," invokes the idea of a foreign incursion, a place where people go to disappear.[45] Jonestown the bar rehearses the memory of the massacre of 914 people led by the charismatic U.S. evangelist and People's Temple leader Jim Jones. This Jonestown, the historical Guyanese site of the massacre, has disappeared under an overgrowth of weeds and vines; Jonestown, as fact and metaphor, is another encroachment of foreigners bringing death and doom through their cultural products—food, oil, and religious fundamentalism. Nonetheless, Tenga and Chofy avail themselves of the drinks in the Jonestown saloon, demonstrating that, even as they recognize the costs of engaging with the outside world, they are seduced by it and drink from its cup.[46]

Deploying feminist rehearsal in order to understand the dilemmas of indigenous people interrogates how these communities have survived and will survive; Tenga's inability to unify or, at least engage with, science and alchemy indicates that he cannot shape a hopeful space from the chaos and despair of the contemporary circumstances of indigenous people. He cannot fashion a mutual space. In the postcolonial space for native peoples—a site that one can argue is still not postcolonial, given the continual colonization Tenga feels he experiences from the

African or Indian Guyanese state—Tenga cannot transcend his Amerindian national space or even transgress, as he would see it, into the national imaginings beyond the image of a time-bound savage of the nation-states that enclose Wapisiana territory.[47]

Constructing narratives, as Benedict Anderson argues, is key to national development and identity formation. Such narratives are a critical component of nationalism and citizenship discourses. Transnationalism is defined as "the process by which immigrants forge and sustain multi-stranded social relations that link together their societies of origin and settlement,"[48] the important factors being "post"-colonialism and deterritorialization. Chofy's stay in the city underscores his transnationality. He, unlike Tenga, sees himself as both Wapisiana *and* Guyanese. Textually, transnationalism is another option for the Wapisiana, though it is clearly one of the most painful and costly choices (i.e., Bla-Bla's death). Chofy's struggles emphasize new and complex representations of Amerindians in a globalized and technologized world while also highlighting groups excised from or romanticized in the construction of the nation—historically and politically.

As for the spaces Chofy shares with the enemy, initially they are centered on the idea of development. Chofy, like Coastlanders and foreign investors, believes there is value in education and mixing. In fact, he argues that it is the only way Amerindians will survive. Yet Chofy recants this position by the novel's end and, because of Bla-Bla's death, returns to the vast and soothing openness of the Rupununi. Chofy's loss of his son, whose choices, had he lived after the Hawk Oil accident, would have been paralysis or slow, torturous death, represents continual depletion of the Amerindian "blood-stock" and, to a degree, Amerindian "choice."[49]

However, Chofy's retreat to the savannahs—and especially vis-à-vis their depiction in such romantic terms—reads a bit too neatly. Upon his return, he is thrown into the creek by his horse and is chided by his wife, Marietta: "'You been away too long. Don' you remember that horse? You have to do his girth up tight because he pushes his belly out when you saddle him. . . . Chofy, soaking wet, stood on the banks . . . while Marietta sat and cried with laughter."[50] Yet, it is Chofy's dilemma as a transnational citizen straddling two different communities with mixed agendas that is intriguing. The position of the transnational, of where to put one's loyalty beyond familial associations, becomes significant. In this transnational world, movement across multiple borders means entrance into systems of exchange in the global order and necessitates the acquisition of money and skills that, in turn, foster the inherent portability in peoples' lives. Transnationalism is shaped by many factors; however, in the novel's scenario, transnationalism is formed by the semi-autonomous Amerindian spaces that endogamous advocates, such as Tenga, would like to be independent.[51] Mainly, characters like Tenga reside permanently or temporarily in the city, a contaminated location removed from the purity and "rotting" romance of the savannahs. Each location—city or savannah—has rotting and romantic traits. The urban characters Rosa and Olly Sampson, the finance minister, share this category of those invested in Western disciplines, structures, and knowledge strategies, while Father Napier, the homosexual priest-cum-missionary, and Alexander McKinnon, the patriarch of Chofy's family and member of the savannah oligarchy, represent this pole in the interior.[52] Tenga claims that Chofy betrayed his people and his family by going to the city; he certainly betrayed his wife, who in some ways is synonymous with the Wapisiana nation.

Reproducing the Nation

As an emblem of the Wapisiana nation, Marietta is described as a ruddy brown, "vibrant, vigorous woman who never stopped working."[53] Chofy characterizes her as a "figure moulded entirely from red Rupununi clay, utterly out of place in these [Georgetown] surroundings."[54] She is stoic and long-suffering in light of her husband's infidelity and her son's death. Her dreams serve as counterpoints to Chofy's narratives of mixing. First, she dreams of foreigners coming to take her away in a Land Rover, though when they arrive, she resists by telling them that she is "married to Chofy."[55] This dream ends with "a plane arriving on the airstrip with a dead person in it," foreshadowing her son's death and his air lifts, to Georgetown for medical treatment and to return his body for burial. Marietta is visited by her son's hearse, a plane, symbolic in its physical form as a transporter of his body and as the vessel of modern-day cargo crossings over seas, landscapes, and transnational borders. Further, the plane as technology enables possibility for the transnational citizen, similar to the way in which rehearsal crosses borders, through the constant interplay and interaction between spaces.

Bla-Bla's burial at the back of Marietta's house is symbolic of her as the mother tied to Amerindian land. Marietta tells the nurse that she cannot bury Bla-Bla in Georgetown, explaining, "This town has nothing to do with us. We do not belong here. He will come home with us."[56] Burying the body of the dead signifies a space of belonging, and

Marietta is clear that her son's remains do not belong to the city or the state it represents. Just as Marina Warner's Sycorax in *Indigo* is buried under her saman tree, emphasizing her belonging to the island, Bla-Bla is buried among the bones of his ancestors, establishing a connection to land and time that predates colonial coming.

Marietta is a native woman married to a native man who loses a child. This loss seems to indicate an end to a purely Amerindian space, though this is slightly mitigated by her dream at the end of the novel. She dreams of eggs, which Aunt Wifreda interprets as "fertility and growth. Food too. It means hope and coming back to life." Marietta dismisses Aunt Wifreda's reading, saying, "Or maybe I was just thinking about eggs."[57] Marietta's refusal to appropriate Aunt Wifreda's reading of the dream as fertility complicates an easy reading of her as a native woman tied to land, fertility, and assumptions of mothering. Though Marietta is a grieving mother, she is the practical one who has to deal with the consequences of her husband's actions, similar to Danticat's Lili. Additionally, like Haiti's Défilée, who gathered the pieces of Dessalines's body, Marietta brings her son's bones home.

Alexander McKinnon, the European progenitor of Chofy's family, simultaneously marries two native sisters—Maba and Zuna. Maba is the mother of Beatrice and Danny and a stark contrast to Marietta. The sexual alliance between this native woman and Alexander produces children who enact the most endogamous of myths—incest. As Maba tells her sister: "It's because they are part white that he [Father Napier] is going [after them]. If they were full Indians he would never make all this fuss. And we would never ask him. We should look after our own affairs."[58] Alexander is undone by his children's relationship and retreats from the savannahs back to Scotland, but Zuna and Maba decide to take control of the situation by focusing on the codes that govern Amerindian communities.

In keeping with the rest of the novel, the Wapisiana national construct does not provide a romantic refuge. The incestuous relationship between Chofy's aunt and uncle, Beatrice and Danny, is emblematic of the lack of romantic answers. They are the ultimate manifestation of Tenga's position: What could be more introspective and endogamous than a sexual relationship between siblings? Their family, the larger Wapisiana community, and other Amerindian communities treat the relationship with various levels of discomfort and horror.[59] Familial and national splits further manifest in their parents' reactions. Alexander McKinnon, Beatrice's and Danny's father, leaves the savannah because, "after twenty-five years, he realized that he did not belong."[60]

In contrast, Maba has perhaps the more complicated response to her children's affair: "I know it's not good, what Danny and Beatrice are doing, but it is not the worst thing in the world. It's happened before."[61] Maba's matter-of-fact response reiterates Amerindian worldviews, in which the incest myth is one of "accepted" contradiction and harbinger of change. In Amerindian folklore and in this family, incest tied to the eclipse is a form of obliteration, which leads, according to Walter Roth, to metamorphosis.[62] As Danny and Beatrice travel through the savannahs, other Amerindians refer to their incestuous relationship as "living close," to the confusion of Father Napier, who does not understand the implication of this phrase. Around the campfire, Wario[63] tells the Wai-Wai version of the incest myth: "'A long time ago, Nuni made love to his sister. Yes, he made love to his own sister. . . . He left his spirit to play the flute and let his body come to her. He came over and over again."[64] Though Danny and Beatrice replay and restage a mythologized incest taboo, it is not simply for the sake of replaying as Wilson Harris might say.[65] Here it is through the multiple stories of incest that the bone flute, the process of consuming the morsel to excavate and distill biases, leads to transformation. The mirroring of the mythology with Danny and Beatrice ruptures time lines and reveals rehearsal as immemorial. One can argue that incest is also a pathway to one's ancestors, the ultimate retreat to one place and one bloodline. Like many aspects of the novel, there is contradiction here—incest is perhaps the opposite embodiment of transnationalism, even as these border-crossing communities ignore state borders and remain essentially transnational.

In *The Ventriloquist's Tale*, the incest and eclipse myths are characterized as deeply internal, endogamous, but also as generative beginnings of the world and of (sexual) awareness. The stories allow characters and tribes to travel inward in order to reveal truths of desire, conflict, and the forbidden. These incest and eclipse narratives reveal what Amerindians have lost and gained. In Shibi-din's tale, the loss of immortality leads to the story, which becomes a way of carrying life, a way to immortality. While incest— the ultimate endogamous position—fractures the family and community, it functions, in the novel, as an effective vehicle for engaging with the questions and rivalries of nations coming to terms with complicated histories forged in desire, conflict, and taboo. These stories of loss bring recognition, but not harmony, for indigenous and non-native people who participate in the story, either through listening to or reading it.

What change does the eclipse signal? First, there is a clear indication that Amerindians, despite policies and assumptions to the contrary, were not obliterated; they did not become museum relics, but they have changed. Within these varied tales of forbidden love (homosexuality, mythical siblings, Danny/Beatrice, and Chofy/Rosa), a process of destruction, exposure, unmasking, separation, and eventually transformation (into stars) is metaphorically rendered, as is a story of belonging through the shared perspectives and common histories of indigenous people. These incest stories—of Wapisiana, Wai-Wai, and Taruma— emphasize the unity among Amerindian peoples and foster an indigenous nationalism. The metaphorical process that uses stories as a gateway to transformation is the most critical component in these tales. These stories also emphasize sacrifice and loss since both Danny and Beatrice leave the Wapisiana community, other indigenous nations, as well as the Guyanese state, abandoning their family and larger communal constructs.

By the novel's end, Sonny, the child of consensual incest, slyly reveals that he is the god Makunima manifesting an Amerindian worldview that is able to find redemption in even the most taboo and unredeemable relationships and situations.[66] "Son"ny, the silent son, disappears into the bush—an unknown territory.[67] The textual weight of an incestuous relationship birthing a god seems to validate endogamy and Wapisiana internalization. However, this trinity eventually leaves the savannah: the brother and sister because their relationship could not be sanctioned in this space, and the son so that he could fully embody his divine Makunima identity.

Sonny's initial silence could be read as idiocy or retardation, a not unexpected consequence of incest. Sonny, as Makunima, is a ventriloquist, undermining expectations and history.[68] In Amerindian lore, the tale told by the idiot, the mute, the possibly retarded Sonny, is valuable because "[i]mbeciles are regarded with awe by the Indians, for according to their traditions, these are in close intimacy with good Spirits, and hence their words and actions are regarded as signs of divinity."[69] The narrator, as device and characters (Chico, Sonny, and Makunima), connects the Amerindian, Western, and mixed value systems.

In the prologue, the narrator, Chico, speaks of his love for the lie and the cream suits he likes to wear—the embodiment of the jet-set gigolo. This is no one's noble savage—staid, naked, and native. The narrator's ability to see the world as a stage, perform, and then return to his origins indicates two things: first, that the trope of performance is as crucial for indigenous people of the Americas as it is for non-Amerindian Caribbean people and, two, that in his soliloquies—the prologue and epilogue—the narrator clarifies that he is rectifying a past of Caribbean, Brazilian (i.e., non-Amerindian), and European distortions and misrepresentations of indigenous people. Sonny's ability to transition beyond the boundaries of his origins means that he transcends local and national identities. He leaves his Wapisiana family, and all that it might suggest, by going into the bush, where he is transformed into or embraces his identity as Makunima. While Chofy left his home and went outward, toward Georgetown, toward the colonial past and the postcolonial present, Sonny entrenches himself deeper in his ancient past, making him, the child born of incest, perhaps the ideal and the answer.

Sonny wears several masks throughout *The Ventriloquist's Tale*, each revealing limited information—at his discretion—and commingling factual lies with ultimate truth. However, Sonny's transcendence of boundaries does not foster connections with nearby Caribbean and postcolonial states; rather, his project seems to be taking on the larger, global postcolonial world. It engages with the political agenda of this adaptable and outrageous being who does not respect constructions of space and time as they are generally understood, who is a master of disguise, a lover of women and his people, and a god. Sonny's crucifixion of history as a discipline, his use of art, culture, and language, are the typical concerns of a postcolonial.

The mutual spaces that Danny, Beatrice, and Sonny rehearse with the enemy are, as is the case with other characters, both internal and external. For this trinity, the internal enemy is most forcefully displayed. Instead of consuming a morsel that will reveal an external enemy, they need to acknowledge that the enemy is already within. It is already within their own cellular makeup, their flesh and bones. Their function is to move beyond consuming to synthesizing and understanding how this enemy operates and how to mitigate its negative influences or convert them to strengths.

These characters are intimately tied to Amerindian epistemologies and ways of knowing the world. In fact, their lives are expressed manifestations of said cosmologies. Yet such stark expressions of internalized traditions do not serve them well. Sonny is the only character who might be said to triumph in this scenario. By virtue of the personification of Wapisiana traditions, the harmony between science and alchemy is not fulfilled, since both Danny and Beatrice have to leave and cannot function in any of the nations in territorial Guyana. They do not transcend; they escape. It is Sonny who claims a broad swath of space that best characterizes the links between science and alchemy.

Because Beatrice and Danny leave, they forfeit their citizenship in the Wapisiana nation. Sonny, though constantly on the move, still claims the South American landscape as his. Though he eschews the hard work of citizenship, his articulation of fiction as a lens or technology that can be used to establish and critique notions of belonging is the clearest and most vociferously stated. Sonny claims that writing, in the Western sense, produces toothless fiction, with heroes too pedantic to enchant and the legacy of triumphal (Western) rationality. His understanding of fiction and the function of heroes is a cultural and political understanding entwined with manifesting his worldview. As he understands and dismisses Western fictions, he celebrates another—the venerated lie.[70] Sonny's explicit articulation of this power is the most exultant in the book and is, ironically, most closely linked to issues of citizenship, transnationalism, and globalization. His migratory movement is that of a deterritorialized citizen, though the "rain forest" is his only home. Critically, this broader construction of homeland is a necessary condition of regional citizenship. As he claims the entire rain forest—no matter where it may lie—he does so because he sees himself beyond Wapisiana boundaries, partly because he embraces the mythic and grandiose manifestations of himself as Makunaima. Rehearsing Sonny/Chico/Makunaima moves one beyond the local to more regional concerns and the ability to see one's environment inside and out.

Conclusion

Pauline Melville's *The Ventriloquist's Tale* is an interesting commentary on the state of the Guyanese nation, as the problem of establishing and stabilizing internal legitimacy plagues not only citizens at the national level but anything on which a government would embark at the regional level.[71] The twofold question Guyana, as well as the rest of the Caribbean, faces is not how to function as an individual nation-state but, rather, what exactly does a Caribbean nation-state look like in a globalized world? Melville's observation that the polemicized nation-state of Guyana is on the verge of collapse locates it within the stereotype of the primitive native, in a space of "pre-nation" and degenerative mimicry, developing no institutions independent of Europe.[72] These varied and multiple inheritances must be rehearsed to reveal regional particularities. While the Guyanese state and, indeed, every Caribbean state might be invested in territorial borders, it is when fictional truth reflects real situations that we are invited to dissolve these borders. It is therefore imperative to then explore cooperative potentials of rehearsal because these strategies can be very effective, not only globally, but at the local, national, and regional levels.

Foundational to the colonial project were the European notions of white supremacy that continue to haunt and corrode these territories. Its absence is particularly glaring in so complex a text with references to history, science, competing cosmologies, and nation building, something Melville's Chico recognizes in Europe: "while I was in Europe I nearly became fatally infected by the epidemic of separatism that was raging there. . . . Sometimes it appears as nationalism, sometimes as racism, sometimes as religious orthodoxy. . . .The Serbs, the Scots, the English, the Basques, the Muslims, the Chechens—everybody was at it."[73] Perhaps as with the romantic depiction of the savannahs, Melville felt the region had problems aplenty without adding this complex discourse. Additionally, in the larger Caribbean context, language reconfigures race, and new racial constructs give way to new challenges; for example, the mulatto class in Haiti functions as a non-black class of people in that space. Racial nuances, but not necessarily racism, are coded differently in the Spanish-speaking Caribbean, which, in the larger Caribbean context, is a majority space.[74]

The Ventriloquist's Tale speaks to issues of definition in an era of globalization that is not new; in fact, it is built on age-old structures that colonized people recognize. This novel calls attention to the provocative nature of art that allows us to imagine beyond our borders and limitations for innovative and creative solutions. Rehearsing with this novel widens the scope of belonging while examining the mutual spaces where enemies and the fatigued citizens of fragmenting states can come together. Amerindian ideas of belonging, citizenship, and sovereignty help the larger Caribbean to interrogate what it means to "belong" to local communities, states, and regional bodies—through various ideological undertakings of the nation, the state, and the transnation. *The Ventriloquist's Tale* utilizes the often unstable in-between space within the text and within the reader's world to suggest that Guyana, and by extension the region, must rehearse simultaneity in power relations, extending its hands inward and outward—like the knot at the center of a tug-of-war rope.

This novel challenges the rhetoric of unity, not because poverty and race are not enough to engender solidarity, but because the connection between these things, survival, and building community is not always overtly stated or dealt with complexly. Cultivating effective coalitions means deeply and consciously acknowledging and working through differences of embedded and imagined power. The novel asks its readers to not lose themselves in easy rhetorical spaces but, using the lens of an ancient technology—fiction—to grasp the differences and deal with them. By beginning the conversation with the story, which puts these issues in the public sphere, two pathways to building consensus emerge: using the characters as tools to discuss the issues and thinking of the characters as ourselves. Here is the platform for discussion and change—the text has created a mutual space that fosters realigning science and alchemy. The question is, where will we, as readers, as state citizens, as members of the global community, go with it? Where we will start our conversation, our rehearsal, and where will it take us together?

Conclusion: Rehearsing and Proxy-formance

Long ago, they were supply fleshed.
But then, all meat fell away
from the bone. Some teeth
and hair remained.
Someone should examine their story.
After all, it's not that they dwindled
into dust altogether. Besides,
these bones could make more than music.
They're a fire-tried instrument.

—Mahadai Das, "Bones"

MY CONCEPTION OF REHEARSAL EMERGED while writing about the three masculinist representations of the Haitian Revolution, two of which are plays, discussed in chapter 2 of this volume. I extended theatrical understandings of rehearsal to help myself understand how we deal with the past. How I dealt with the past. These three texts written by twentieth-century, non-Haitian Caribbean men, who in their own ways defined Caribbean studies, were instrumental in developing my initial interest in rehearsal as a potential methodology for exploring Caribbean pasts.

Each text revisits the event of the Haitian Revolution from various perspectives. These differences expose the rich details of this historical moment. The novels and the play explore men as founding fathers, as part of a twentieth-century recuperation of Caribbean masculinity, with women as peripheral, though sometimes complex, characters who complicate male lives and leadership. The kaleidoscopic shifts from one text to the next helped me see the dynamism of Haiti's revolution not just in and of itself but as a Caribbean revolution, given that it shares, in hindsight, similarities with revolutions to come, such as Cuba (1959–present) and Grenada (1979–1983). These texts raised exciting questions on the transactional or negotiated nature of belonging while exposing important analytical gaps regarding gender and sexuality in regional representations.

When actors rehearse a play, they generally work with a set text. What actors do to transform the text is rehearse. They transform meaning through pauses, inflections, and/or body movements. These subtle shifts alter the text, often giving it numerous meanings. Rehearsing the Haitian Revolution through these texts not only reveals differing interpretations, foci, and investments in or attachments to particular notions of history but also exposes the paradox of rehearsal as that of preparing for an ideal (the horizon) and embodying and cultivating a different way of being and belonging, while existing in the status quo of colonial (neocolonial and globalized) economic structures. Rehearsal became an engrossing way of distilling the legacies of the past.

When reading Césaire's play, which characterizes Christophe as a fatherly autocrat, I was able to make connections to other Caribbean leaders such as François "Papa Doc" Duvalier (Haiti) and Eric Williams, "father" to the independent nation of Trinidad and Tobago. Duvalier began his career as a medical doctor, which earned him the sobriquet "Papa Doc," while Williams, trained as a historian, left his academic post and worked to ameliorate the consequences of colonialism in his native Trinidad. Duvalier ascended to power in 1957 on a wave of populist goodwill and remained head of state until his death in 1971; Williams transitioned from leader of the People's National Movement, the party he founded, to the first prime minister of an independent country, remaining in power from 1962 to his death in 1981. Ultimately, Duvalier's benevolence was undermined by his cult of personality, ambition, and state terror, but Williams, as Rex Nettleford comments, governed with intellectual and academic acuity, wit, and gossip. The knowing hand of the father is embedded in each example, and while Williams did not condemn twenty thousand of his compatriots to their deaths with the building of Citadelle La Ferrière as did Christophe, nor execute thirty thousand of his own citizens like Papa Doc, he is indeed a rehearsal of the stern sometimes misguided father of Césaire's play. These are men of undeniable strength and fortitude, though they are not always wise. Their potency and vigor, fused with a paternalistic philosophy of governance, cements the notion of the nation as a family guided by a stern and knowing father. The revolutionary idea, in this case, is that the father is black. Black Caribbean patriarchy is a contested endeavor, since most households are not structured as a mating couple but as family systems. These layers indicate that representations of family and governance repeatedly reproduce gendered hierarchies of belonging.

As my work progressed, I became more interested in building on the ideas in Wilson Harris's essay "Judgment and Dream" and his novel *The Infinite Rehearsal*, which uses the ideas of repeating and rehearsal to understand the "ghosts relating to the conquistadorial and victimized bod[ies]."[1] Similarly, Antonio Benítez-Rojo's characterization of the Caribbean as a repeating island, but one that repeats with a difference, was influential. These two—Harris and Benítez-Rojo— became touchstones for my characterization of rehearsal. The more I explored James's, Carpentier's, and Césaire's representations of Haiti's revolution, the more rehearsal's generative power for thinking and rethinking Caribbean temporalities emerged. I was particularly excited with rehearsal's potential for helping me understand a broad range of perspectives through a multitude of genres. This idea proved a catalyst for me personally as I saw the dimensionality of it. Furthermore, I saw that being solely or only repetitive could lead to a rut or chaos, but rehearsal, with its emphasis on revision, its attention to the ways in which one might change the voice or twitch the body, its appreciation for the details of the body and the stories bodies tell, makes narratives of the flesh essential to actually moving women and men beyond the patriarchal frames most of us have inherited. Thus, using the attentiveness inherent in rehearsal's concern with the body means developing empathy in those details, and empathy leads to shifts in consciousness that create something different. Feminist rehearsal as a methodology proves essential to my personal interests in fusing art, scholarship, and activism.

Bodies and bones have been a tangible reminder of the material realities of Caribbean lives and the specific impact of history and gender on bodies in this location. The bone flutes, the bones of ancestors, and the bones of history emphasize the concrete traces of the physical presence of the culture, history, and fact. These bones amplify the flesh and bodies that lived and live with the realities of plantation structures. As Mahadai Das indicates, "these bones could make more than music. They're a fire-tried instrument."[2]

Wilson Harris's work on the Carib bone flute led me to the idea of rehearsal and the ways in which replaying history and gendered expectations can remake the region. Though my work departs from Harris's, the theoretical framework of feminist rehearsal advocates multivalent readings that encourage unity and cohesion through confrontation with local and global histories of knowledge, power, and freedom. The transactional nature of national belonging has meant interrogating both the aesthetic and the sociopolitical manifestations of Caribbean cultural production. Feminist rehearsal as an analytic frame makes legible the power of this dynamic on and off the page because it allows readers of visual and scribal texts to be proxies in cultural production.

A feminist notion of rehearsal and belonging helps us realize the extent to which Harris's and Benítez-Rojo's work assumes the masculine subject as the representative of Caribbean identity and community. The constant refashioning of Caribbean cultural production has privileged masculinist narratives. The typical masculine citizen-subject central in Caribbean literature and history has been its own kind of rehearsal on writing women out of transactional citizenship. In contrast, *Bodies and Bones* applies feminist rehearsal to concretize the sometimes visible but voiceless (or with voice and dismissed) and overlooked women and communities on the Caribbean national stage.

Caribbean peoples share the commonalities of European colonization: imported labor (i.e., enslavement and indenture) and the plantation systems that led to neocolonial development patterns economically and politically across four European linguistic groupings and innumerable Creole languages. Given these factors, the Caribbean has been a fragmented space whose commonalities, as characterized by Edward Kamau Brathwaite, are submarine. Globalization has both reduced the world in real time and united fragments across disjointed history and geography. Derek Walcott has said that repairing broken pieces is an indication of love of the whole: "Break a vase, and the love that reassembles the fragments is stronger than that love which took its symmetry for granted when it was whole."[3] Political and economic attempts at fully belonging have a patchy and tortuous history. Therefore, *Bodies and Bones* uses the method of feminist rehearsal to debate through art—particularly literature—and to more concretely unite fragmented, latent, submarine connections. Furthermore, feminist rehearsal proposes direct engagement with these contradictions, fashioning mutual spaces that create more democratic and participatory models for Caribbean belonging.

Feminist rehearsals in this book have revealed the negotiations for belonging across space and time. Employing rehearsal as epistemological mode has revealed moments of affinity and empathy that can lead to communities of consensus and intellectual and political selfhood. As an intermediary, the creative text provides a safe space in which to challenge and transform narrow group differences. Though, as Edwidge Danticat warns, creating dangerously and reading dangerously can have perilous consequences, the creative text still functions as a valuable proxy in processing difficult ideas and realities.[4] The imaginative capacity of the creative text is a space of alchemy. These creative texts, particularly those analyzed in this book, provide the room for discovery, engagement, and problem solving and, ergo, facilitate emancipatory projects. We think and talk "in story," and it is only through the process of reflection (rehearsal), in which we replay and adapt the story, that we can affix new meanings, new prompts, and new calibrations to our histories and experiences. Locating ourselves in stories makes us visible and confers a type of legitimacy, one we can use to radically shift our relationships to one another and to the places of our belonging. To truly integrate this belief at the personal, often financially straitened level involves using artistic deployments in ways that embed at the core of one's being and imbue citizens with the overall notion that working through differences—which are tremendous, terrifying, and often traumatizing—is the only way forward.

As indicated in the introduction, the framework of feminist rehearsal is full of possibilities for building new, self-sustaining, and self-defined communities of consensus through the bones and bodies of indigenous, African, Asian, European, and mixed Caribbean bodies. Chapter 1 applies the idea of rehearsal to different types of texts in order to illustrate the ways in which rehearsing the Middle Passage can lead to communities of consensus. That connection between representations of the past and the present is the basis for building communities of consensus because, in this manner, the past is neither avoided nor flattened into a celebratory narrative devoid of the hearse, or body, or bones of history. Instead, these bloody, exclusionary, and complex histories are embraced and integrated into the present.

Chapter 2 continues the work of chapter 1 and rehearses a pivotal event in the life of the Caribbean as a region—the success of the Haitian Revolution, which threw off the bonds of slavery and founded/formed a free state of/for black people in the Americas. Replaying the Haitian Revolution constructs communities of consensus in several ways. First, making the history tangible, as does every rehearsal in this book, is valuable in understanding, through various representations, the revolutionary leaders, namely representations of Toussaint and Christophe. Second, using these texts in the rehearsal, we see how men who shaped Caribbean studies, specifically C. L. R. James, Aimé Césaire, and Alejo Carpentier, used the Revolution to mount their own challenges to European and imperial masculinity. Third, the historical representations and those made by the twentieth-century writers reveal multiple biases, from the types of leaders valued to the types of masculinity that held, and still do, hold sway.

Chapter 3 leads us to communities of consensus by using the roles of women as proxies for understanding the Haitian Revolution from the perspective of the country's majority. This chapter reveals the competing and gendered interpretations of the Revolution and also highlights the role of religion and the domestic sphere in nation formation. The Haitian and Haitian American voices in this chapter produce complex and contradictory responses to the Revolution by Haitian women.

Chapter 4 rehearses two versions of the character Sycorax—the original as created by Shakespeare in *The Tempest* and the recuperated Sycorax defined by postcolonial writers and artists. Rehearsing Sycorax creates a mutual space for the imperial past and an independent present. The archetypes generated from this play inform Caribbean relationships with their colonial masters. As in the previous chapter, rehearsing Sycorax produces an alternative way of reading and utilizing the archetypes inherited in the colonial process, meaning that it reiterates the possibilities of the spaces shared with the "enemy."

Chapter 5 is perhaps the most difficult rehearsal since it replays the ways in which an indigenous and transnational community considers belonging to an independent Caribbean state. Here there are several proxies with which to rehearse belonging—Chofy, Tenga, Marietta, Beatrice, Danny, and the city of Georgetown. These rehearsals reveal the very contentions and reality of postcolonial states from the perspective of the often-erased native populations. Centering indigenous perspectives in this manner aspires not only to fashion a mutual space with a population thought of as "lost" but to critique gender and sexual roles that have been entrenched since colonialism as well. Ending the stranglehold of the colonial adventure and the real consequences of its violence means never forgetting the manner in which communities can be decimated.

For me, it is imperative to make intellectual discourse relevant and important to physical bodies. In *Bodies and Bones*, my goal has been to consider the ways in which what I do, teach literary and cultural studies, can make use of the power of Caribbean cultural production to transform that space from one perceived of as "inadequate and lacking" to one that can be recognized as a model for living in the twenty-first century. I believe these positive aspects of the Caribbean experience exist, but because those inside and outside the region give its history a cursory reading, these possibilities are lost. So how does feminist rehearsal offer a resolution to or amelioration of contemporary debates? And what are the political or social possibilities of empathetic consensus communities?

The dynamic social and political circumstances of Caribbean people continue to be part of my professional and personal concerns, suggesting opportunities for performing feminist rehearsals. A current topic that would benefit from feminist rehearsal methodology is immigration. Rehearsing histories of intra-Caribbean migration—the movement of people, mostly men, to Guyana and Panama and the shifts of mostly women from the Dominican Republic to Curaçao—might reveal familiar stories of belonging and unbelonging in the migratory process.

Rehearsing immigration reminds us to be attentive to bodies, not in the abstract but concretely. In the United States, there is vigorous debate on immigration, centered largely on notions of whose bodies have value and for what. Some bodies cannot belong because they are manual rather than intellectual laborers. Other bodies might believe they belong, but their lack of documents makes their unbelonging obvious. And bodies outside of heteronormative practices continue to be challenged in terms of their belonging. Intra-Caribbean immigration debates have a similar tone. As Annalee Davis's short film *On the Map* reveals, Barbados is a no-man's land for undocumented Guyanese immigrants who are disparaged and vilified, though Guyana had been a haven for Barbadian immigrants seeking opportunities in the mid-twentieth century. But it is not just Barbados. Bahamians speak of the "Haitian Problem," Puerto Ricans complain about Dominicans and Cubans, Guadeloupeans express dissatisfaction about Haitians and Dominicans, and Antiguans seek to crack down on "illegal aliens." Rehearsing (im)migration would allow thinking through the conflicts of migratory flows from the time of slavery to today, exploring the transactions of the migratory process, and understanding the hearse implications of bodies moving across borders. Thus, rehearsal seems to offer a way of accessing these frictions, not only to understand them in the broader dynamics of the Atlantic world, but to make them concrete and comprehensible in a political project.

Feminist rehearsal provides the space for open dialogues that keep building communities and allowing more discussion to occur, with the subject matter deeply rooted in the bones of the Caribbean. I believe in the power of feminist rehearsal to help us reflect on the past and the present and craft a future that is not limited to colonial inheritances and structures but is vital and makes another world possible.

Notes

Introduction

1. Walcott, *Star-Apple Kingdom*, 25–28.

2. See Schutzman and Cohen-Cruz, 2. The "spect-actor," as this person would become in Boal's evolution, has to arrange three poses: actual, ideal, and, most important, transitional (Boal, 132–142). In the Forum Theatre, the spectator/participant "has to intervene decisively in the dramatic action and change it. This begins by performing an entire scene uninterrupted, then staging that scene exactly as it had been the first time, but now each spectator-participant would have the right to intervene and change the action, trying out his or her proposal for change" (Boal, 139–140).

3. *Oxford English Dictionary*, accessed January 2012, www.oed.com; see also the discussion of the Cauvin painting in chapter 1.

4. Morrison, *Beloved*, 88–89.

5. See Karla F. C. Holloway's *Private Bodies, Public Texts* in which she discusses Lacks, Terri Schiavo, and the ways in which privacy and personhood are racialized and gendered in the law.

6. "'Immortal Cells' of Henrietta Lacks Live On in Labs," accessed February 19, 2013, http://wunc.org/post/immortal-cells-henrietta-lacks-live-labs.

7. Skloot, *The Immortal Life of Henrietta Lacks*, 13.

8. "The Pill," *American Experience*, directed by Chana Gazit and David Steward (2003; Alexandria, VA: Public Broadcasting Service, 2005), television program.

9. Lopez, *Matters of Choice*, x–xiii.

10. Skloot, 7.

11. Ibid., 2.

12. Skloot reports that Lacks's cells "could float through the air on dust particles. They could travel from one culture to the next. . . . And they were strong: if just *one* HeLa cell landed in a culture dish, it took over, consuming all the media and filling all the space" (153).

13. Koff, *The Bone Woman*, 8–9.

14. *One Million Bones*, accessed April 2013, http://www.onemillionbones.org/the-project/.

15. "Storytelling Grant Highlights," accessed March 2013, http://www.comptonfoundation.org/grants-awarded/grant-highlights/storytelling-grant-highlights/.

16. Spillers, 68.

17. Ibid., 67.

18. Ibid.

19. See also Kimberly Nichele Brown's *Writing the Black Revolutionary Diva*, 156–157.

20. Koff, 8–9.

21. Hartman, "Seduction and the Uses of Power," 552.

22. Blouet, *The Contemporary Caribbean*, 48–54. Furthermore, these visible aggressions mute other interventions such as the suspension of the Guyanese constitution by the British in 1953.

23. Spillers, 67.

24. Omolade, "Hearts of Darkness," 6–7.

25. See Mimi Sheller's *Consuming the Caribbean* for a discussion of the products the British and other Europeans craved from the Caribbean. See also Sidney Mintz's *Sweetness and Power* for a discussion of sugar and the development of Caribbean colonial economies.

26. Antonio Benítez-Rojo, Édouard Glissant, and Paul Gilroy note the importance of ships in creating the Caribbean.

27. I am indebted to political scientist David Hinds for his discussion of "communities of reason," which sent me down the path to articulating "communities of consensus."

28. Glissant, *Poetics of Relation*, 29–30.

29. Ibid., 27.

30. Frank Stasio and Shawn Wein, "How Does Empathy Make Us Uniquely Human?" WUNC Radio. In fact, one of the show's guests argued that "the cost of helping mitigates empathy, but guilt is a more valuable emotion" for societal change. See also Sara Ahmed, *The Cultural Politics of Emotion*, 39.

31. Raymond Williams, "Structures of Feeling," 128–129, 132.

32. Ibid., 130–131.

33. Ibid., 132.

34. Tinsley, "Black Atlantic, Queer Atlantic," 192.

35. Marina Sitrin chronicles the *horizontalismo* movement in Argentina as one of consensus building in which social movements are "constructing new types of networks that reject the hierarchical template bequeathed to them by established politics" (3).

36. McClintock, "'No Longer in a Future Heaven,'" 112.

37. Ibid., 122, 104–105.

38. Chapter 3 discusses nationalism as simultaneously regressive and central to providing a sensibility, which characters use as a positive force.

39. See Benedict Anderson's *Imagined Communities* and M. Jacqui Alexander and Chandra T. Mohanty's *Feminist Genealogies and Colonial Legacies.*

40. McClintock, 112.

41. Ibid.

42. Eisenstein, *The Color of Gender,* 2–13.

43. Saunders, *Alien-Nation,* 2.

44. Ibid., 3.

45. Rosenberg, *Nationalism and the Formation of Caribbean Literature,* 2–3.

46. Pearce, *Devolving Identities,* 5.

47. See Shalini Puri's *The Caribbean Postcolonial* for a discussion on hybridity and nationalism as political forces and in literature.

48. For example, Jamaica's motto is "Out of Many, One People"; Haiti's is "Unity Is Strength"; Suriname's is "Justice, Piety, Fidelity"; Guyana's is "One People, One Nation, One Destiny"; Trinidad and Tobago's is "Together We Aspire, Together We Achieve"; Cuba's national motto is "Our Homeland or Death"; Grenada's is "Ever Conscious of God We Aspire, Build and Advance as One People"; Bahamas's is "Forward, Upward, Onward Together"; and Antigua and Barbuda's is "Each Endeavouring, All Achieving."

49. Hartman, 544.

50. Omolade, 7.

51. See Benítez-Rojo's *The Repeating Island.*

52. Harris, *The Infinite Rehearsal,* 1.

53. Harris, "Judgment and Dream," 30–31.

54. Ibid., 22.

55. Ibid., 22–24.

56. Taylor, *The Archive and the Repertoire,* 4, 7–13.

57. Ibid., 12.

58. Di Cenzo and Bennett, "Women, Popular Theatre, and Social Action," 82.

59. See Honor Ford-Smith's "Ring, Ding, Ding in a Tight Corner: Sistren, Collective Democracy, and the Organization of Cultural Production" and Sharon L. Green's "Sistren Theatre Collective: Struggling to Remain Radical in an Era of Globalization."

60. Sharon L. Green, "Sistren Theatre Collective," 481.

61. Ibid.

62. Ibid., 488.

63. C. L. R. James, "The Artist in the Caribbean," 188–189.

64. Ibid., 188.

65. Conquergood, "Performance Studies," 145.

66. Butler, *Undoing Gender,* 1.

67. For two examples, see the works of Earl Lovelace and Sam Selvon; see also Curdella Forbes's *From Nation to Diaspora*.

68. For a discussion of aspects of rehearsal and history, see Joan Dayan's discussion in *Haiti, History and the Gods*.

69. Ibid., xv.

70. Ibid., 54.

71. Glissant, "The Quarrel with History," 61–71.

72. Shannon Sullivan, *Living Across and Through Skins*, 1, 3.

73. Ibid., 4.

74. Earl Lovelace's novel *The Dragon Can't Dance* portrays one experience of Indian indenture. In the story, Aldrick, searching for himself as the inheritor of heroic male privilege in the Caribbean, is destabilized by the presence of Pariag (aka Boya), the Indian character who migrated from rural Trinidad to the capital, Port-of-Spain. Boya is a competitor and threatens the sense of African-descendant communities that they are the natural inheritors of the postcolonial state. Boya's Indianness and maleness are at the nexus of the peril he poses to Aldrick. Since Aldrick does not consider Dolly, Boya's wife, or any other Indian woman as a viable inheritor of the colonial space, it is the Indian man as threat that concerns him. Indian women, similar to black women, are relegated to the background. Dolly, therefore, does not contribute to the tensions that Aldrick feels toward the relative newcomer to the Caribbean space.

75. Bahadur, "Coolie Women Are in Demand Here," 50.

76. Ibid., 53.

77. Ibid., 54.

78. Senior, "Arrival of the Snake Woman," 1–15.

1. Rehearsing with Ghosts

1. Collingwood told his officers that "'if the slaves died a natural death, it would be the loss of the owners of the ship; but if they were *thrown alive into the sea, it would be the loss of the underwriters.*' As a humane, though obviously specious, justification, he suggested that 'it would not be so cruel to *throw the poor sick wretches into the sea, as to suffer* them to linger out a few days, under the disorders with which they were afflicted.' No such proposal was made to put an end to the suffering of sick crewmen" (Walvin, *Black Ivory*, 14–15).

2. Ibid., 15; Baucom, *Specters of the Atlantic*, 129; and Vincent Brown, *The Reaper's Garden*, 159. All discuss the impact of the *Zong*. Walvin's and Brown's works discuss the historical impacts, while Baucom's work reads fictional and historical representations of the *Zong*'s journey and the legal proceedings that followed.

3. D'Aguiar, *Feeding the Ghosts*, 229.

4. Ibid., 61.

5. Ibid., 63.

6. See Elizabeth DeLoughrey's discussion of tidalectics in *Routes and Roots*.

7. Alexander and Mohanty, *Feminist Genealogies*, xlii.

8. The figure can be read as ambiguous, though Cauvin imagines the text as depicting female support systems (interview, June 2011). I initially read the submerged body as female, but to read it as male would yield another dynamic. If the central figure is running on a male body, this inverts the normal constructs of men walking on women. The image then offers a balance of sorts in that both the male and female figures are united against the white-sailed ship and the economic and political system it represents. It is precisely this ambiguity that makes viewers take another look and reread/rehearse the image.

9. Antonio Benítez-Rojo, Édouard Glissant, and Paul Gilroy recognize the importance of ships in Atlantic discourses, with Benítez-Rojo and Glissant focused particularly on Caribbean development. Benítez-Rojo characterizes *la flota*, "the fleet," made up of several ships, as the machine of the Americas and the Atlantic world. The ship, in conjunction with other machinery, makes the plantation machine possible (Benítez-Rojo, *Repeating Island*, 6–7). Glissant describes three instances of the abyss, one of which is the boat as "a womb abyss" (Glissant, *Poetics*, 6). Gilroy uses the metaphor of the ship to invoke it as a complicated site of terror and "a living, micro-cultural, micro-political system in motion" that circulated people, goods, and ideas (Gilroy, *The Black Atlantic*, 4).

10. Benítez-Rojo describes the plantation as a "family of machines" (naval, military, bureaucratic, commercial, legal, religious, etc.) united in production of colonial commodities that not only indicated an economic rationale but also resulted in a type of society (Benítez-Rojo, *Repeating Island*, 7–9).

11. Cauvin's runner flees in the tradition of the flying Africans who left the misery of the plantation once they had not eaten salt (Lovelace, *Salt*, 3). Similar to the flying Africans are the Igbo, who walked back to Africa upon realizing the horrors of slavery. As Aunt Cuney relates in *Praisesong for the Widow*: "It was here that they brought 'em. They taken 'em out of the boats right here where we's standing. . . . And the minute those Ibos was brought on shore they just stopped, my gran' said, and taken a look around. A good long look. . . . And they seen things that day you and me don't have the power to see. 'Cause those pure-born Africans was peoples my gran' said could see in more ways than one. The kind can tell 'bout things happened long before they was born and things to come long after they's dead" (Marshall, 37–38). See also Meredith Gatsby's discussion of flying Africans and the consumption of salt in *Sucking Salt: Caribbean Women Writers, Migration and Survival* (Gatsby, 20–29).

12. Kempadoo, *Sexing the Caribbean*, 53–54.

13. Ibid., 55.

14. In an e-mail exchange on October 13, 2012, Merle Collins revealed that this section of "Rehearsing with Ghosts" reminds her of her poem "Up and Down the Deck," which is also a children's game: "One person calls 'Up and down the deck' and everyone else answers, 'Keep Moving.' The children all move about the

yard with this call and response until the caller says, 'Boom overhead' and everyone ducks so that the boom (which is described in dictionaries as a spar or long
rod pivoting above the mast of a ship) won't hit them and throw them overboard
as it pivots. This means, then, that the yard is imagined as the sea/the ocean. In
my poem, the game is imagined as a recreation of the dangers of the middle passage, and explains why island Caribbean people often fear the sea, warning their
children to be careful when they go the sea because 'seawater have no branch.'
This section of your work makes me think about this and how the poem focuses
on memory, so that, I guess, the poem insists on a rehearsal to explain caution
regarding an experience seen by tourist visitors as all pleasure."

15. The importance of the womb returns; see the discussion of Henrietta
Lacks in the introduction to this volume.

16. Moitt, *Women and Slavery in the French Antilles*, 89.

17. D'Aguiar, 84, 89–91.

18. Ibid., 103.

19. Goodison, "Nanny," CD.

20. Maroons, also called *cimarrones* in Spanish-speaking territories, were
people who freed themselves by escaping from plantations. They normally
developed communities in forested or mountainous areas and maintained their
freedom through guerrilla warfare and by looting plantations. Maroons still
exist as a cultural and ethnic identity throughout the Caribbean, particularly in
Jamaica and Suriname.

21. D'Aguiar, 93.

22. Ibid., 209.

23. Ibid., 223–226.

24. Ibid., 75–76.

25. Benítez-Rojo, 5.

26. D'Aguiar, 226.

27. Ibid., 19–37.

28. Ibid., 200.

29. No ledger was presented during the actual court proceedings: "The
Zong's logbook and other papers were neither presented at the original trial nor
at the appeal, much to the displeasure of the lead attorney for the underwriters,
Mr. Davenport" (Baucom, 127).

30. In reality, Captain Luke Collingwood died before the *Zong* case went to
trial (Walvin, *Black Ivory*, 16).

31. D'Aguiar, 155.

32. Ibid., 169.

33. Ibid., 170.

34. Anderson, *Imagined Communities*, 45, 61.

35. Philip, *Zong!*, 190.

36. Ibid., 194.

37. Jenkins, *The Language of Caribbean Poetry*, 171–172.

38. Ibid., 172.

39. Philip, *Zong!*, 196, 200.

40. Philip indicates that the number killed on the *Zong* varies between sources, but she uses the number 150 and explains that "the exact number of African slaves murdered remains a slippery signifier of what was undoubtably a massacre" (Ibid., 208). Furthermore, in the court documents that are the basis for the text, the decision reads that "sixty negroes died for want of water . . . ; and forty others . . . threw themselves into the sea and were drowned; . . . and the lives of the rest of the negroes, which for want of water they could not otherwise preserve, were obliged to throw overboard 150 *other* negroes" (210; emphasis added).

41. Ibid., 198.

42. Philip suggests that the form of the poem is one that helps the reader find voice through relation, and that "every word or word cluster is seeking a space directly above within which to fit itself and in so doing falls into relation with others either above, below, or laterally" (Ibid., 203).

43. Jenkins, 170.

44. Baucom, 332.

45. D'Aguiar, 230.

46. Baucom, 332.

47. Another rehearsal is the *Kali Pani*, the journey of indentured workers across "dark and bitter waters" from India to the Caribbean. Like other voyages to the region, Indians began their membership negotiations, sometimes mitigated by their home country's policies, on ships that traversed the Indian and Atlantic Oceans before reaching the Caribbean Sea.

48. D'Aguiar, 4.

49. Polly Patullo characterizes the sea as an economic highway and battleground on which cruise ships are "giant white whales" that pollute Caribbean waters in the name of pleasure (*Last Resorts*, 193, 198).

50. Ibid., 198.

51. Gibson, "Cruising in the 21st Century," 43; and Patullo, 195–196.

52. Patullo, 208.

53. Ibid., 199.

54. Shemak, *Asylum Speakers*, 184.

55. Klein, "High Seas, Low Pay," accessed May 2011, http://www.cruise-junkie.com/ot.html.

56. "Thus, as the president of the Carnival Corporation, whose ships are registered in Panama, wrote in his book, *Selling the Sea*: 'Of course, ships are registered in these flag-of-convenience nations pay lower wages and taxes on an aggregate bases than those registered in the United States (or Norway or Italy for that matter). But that makes it possible for them to offer cruises at a much lower cost than if their ships were registered in countries with restrictive hiring policies'" (Patullo, 199).

57. "Job description," accessed July 2011, http://www.cruiselinesjobs.com/job-descriptions-entertainment -jobs/.

58. "Brown," personal interview, July 17, 2011.

59. The site http://www.cruiserape.com/ shares stories and statistics of women, primarily passengers, raped on cruise ships. Women on these ships, whether Caribbean or not, and whether asked to perform Caribbeanness or not, can find themselves in great peril. Elsewhere, female crewmembers (and some passengers) have chronicled various indignities and violence ranging from sexual harassment by passengers and crew members to rape.

60. The Big Drum Ceremony is part of ritual memory in Carriacou, Grenada, and is now staged for tourists.

61. This performance is similar to Marpessa Dawn's performance of Brazilianness as Eurydice in the 1959 film *Black Orpheus*.

62. Island Windjammer Cruises, accessed April 15, 2011, http://www.islandwindjammers.com/.

63. See "Windjammer Specials," accessed April 15, 2011, http://www.islandwindjammers.com/island-windjammers-cruise-specials.aspx.

64. Walvin chronicles John Newton's career and transformations through his calculating work as the captain of the slave ship *Duke of Argyle*, as well as through the letters filled with tenderness and religiosity that he sent to his wife. Walvin, *Black Ivory*, 36–51.

65. "We encourage you to join the Island Windjammers crew by lending a hand to help hoist the sails—or by shouting encouragement as you relax with a cool drink. . . . Have your photo snapped as you take your turn at the helm of a majestic tall ship. The friendly crew, hailing from all corners of the Caribbean, is eager to help you learn about the ship, the islands, and their people." Island Windjammers, accessed April 15, 2011, http://www.islandwindjammers.com/what-to-expect.aspx.

66. See Edwidge Danticat's "Children of the Sea," in which the male protagonist drowns and connects his experience to the Middle Passage: "I go to them now as though it was always meant to be, as though the very day that my mother birthed me, she had chosen me to live life eternal, among the children of the deep blue sea, those who have escaped the chains of slavery to form a world beneath the heavens and the blood-drenched earth where you live" (*Krik? Krak!* 27). April Shemak analyzes the multiple "inter-dictions" and inhospitalities that refugees face in Danticat's short story in her book *Asylum Speakers* (72–77).

67. "Migration has historically been central in the formation of Caribbean countries. Throughout the region, migration patterns have, over time, responded to economic and political developments within the islands and to the impact of international forces ranging from investment and trade regulations to changes in the character of immigration policy in receiving countries including the United States, England, and France. . . . These pressures culminated in open protests and waves of boat people and rafters leaving Cuba in the summer of

1994. Most of these migrants were young men (20–35 years old) whose decision to leave Cuba was grounded above all in economic motives: a desire to 'make their destiny' somewhere else." Celia Green, in Daniel Levine, "Migration from the Caribbean," *Migration from the Caribbean: Issues for the 1990s*, vol. 3, no. 1 (Fall 1995).

68. Ibid.

69. Ibid.

70. Shemak, *Asylum Speakers*, 46.

71. Ibid.

72. Olmos and Parvisini-Gebert, *Sacred Possessions*, 92.

73. Fleurant, *Dancing Spirits*, 29.

74. In her discussion of Vodou altars, Karen McCarthy Brown reveals that "because the power of the altar is below the earth where it cannot be seen, and the dead and the spirits live below the mirror surface of the water, which also thwarts the human gaze, the products of the earth, the things that push up from down under, as well as the surface conditions of earth and water, are loaded with meaning" (*Tracing the Spirit*, 16).

75. VèVè Clark, "Developing Diaspora Literacy," 12.

76. Doerner, quoted in Crichlow, "Making Waves," 1.

77. Mordecai and Wilson, *Her True-True Name*, 107.

78. Ibid., 108.

79. Ibid., 109.

80. "Haitian Migrants Apprehended," June 3, 2013. Similar to U.S. Coast Guard interdictions of Caribbean migrants, the Royal Bahamas Defence Force routinely apprehends Haitian migrants many of them in unstable sloops under dangerous conditions. *The Nassau Guardian*, accessed June 20, 2013, /index. php?option=com_content&view=article&id=39606:haitian-migrants-apprehended&catid=3:news&Itemid=27.

81. CNN recently reported that twenty-three Cubans had been rescued by Royal Caribbean's *Oasis of the Seas*. The crew provided food and medical treatment while "passengers videotaped the rescue," further linking the various Middle Passage rehearsals to the cruise ship. Todd Sperry, "Cruise Ship Rescues 23 Cubans at Sea," April 6, 2012, accessed April 10, 2012, http://www.cnn. com/2012/04/06/travel/cruise-ship-rescue/.

82. Mordecai and Wilson, 110–111.

83. Glissant, *Poetics*, 7–8.

84. The *Nassau Guardian* and other regional outlets have published countless articles on regional migration and the problems—perceived and real—of the movement of people in the Caribbean, for example, http://www.thenassauguardian.com/index.php?option=com_content&view=article&id=10752:the-haitian-problem&catid=49:op-ed&Itemid=86, accessed July 5, 2011. Others include, on Barbados, http://www.nationnews.com/index.php/ articles/view/our-caribbean-health-care-and-immigrants-in-barbados/, and on Trinidad, http://www2.

guardian.co.tt/letters/2011/06/21/underachievement-came-immigrants-other-islands.

85. See "Underwater Sculpture," accessed June 2011, https://freeartlondon.wordpress.com/2010/02/10/ underwater-sculpture/ (site discontinued).

86. A current installation at the site features sculptor Troy Lewis's work, which is based on Amerindian inheritances. Ian George, "Grenadas Underwater Sculpture Park Unveils New Sculpture," October 27, 2010, accessed June 2011, http://www.barnaclegrenada.com/index.php/component/content/article/17-travel-a-tourism/1773-grenadas-underwater-sculpture-park-unveils-new-sculpture.

87. Interview with Jason deCaires Taylor, May 22, 2012.

88. George Brizan, *Grenada—Island of Conflict*, 22–23.

89. Grenada does have a fraught history with monuments, particularly the one that commemorates Operation Urgent Fury of 1983. This concrete structure near the airport, populated by goats, pays tribute to U.S. troops who invaded the country, rather than the Grenadians who fought and died in the conflict.

90. Civ Jones, "'The Vicissitudes': An Underwater Sculpture That Honors the African Ancestors Lost at Sea during the Middle Passage," March 23, 2012, accessed July 6, 2012, http://magicbaltimore.com/3278378/the-vicissitudes-an-underwater-sculpture-that-honors-the-african-ancestors-lost-in-the-sea-during-the-middle-passage/.

91. Jason deCaires Taylor, e-mail to author , July 6, 2012.

92. Interview with Jason deCaires Taylor, May 22, 2012.

93. "Underwater Sculpture Park Action Group Strategy and Plan," 9–10.

94. Ibid., 12.

95. Rediker, *The Slave Ship*, 19.

96. Ibid., 20.

2. Their Bones Would Reject Yours

1. After a series of cremations (burning the flesh, sifting through it, removing the bones, burning again), the Yanomamö crush the bones of the deceased several times; the ground ashes mixed with boiled plantain soup are then eaten (Chagnon, 50).

2. Dubois and Garrigus, *Slave Revolution in the Caribbean*, 188–191.

3. Quoted in Nicole King, "Double or Nothing," 31.

4. Dash, *The Other America*, 2.

5. Black Caribbean patriarchy is a contested endeavor that is always constructed in relation to race, color, and class. Since most households are structured not around a mating couple but rather as family systems, black Caribbean patriarchy is challenged somewhat. As Merle Hodge argues, the desire to represent Caribbean households as "isolated nuclear units" is a historical contradiction, particularly in the anglophone region (476). These layers indicate that

representations of family and governance repeatedly reproduce gendered hierarchies of belonging.

6. Christian Hogsbjerg's recent book *Toussaint Louverture: The Story of the Only Successful Slave Revolt in History* includes the original play *Toussaint Louverture* (1936), production notes, reviews, and photographs.

7. Regarding Sycorax's character in Shakespeare's *The Tempest*, see chapter 4 in this book.

8. Jeannette Allsopp, "History Re-interpreted," 21.

9. Anderson, *Imagined Communities*, 11.

10. "Declaration of the Rights of Man and the Citizen," accessed August 15, 2004, http://www.hrcr.org/docs/frenchdec.html.

11. Ibid.

12. Peabody, *"There Are No Slaves in France,"* 8–9.

13. Eze, *Race and the Enlightenment*, 11.

14. Ibid., 11–13.

15. Leclerc, "The Geographical and Cultural Distribution of Mankind," 21–23.

16. Hume, "Of National Characters," 33.

17. Ibid.

18. Kant, "On National Characteristics," 53, 57.

19. Linden Lewis, "Caribbean Masculinity," 95.

20. Edmonson, *Making Men*, 5.

21. Bush, *Slave Women in Caribbean Society*, 91–93.

22. Edmondson, 20–35.

23. Ibid., 23.

24. Ibid., 28.

25. Burton and Reno, eds., *French and West Indian*, 2.

26. Senghor, "Négritude," 45. Negritude is often criticized as "essential" because it places black difference at the level of biology rather than situating it in social factors (Burton and Reno, 141).

27. Wilson-Tagoe, *Historical Thought and Literary Representation*, 28.

28. James, *The Black Jacobins* (play), 418–419.

29. Gaspar and Geggus, *A Turbulent Time*, viii.

30. James, *The Black Jacobins* (play), 427.

31. Ibid., 426.

32. Ibid., 428.

33. Peter Hitchcock, "Revolutionary Violence," in *Symploke*, vol. 20, nos. 1–2: 9–10.

34. James, *The Black Jacobins* (play), 417.

35. Fick, *The Haitian Revolution from Below*, 114.

36. James, *The Black Jacobins* (history), 395.

37. James, *The Black Jacobins* (play), 425.

38. Ibid., 401.

39. Ibid., 421.

40. Ibid.

41. Haiti Grassroots Watch, "Monsanto in Haiti," May 5, 2011, accessed July 2013, http://www.truth-out.org/news/item/917:monsanto-in-haiti. Tory Field and Beverly Bell, "Farmers and Consumers versus Monsanto: David Meets Goliath," in *Other World*, April 8, 2013, accessed July 2013, http://truth-out.org/news/item/15601-farmers-and-consumers-vs-monsanto-david-meets-goliath.

42. Many neoliberal policies were instituted before the earthquake and as post-earthquake relief initiatives. Two arresting examples of the ways in which international interests continue to undermine Haitian democracy and prosperity are challenges to increasing the minimum wage from roughly two dollars per day to five dollars per day and the donation of genetically modified grain to Haitian farmers. In June 2009, before the earthquake, international companies including Levi's and Hanes attempted to block the increase of the minimum wage (see Coughlin and Ives). In June 2010, Haitian farmers protested against donated genetically modified grain from Monsanto, arguing that the company's hybrid would undermine local grain stocks and create dependency on Monsanto for seeds (see GRAIN).

43. James, *The Black Jacobins* (play), 446.

44. Fanon, *The Wretched of the Earth*, 35–106.

45. Ibid., 52–55.

46. James, *The Black Jacobins* (history), 370–372.

47. Ibid., 373–374.

48. Ibid., 373. Joan Dayan supports the claims of a vengeful Dessalines by quoting him: "We have rendered to these true cannibals, war for war, crime for crime, outrage for outrage; yes, I have saved my country; I have avenged America" (Dayan, 4).

49. Dayan, 24.

50. Ibid., 17.

51. Ibid., 18.

52. Ibid., 17.

53. Ibid.

54. Edmondson, 8–10, 13.

55. Ibid., 106.

56. Paravisini-Gebert, "The Haitian Revolution in Interstices and Shadows," 126.

57. Césaire, *The Tragedy*, 48.

58. Ibid., 72.

59. Bellegarde, "Alexandre Pétion," 171.

60. The historical reality is that Pétion died in 1818 of yellow fever, two years before Christophe's suicide.

61. Césaire, 17.

62. Ibid., 21.

63. Ibid., 18.
64. Ibid., 17, 21.
65. Ibid., 28.
66. Ibid., 12.
67. Ibid.
68. The senate elected Pétion in March 1807 after Christophe rejected the presidency. Pétion was reelected in 1811 and 1815. His 1816 constitution "reorganized the legislative body, established a life term for the Presidency, giving the head of State the right to nominate his successor; as well as providing free elementary education for boys, redistributing national lands and creating a landed peasantry; and supporting Simón Bolívar's independence dreams" (Bellegarde, 170–172).
69. The Code Henri (1812) mandated fieldwork and other draconian measures reminiscent of France's Code Noir, which Haitians viewed as a reimposition of slavery.
70. Césaire, 41.
71. Ibid., 54.
72. Michel-Rolph Trouillot, *Silencing the Past*, 32.
73. Césaire, 18.
74. Ibid., 43.
75. Michel-Rolph Trouillot, 36.
76. Ibid., 65
77. Michel-Rolph Trouillot writes that "Dahomy was founded by Tacoodonou after a successful war against Da, the ruler of Abomey. Tacoodonou 'put Da to death by cutting open his belly, and placed his body under the foundation of a palace that he built in Abomey, as a memorial of his victory; which he called Dahomy, from Da the unfortunate victim, and Homy his belly: that is the house built on Da's belly.' . . . [C]hances are that Christophe knew this story. He praised Dahomans as great warriors" (65). This is also similar to Wilson Harris's characterization of why Amerindians would eat a morsel of their enemies' flesh. It was to understand and ultimately defeat them.
78. Barrett H. Clark, as quoted in VèVè Clark, "Haiti's Tragic Overture," 250.
79. Ibid., 247.
80. *Zemi* is the Taino term for "gods," but more commonly "the idols and fetishes representing them, which were made from the remains of ancestors or from natural objects believed to be inhabited by powerful spirits" (Rouse, 13).
81. Césaire, 48.
82. Ibid., 49.
83. Ibid., 71.
84. Carpentier, 120.
85. Ibid., 101.
86. Ibid.

87. Paravisini-Gebert, "The Haitian Revolution in Interstices and Shadows," 125.

88. Dayan, *Haiti, History, and the Gods*, 31.

89. Carpentier, 55.

90. Natasha Barnes's introduction to her book *Cultural Conundrums* is an excellent discussion of Josephine's rehearsals.

91. According to VèVè Clark's study of the approximately sixty-three plays written on the Haitian Revolution from 1796 to 1975, about four are written by women and two deal with the daughters of Toussaint and Christophe (Clark, "Haiti's Tragic Overture," 240, 255–56). Evelyne Trouillot's novel *Rosalie l'infâme* and Nalo Hopkinson's *The Salt Roads* have been included among the more recent texts that foreground women and the Revolution.

92. Garraway, *The Libertine Colony*, 246–247.

93. James, *The Black Jacobins* (play), 410.

94. Ibid., 414.

95. Ibid., 441.

96. Ibid.

97. Ibid., 415–416.

98. I make note of their twins, Jacques Bien-Aimé and his sister, Célestine Dessalines, born in April 1793, because twins and the idea of doubleness— La Marasa, "the twins"—are crucial parts of the Vodou worldview; http://www.4dw.net/ royalark/Haiti/haiti2.htm. According to Olmos and Paravisini-Gebert, La Marasa "are endowed with special powers and hold a privileged position. . . . They are invoked and greeted after Legba [and] are often depicted as three, because twins represent abundant life, and triplets mark exceptional fertility" (Olmos and Paravisini-Gebert, *Creole Religions*, 116–117).

99. Christopher Buyers, "Haiti Monarchy," accessed May 2012, 4dw.net/royalark/haiti.php.

100. In his eulogy for Malcolm X, called "On Malcolm X," in *The Autobiography of Malcolm X*, as told to Alex Haley, Ossie Davis uses this phrase.

101. Césaire, 56–57. This policy is remarkably like those in many, often fascist nations, including the latest Republican marriage policy, the Healthy Marriage Initiative, in the United States, which "encourages" women to marry their children's fathers so that they will be eligible for government benefits.

102. Dayan, xv.

103. Cosentino, *Sacred Arts of Haitian Vodou*, 430.

104. Césaire, 94.

105. Ibid., 26.

106. Nicole King makes a similar argument about James's play and the role of Vodou in *C.L.R. James and Creolization: Circles of Influence*: "But by drowning out both 'La Marseillaise' and 'La Liberté' with the ritual Vodun drumming, James anchors the political posturing of the masses in African custom and ritual memory, which suggests a hesitancy on James's part to understand

fully the revolutionary activity as creolized formation and foreshadows the dip-lomatic isolation inflicted on Haiti after its self-liberation" (39).

107. Césaire, 78–79.

108. Ibid., 80.

109. Ibid., 84–85.

110. Ibid., 86.

111. Ibid., 43.

112. Michel-Rolph Trouillot, 59–60. "Christophe's reliance on transforma-tive rituals, his desire to control both humans and death itself are epitomized in his last moments. Having engaged unsuccessfully in various rituals to restore his failing health and knowing that he had lost the personal magnetism that made his contemporaries tremble, . . . a paralyzed Christophe shot himself, report-edly with a silver bullet."

113. Olmos and Paravisini-Gebert, *Creole Religions of the Caribbean*, 113.

114. Césaire, 17.

115. Murphy, *Working the Spirit*, 15–16.

116. Ibid., 26.

117. Ibid., 12.

118. Ibid., 17.

119. Ibid., 16.

120. Ibid., 15–16.

121. Ibid., 12.

122. Ibid., 27.

123. Carpentier, 86.

124. Webb, *Myth and History in the Caribbean*, 17–18.

125. Ibid., 18.

126. Paravisini-Gebert, "The Haitian Revolution in Interstices and Shad-ows," 126.

127. Ibid., 121.

128. Carpentier, 14.

129. Ibid.

130. Ibid., 16–17.

131. Paravisini-Gebert, "The Haitian Revolution in Interstices and Shad-ows," 118.

132. Ibid., 124.

133. Carpentier, 32.

134. Paravisini-Gebert, "The Haitian Revolution in Interstices and Shad-ows," 126.

135. Carpentier, 156.

3. Hope and Infinity

1. There are representations of the Revolution by Haitian men, but I thought it important to examine the work of Haitian women. Additionally, many of

these narratives are written in Haitian Kreyol, a language in which I am not fluent.

2. Dayan, *Haiti, History, and the Gods*, 44.

3. "Though Défilée was helped to carry the sack by a well-known madman named Dauphin, most accounts choose to ignore what is possible in favor of the miraculous: Défilée's lone journey with the hero's remains" (Dayan, 41).

4. Jana Evans Braziel, "Remembering Défilée," 65.

5. Ertha Pascal-Trouillot, as quoted in Dayan, 44.

6. Dayan, 44.

7. Ibid.

8. Chatland, "Descriptions of Various Loa of Voodoo," accessed April 2, 2013, http://www2.webster.edu/~corbetre/haiti/voodoo/biglist.htm.

9. Dayan, 40.

10. Ibid.

11. Myriam Chancy, *Framing Silence*, 5–6.

12. Ibid., 10.

13. Dayan, 47.

14. McClintock. See her discussion of "The Second Trek," 109.

15. Alexis, *Peintres Haïtiens*, 56.

16. Poupeye, *Caribbean Art*, 65–66.

17. Alexis, "All Mankind."

18. Ibid.

19. "Primitive" is a term deployed in Haiti to denote untrained artists; these artists have also been called "intuitive." Both of these terms are loaded and continue to be debated, but because "primitive" was used to characterize a generation of painters, I use it here.

20. Poupeye, 65. Though I spell "Vodou" in this way throughout this text, some authors use an "a" as in "Vaudou" or "oo" as in "voodoo"; I have maintained the authors' spellings in direct quotes.

21. Ibid., 67.

22. Alexis, *Peintres Haïtiens*, 216.

23. Alexis, "All Mankind."

24. Alexis, "Caribbean Art and Culture," 59.

25. Ibid.

26. Hoffman, *Haitian Art*, 53.

27. Ibid., 52.

28. Ibid., 53.

29. Mintz and Trouillot, "The Social History of Haitian Vodou," 141–142.

30. Poupeye, 64–65.

31. André Juste, "Review of *Saving Grace* Exhibition," in *Haiti Liberté*, vol. 4, no. 23 (December 22–28, 2010).

32. Mintz and Trouillot argue that the Haitian elite and Haitian politicians exploit Vodou for their own ends, but François Duvalier, more than

other politician, systematically used cultural nationalism to undermine the country (Mintz and Trouillot, 142–146). They conclude that "Vodou has become less and less the people's religion, and more and more something else. Its sociology today is a function not only of the meaning of life for the peasantry and the urban poor, but also of Haiti's present and future as a tourist retreat, of its capacity to attract the jaded with exotica. What was once a people's religion is now two other things besides: a political divertissement for Haitian political leaders, and a side show for tourist hotels" (Mintz and Trouillot, 147).

33. Hoffman, 51.

34. Mintz and Trouillot, 142.

35. Poupeye, 65.

36. Mintz and Trouillot, 138.

37. Alexis, "Contemporary Haitian Art," 59.

38. Mintz and Trouillot, 142.

39. A Poto-Mitan artistic school emerged in 1968, and its members use "Vodou cosmology and Prehispanic culture as the basis of their aesthetic investigations" (Poupeye, 88).

40. Karen McCarthy Brown, "The Art of Transformation," 15–16.

41. Ibid., 16.

42. Arthur and Dash, *A Haiti Anthology*, 139.

43. Renda, *Taking Haiti*, 140.

44. Tann, *Haitian Vodou*, 17, 136–138.

45. Ibid., 138–141.

46. Fred D'Aguiar, 90. Through ritual action, bones become part of Morrison's character Baby Suggs's admonition to love the flesh and to acknowledge the suffering of the bodies and bones.

47. Alexis, *Peintres Haïtiens* , 56.

48. Blood ritual has been negatively characterized as devil worship as it relates to Vodou, but it is important to note that blood is a symbol of redemption in Christianity and other religious practices.

49. As Kimberly Brown observes, Toni Cade Bambara "argues for a more inclusive definition of the black revolutionary that lies in the rejection of rigid notions of femininity and masculinity that not only tend to be a barrier to achieving political consciousness, but a hindrance to 'self-autonomy' or self-actualization" (*Writing the Black Revolutionary Diva*, 85).

50. Dayan, 29.

51. Dubois, *Avengers of the New World*, 100.

52. Tann, 24.

53. Fick, 94.

54. The Vatican recalled its priests from Haiti after some of them were killed during the revolutions. From 1804 to 1860, the Catholic Church was not officially part of the Haitian nation. Various Haitian presidents had Vodou advisers

and some were Vodouists themselves. When the church returned to Haiti in the 1860s, it waged a campaign against Vodou that lasted until 1943.

55. Regarding Pat Robertson's comments, see discussion of evangelical discourse, the Bois Caïman ceremony, and rehearsing the Haitian Revolution in Angela Naimou's "'I Need Many Repetitions': Rehearsing the Haitian Revolution in the Shadows of the Sugar Mill." Also see Elizabeth McAllister's two *Washington Post* articles, "Voodoo's View of the Quake," January 15, 2010, and "Haiti Mobs Lynch Voodoo Priests over Cholera Fears," December 24, 2010.

56. Dayan, 54.

57. Desruisseau, *La Rencontre des Trois Mondes* exhibition, Paris, 1992

58. Edwidge Danticat, "A Wall of Fire Rising," 57.

59. Ibid., 55.

60. Ibid., 56.

61. Ibid., 71, 79–80.

62. Ibid., 59, 68.

63. Ibid., 56, 78–79.

64. Ibid., 59–60.

65. Ibid., 62.

66. Ibid., 64.

67. Ibid., 60.

68. Ibid., 66.

69. Ibid.

70. Ibid., 72.

71. Ibid., 74.

72. Ibid., 67.

73. Ibid., 73.

74. Ibid., 76.

75. Ibid., 77.

76. Ibid., 75.

77. Dayan, 50.

78. Naimou, "'I Need Many Repetitions,'" 179.

79. Ibid., 174.

80. Nicholls, "Economic Dependence and Political Autonomy," 218–219.

81. Arthur and Dash, 210.

82. Danticat, "Between the Pool and the Gardenias," 94.

83. Dayan, 48.

84. Chancy, *Framing Silence*, 9.

85. Braziel, 65.

4. Signs of Sycorax

1. The same torture described in "Ala" is rehearsed in *A Woman Named Solitude*, in "the public execution of the Bambara wild woman who had thrust

a needle into the skull of her newborn baby. They had tied her to the doorpost of one of the huts and coated her naked body with molasses. It took the manioc ants several hours to finish her off, and all that time, her eyes blazing like torches, she had screamed insults at the masters" (59).

2. Hilary Beckles distinguishes between the "rebel woman" and the "natural rebel." He characterizes the rebel woman, on the one hand, as a "cultural icon invested with political leadership, magical and spiritual powers, around whom the community rallies." The natural rebel, on the other hand, is the "typical woman in the fields, who possesses no claim to distinct individuality and is therefore one of the masses. Her identity, and the level of consciousness that informs her politics, have been conceptualized and defined by . . . the everyday experience of her enslavement [and] represents the basis of a culture of refusal and resistance through which she claims a 'self' and an 'identity.'" Beckles's desire to reclaim as many of women's everyday experiences as possible accomplishes two objectives: it provides contemporary women with "real" role models, and it challenges the tendency to deify the common in reclamation work. Beckles argues that a dependence on heroines developmentally disables feminist consciousness and scholarship (xxii, 186).

3. See Schwarz-Bart and Schwarz-Bart, *In Praise of Black Women*.

4. In 2007, a statue was erected in Bagneux (Hauts-de-Seine), Abymes's sister city, to commemorate the abolition of slavery and the slave trade. This work, composed of African wood (iroko) and metal, is, according sculptor Nicolas Alquin, "the first memorial in the world dedicated to all resisting slaves." The work recalls the "Negro iron to put iron in his own skin."

5. *Solitude* exhibit, La Médiathèque Caraïbe, Basse-Terre, Guadeloupe, French West Indies.

6. The levels of names and naming are not only part of the colonial process of claiming but also part of the decolonizing process of reclaiming, and Solitude's name changes several times over the course of the novel.

7. Schwarz-Bart, *Solitude*, 65.

8. Ibid., 130.

9. Benítez-Rojo, *The Repeating Island*, 7–8.

10. Barrow, *Caribbean Portraits*, 4.

11. Ibid., 5.

12. Barrow, "Charting Futures," 353–354.

13. Mohammed, "Writing Gender into History," 29.

14. Beckles, *Centering Woman*, ix.

15. Mohammed and Shepherd, *Gender and Caribbean Development*, 10.

16. Bailey et al., *Gender*, xiii.

17. Shakespeare, *The Tempest*, act 1, scene 2.

18. Torres-Saillant, *Caribbean Poetics*, 153; and Mehta, *Notions of Identity*, 44–45.

19. Cliff, "Caliban's Daughter," 47–48.

20. Ibid., 36–37.

21. Ibid., 48.

22. Chancy, *Searching for Safe Spaces*, 26.

23. Ibid., 25.

24. Ibid., 27.

25. Mehta, 157–159. In addition to Sycorax, many articles discuss Miranda, a key figure in postcolonial power asymmetries. While I do address this character, specific articles of interest are Sylvia Wynter's dense afterword "Beyond Miranda's Meanings: Un/Silencing the 'Demonic Ground' of Caliban's 'Woman,'" which discusses the ways in which Miranda creates an unstable or "demonic" ground on which to challenge patriarchy; and Coco Fusco's "Miranda's Diary," which works in conjunction with Chancy's discussion of exile, since Fusco chronicles her own transnational experiences as Cuban, American, and "displaced." Fusco argues that displacement or exile is fundamental to Miranda's story, as is her rejection of or challenge to the symbolic power of the father. Fusco sees Miranda as the daughter of the colonial and symbolic father rather than as the elite white woman in the colonial enterprise. Thus she identifies with Miranda, not only for her "wonder" when initially encountering the island, but also for her journey, "straying far from the fictions of identity imparted by a symbolic father" (6).

26. Fusco, 7.

27. Mehta, 170.

28. Joseph, "The Scream of Sycorax," 128.

29. Ibid., 131.

30. Ibid., 131–132.

31. Ibid., 138–139.

32. Anderson, *Imagined Communities*, 11.

33. Nichols, *I is a Long Memoried Woman*, 23.

34. Ibid.

35. Ibid., 23–24.

36. Paravisini-Gebert, "Decolonising Feminism," 7.

37. Spillers, "Mama's Baby, Papa's Maybe," 67.

38. DeCaires, "Body Talk," 256.

39. McKinley, *Indigo*, 1.

40. Ibid., 1–11.

41. Shakespeare, *The Tempest*, act 1, scene 2.

42. Hopkinson, *Salt Roads*, 331.

43. Warner, *Indigo*, 207.

44. Hopkinson, 69.

45. Ibid., 299.

46. See Merle Hodge, "The Challenges of the Struggle for Sovereignty."

47. Warner, 129.

48. Fernández Olmos and Paravisini-Gebert, *Creole Religions of the Caribbean*, 9.

49. Hill Collins, *Black Feminist Thought*, 1.

50. Welter, "The Cult of True Womanhood," 151–174.

51. Reddock, *Women, Labour and Politics in Trinidad and Tobago*, 10; Senior, *Working Miracles*, 108, 189.

52. Verene Shepherd, *Women in Caribbean History*, 15.

53. Both enslaved African women and indentured Indian women came from patriarchal societies in which work was divided by sex, a "norm" women embraced post-emancipation. Additionally, "the essentially patriarchal basis of African societies, which can result in the social oppression of women, despite their relative economic independence," remained largely intact in the Americas (Bush, 92–93).

54. Mohammed, "Writing Gender into History," 28.

55. Senior, *Working Miracles*, 190.

56. Ibid.

57. Warner, *Indigo*, 91.

58. Ibid., 94.

59. Ibid., 97.

60. Ibid., 97.

61. Ibid., 99.

62. Joseph, 129.

63. Warner, *Indigo*, 93.

64. Hopkinson, 42.

65. Beckles, *Centering Woman*, 89.

66. Shepherd, *Women in Caribbean History*, 30.

67. Wynter, "Beyond Miranda's Meanings," 307–309.

68. Warner, *Indigo*, 263.

69. Ibid., 314.

70. Ibid., 301.

71. Zabus, *Tempests after Shakespeare*, 145. Serafine's journey is certainly reminiscent of the women who have to leave their children and their own homes to labor in other people's homes, whether in the country or abroad.

72. Shakespeare, *The Tempest*, act 1, scene 2.

73. Ibid.

74. Roberto Fernández Retamar, *Caliban and Other Essays*, 5.

75. Hodge, "The Shadow of the Whip," 116.

76. Bob Corbett, "The Spelling of Voodoo," accessed April 25, 2013, http://www2.webster.edu/~corbetre/haiti/voodoo/spelling.htm.

77. Hopkinson, 336.

78. Patricia Hill Collins argues that there are four controlling images of black women, which, together with class and other factors, reinscribe black women's oppression (67–93).

79. Patricia Hill Collins, 77; and Bush, 94–97.

80. Patricia Hill Collins, 74.

81. Shepherd, *Women in Caribbean History*, 13.

82. Ibid., 14.

83. Warner, "Siren/Hyphen," 362. In the novel, Ariel regains her voice and attempts to poison Kit. She fails, but her actions inform him that something is amiss, and he and his men are able to subdue the native insurgency.

84. Warner, *Indigo*, 173.

85. Zabus, 153.

86. Warner, "Siren/Hyphen," 364.

87. Beckles, 184.

88. Lucille Mathurin Mair, *Rebel Woman*, 8–12; and Shepherd, *Women in Caribbean History*, 60–62.

89. Mair, *Rebel Woman*, 13.

90. Sycorax's relationship with Ariel is another point of complexity. Ariel's subjugation of a woman by a woman illustrates part of the dynamic of free colored people who owned slaves.

91. Hopkinson, 392.

92. Ibid., 310.

93. Ibid., 317.

94. Patricia Powell's novel *The Pagoda* is the story of Lowe, a Chinese woman masquerading as a man so that she can enjoy the fruits of her labor in nineteenth-century Jamaica. This story foregrounds not only a Chinese experience in the Caribbean but also the experience of sexual minorities and others who have had to don disguises (race, class, and, here, gender performance) in order to exercise power and to survive.

95. Mohammed, "Writing Gender into History," 21, 27.

96. Hopkinson, 16–17.

97. Wallace, "'I Will Pay for This Fearlessness'" (unpublished manuscript).

98. Sheller, *Citizenship from Below*, 241.

99. Cliff, 36–37.

100. In Lauren Berlant's words, they are part of the "intimate public sphere." Berlant defines this in the U.S. context as citizenship no longer based on personhood and public life; rather, this type of belonging is situated in notions of family and "renders citizenship as a condition of social membership produced by personal acts and values, especially acts originating in or directed toward the family sphere. . . . In the new nostalgia-based fantasy nation of the 'American way of life,' the residential enclave where 'the family' lives usurps the modernist promise of the culturally vital, multiethnic city; in the new, utopian America, mass-mediated political identifications can only be rooted in traditional notions of home, family, and community" (Berlant 5).

101. Bush, 92.

102. Barrow, *Caribbean Portraits*, xxxvi.

103. See also George W. Bush's rationale for war with Iraq in 2003. Bush did not gain public legitimacy until he found an entity, amorphous though it may have been, to otherize and attack.

5. Rehearsing Indigeneity

1. Peter Hulme and Neil Whitehead have contributed greatly to (re)reading the indigenous experience in the Americas, and their work continues to be invaluable to understanding indigenous conditions, particularly Hulme's *Colonial Encounters*.

2. Paula Burnett claims that Melville constructs these two poles—endogamy (incest) and exogamy (trans-racial interaction)—in a zone of exchange (24–25).

3. Melville, *Ventriloquist's Tale*, 34.

4. Gordon Lewis, "Emergence of National Society: Guyana," 262–266.

5. "The Bookers Empire," accessed May 2013, http://www.guyana.org/features/guyanastory/chapter112.html.

6. Lewis, "Emergence of National Society," 266.

7. Brackette F. Williams, *Stains on My Name*, 140.

8. In fact, Melville takes on several texts that represent either Guyana (Waugh's travelogue) or Amerindians (*Macunaíma*).

9. Melville, *Ventriloquist's Tale*, 31.

10. It would be fascinating to put the novel's finance minister Olly Sampson's version of the failure of the Guyanese state in conversation with "Bookers' Guiana."

11. Melville, *Ventriloquist's Tale*, 34.

12. Ibid., 31.

13. Ibid., 54.

14. See Shona N. Jackson's discussion of indigenous poet and cultural warrior Basil Rodrigues, who is concerned about cultural retention, as is Melville, who has written a dictionary to preserve Amerindian languages (Jackson, *Creole Indigeneity*).

15. Burnett, 25.

16. Amerindian cultures, like all others, are ever evolving. Samuel Wilson characterizes the idea that indigenous people are inauthentic for changing as a "damaging myth." Focusing his comments on Island Caribs, he writes that to argue "that modern Island Caribs somehow are not 'real' Caribs . . . is a peculiar way of looking at things, and one that does not make sense: human cultures are constantly changing, and if Island Caribs today do not live as their ancestors did five hundred years ago, neither do people who came from Africa or Europe" (197). Maximilian C. Forte explores how native peoples around the world are using emerging technologies, like the Internet. "In the case of Guyana, the Amerindian Peoples Association has a Website (APA 2001) which was produced and is maintained as a result of an initiative between the Government of Guyana and the United Nations Development Program—and this is a site with a strong political and economic focus that is not centered on the 'we are not extinct' since this is not a predominant perception of the state of Guyana's Amerindians" ("We Are Not Extinct: The Revival of Carib and Taino Identities, the Internet, and the Transformation of Offline Indigenes into Online

'N-digenes,'" Sincronía 2002, accessed May 2012, http://sincronia.cucsh.udg.
mx/CyberIndigen.htm).

17. See April Shemak's excellent discussion of this in "Alter/Natives: Myth,
Translation and the Native Informant."

18. Ibid.

19. Melville, *Ventriloquist's Tale*, 345.

20. Ibid., 343–344.

21. Ibid., 349.

22. Shemak, "Alter/Natives," 367.

23. Melville, *Ventriloquist's Tale*, 346–347.

24. "Current Policies toward Amerindians," Guyana National Development
Policy, accessed January 2007, http://www.guyana.org/NDS/chap22.htm.

25. Melville, *Ventriloquist's Tale*, 54.

26. Brackette Williams, *Stains on My Name*, 137.

27. Ibid.

28. Ibid., 136–138.

29. Robert Manley, *Guyana Emergent*, 51; and Forbes Burnham, *A Destiny
to Mould*, 172–174.

30. In 1999, the South African mining company Migrate Mining received
permission from the Guyanese government, over the objections of Amerindian
people, for "a three-year concession to prospect for minerals over more than
three million hectares of the Roraima Formation on Guyana's Pakaraima Pla-
teau, bordering Venezuela." "Guyana Privatization Evokes Local Interest,"
August 1999, accessed November 20, 2006, http://www.miningweekly.com/
article/guyana-privatisation-evokes-local-interest-1999-08-06-1.

31. Colchester, *Guyana Fragile Frontiers*, 135.

32. Manley, 53.

33. Cheyfitz, *Poetics of Imperialism*, 8.

34. Melville, *Ventriloquist's Tale*, 77–78.

35. Ibid., 80.

36. Ibid., 78.

37. Ibid.

38. Ibid., 79.

39. Ibid., 54. In the next sentence, Tenga "suddenly" asks about Marietta,
the woman most tied to Amerindian ways of being in their discussion of where
they belong.

40. Because of their special status as indigenous people, Amerindians are
entitled to make claims on these states.

41. Colchester, 129–130. Sociologist Desrey Fox and members of the
Akawayo aboriginal community believe that indigenous people should organize across borders to combat their minority status. Fox observes that organizing across boundaries is the way to Amerindian empowerment, and her
project incorporates the global South, not just Guyana or Central America. In

reconfiguring indigenous identities in a global framework, her solution to the potential marginalization, or in-between status, of Amerindian cultures is to find spaces of accommodation. Fox posits that Amerindian cultural abandonment has been an impediment: "We tend to see it a little wrong, I mean my own people too. After they have been introduced to this modern, contemporary education [and lifestyle] they tend to go aside with the dominant culture, leave their own culture . . . and try to develop that way, but then you realize that you are neither here nor there" (Fox, 1989 interview).

42. Melville, *Ventriloquist's Tale*, 55.

43. Ibid.

44. Melville visited the "Caribbean Experience in London" class at the University of London and gave an informal talk.

45. Melville, *Ventriloquist's Tale*, 53.

46. Ibid.

47. Because Amerindians vacillate between being characterized as native minority groups within the states they inhabit, as autonomous states, and as independent enclaves within larger states, integration into the larger society has been a struggle. One example is Dominica. See Anthony Layng's "The Caribs of Dominica: Prospects for Structural Assimilation of a Territorial Minority."

48. Basch et al., *Nations Unbound*, 7.

49. In the epilogue, Melville's narrator recognizes European ethnic and racial violence, but not in the Caribbean (355).

50. Melville, *Ventriloquist's Tale*, 350.

51. Basch et al., 9.

52. Rosa, while like Wormoal in her pursuit of knowledge, is uncomfortable with the idea of *possessing* knowledge, control, and the colonial project. Rosa characterizes Wormoal's ideas on knowledge as the "new" colonial project (Melville, 80). However, control of knowledge in accumulation, distribution, and characterization is an old mainstay of imperial and colonial powers. Because Rosa's knowledge accumulation focuses on citizens of the empire rather than subjects, her research seems less nefarious. But she too shares a sense of possessing Chofy (through sex) that Wormoal gets from books. See also the passages on Alexander McKinnon, whose pride in his rationality is fractured by the incestuous relationship between his children, Danny and Beatrice (Melville, 213).

53. Melville, *Ventriloquist's Tale*, 17.

54. Ibid., 342.

55. Ibid., 18–19.

56. Ibid., 346.

57. Ibid., 352.

58. Ibid., 215.

59. Ibid., 200.

60. Ibid., 210. McKinnon, based on the "fertile person of H.P.C. Melville" and the most liberal incarnation of a European, is ruptured by his children's relationship (Swan, 125). Swan, in his 1950s search for El Dorado, recounts with relish the story of H. P. C. Melville, who starts as a prospector and becomes a land and cattle baron in the late nineteenth century. The Rupununi made him "Chief of the Wapisianas." Characterizing Melville's relationship with his wife, Swan writes, "[She] had borne him fine children. He treated her with a certain indifference, I gathered, and their relationship had little in it of Captain Smith's idyll with the Princess Pocahontas. He taught the Indians many things that were of use to them, and they, besides giving him their allegiance, sharpened arrow points so fine . . . he was able to use them as gramophone needles. He found them a meek, utterly passive people who accepted whatever fate brought them" (125). Chronicling Melville's relationship with his two partners, Mamai Mary, his Wapisiana wife, and an unnamed Patomona wife, Swan illustrates Mamai Mary's lack of resentment with her reported statement, speaking of Melville's Patomona wife, "She can have him. I had the best of him" (126). Swan concludes Melville's history, which like McKinnon's does not end in the savannahs: "Old Melville did not die on the savannahs; in fact, the end of his story is a little disappointing, an unromantic acceptance of the values of civilization. No wonder there is a slight mystery about it. He put his two wives to live with their children and sailed away to the Scotland his father left so many years before. Here he married at the kirk, and here, in or about the year 1930, he died. . . . It was interesting, as I traveled all over the savannahs and met the Melville children and many of the hundred or so grandchildren of the old man, to see the Mendelian sports that the mixed bloods had played. And I felt at the end that those powerful Scottish genes would be active till the end of time" (127).

61. Melville, *Ventriloquist's Tale*, 215.

62. Roth, *An Inquiry into the Animism and Folklore of the Guiana Indians*, 198.

63. This young Wai-Wai narrator is perhaps another incarnation of Makunima.

64. Melville, *Ventriloquist's Tale*, 191.

65. Harris, "Judgment and Dream," 30–31.

66. The name Makunima means "one that works in the dark" (Roth 130), which makes sense for a child of the eclipse.

67. It is interesting to note that Bla-Bla, vernacular for "too much chatter," and Melville's loquacious cousin (Burnett, 13) are visited by and talk "to a man he could see in the corner of the room, who had a parrot sitting on his shoulder" (Melville, 344).

68. Shemak, "Alter/Natives," 368.

69. Roth, 166.

70. Shemak also discusses the veneration of the lie in her presentations and publications about this novel.

71. Girvan, "Reinterpreting the Caribbean," 16.

72. Derek Walcott, "The Caribbean: Culture as Mimicry?" 3–13. Walcott addresses this idea as both a positive and a negative. In addressing Naipaul, Walcott says that "our pantomime is conducted before a projection of ourselves which in its smallest gestures is based on metropolitan references. No gesture, according to this philosophy, is authentic, every sentence is a quotation, every movement either ambitious or pathetic, and because it is mimicry, uncreative" ("The Caribbean: Culture as Mimicry?" 6). He acknowledges that this would indeed be a paralyzing phenomenon, one he characterizes as not just West Indian but American. Walcott goes on to argue that mimicry, but mimicry by design, is what the Caribbean needs: "Mimicry is an act of imagination, . . . endemic cunning. . . . Camouflage . . . is mimicry, or more than that, it is design. What if the man in the New World needs mimicry as design, both as defense and as lure . . . ?" (10). "Degenerative mimicry would be that imitation without design. That imitation that is neither a tool nor a weapon, but the crippling . . . uncreative . . . pantomime" (6).

73. Melville, 355.

74. Girvan, 19–20.

Conclusion

1. Harris, *The Infinite Rehearsal*, 1.
2. Das, *Bones*, 48.
3. Walcott, "The Antilles," 8.
4. Danticat, *Create Dangerously*, 8–13.

Bibliography

Ahmed, Belal. "The Impact of Globalization on the Caribbean Sugar and Banana Industries." In *The Society for Caribbean Studies Annual Conference Papers*. Vol. 2. Ed. Sandra Courtman. Nottingham, UK: The University of Nottingham, 2001. http://www.scsonline.freeserve.co.uk/olvol2.html.

Ahmed, Sara. *The Cultural Politics of Emotion*. London: Routledge, 2004.

Alexander, M. Jacqui, and Chandra Talpade Mohanty. *Feminist Genealogies, Colonial Legacies, Democratic Futures*. New York: Routledge, 1997.

Alexis, Gérald. "All Mankind." *La Rencontre des Trois Mondes*. Exhibition catalog. Paris: Éditions Henri Deschamps, 1992.

———. "Caribbean Art and Culture from a Haitian Perspective." *Caribbean Visions: Contemporary Painting and Sculpture*. Alexandria, VA: Art Services International, 1995.

———. "The Caribbean in the Hour of Haiti." *Caribbean Art at the Crossroads of the World*. New York: El Museo Del Barrio in association with Yale University Press, 2012.

———. "Contemporary Haitian Art: Private Collections—Public Property." *Museum International*, vol. 62, no. 4 (2001): 55–64.

———. *Peintres Haïtiens: English Edition*. Paris: Éditions Cercle d'Art, 2000.

Allsopp, Jeannette. "History Re-interpreted in Carpentier's *El reino de esta mundo*." *History and Time in Caribbean Literature: Proceedings of the XI Conference on Spanish Caribbean Literature April 1988*. Claudette Williams, ed. Institute of Caribbean Studies. Mona, Jamaica: University of the West Indies, 1992.

Allsopp, Richard. *Dictionary of Caribbean English Usage*. Oxford: Oxford University, 1996.

Amin, Samir. "Imperialism and Globalization." *Monthly Review*, vol. 53, no. 2 (June 2001). Accessed January 2005. http://monthlyreview.org/2001/06/01/imperialism-and-globalization.

Andaiye. "The Angle You Look from Determines What You See: Towards a Critique of Feminist Politics in the Caribbean." The Lucille Mathurin

Mair Lecture, delivered March 6, 2002. Mona, Jamaica: University of the West Indies.

Anderson, Benedict. *Imagined Communities: Reflections on the Origin and Spread of Nationalism*. London: Verso Press, 1983.

Andrade, Mário de. *Macunaíma*. E. A. Goodland, trans. New York: Random House, [1928] 1984.

Arion, Frank Martinus. "The Great Curassow or the Road to Caribbeanness." *Callaloo*, vol. 21, no. 3 (1998): 443–456.

——. "The Victory of the Concubines and the Nannies." *Caribbean Creolization*. Kathleen M. Balutansky and Marie-Agnès Sourieau, eds. Gainesville, FL: University of Florida Press, 1998.

Arthur, Charles A., and Michael Dash, eds. *A Haiti Anthology: Libète*. London: Latin America Bureau, 1999.

Aub-Buscher, Gertrud, and Beverley Ormerod Noakes, eds. Introduction. *The Francophone Caribbean Today*. Kingston, Jamaica: University of the West Indies Press, 2003.

Bahadur, Gaiutra. "Coolie Women Are in Demand Here." *Virginia Quarterly Review*, vol. 87, no. 2, (Spring 2011): 48–61.

Bailey, Barbara, et al. *Gender: A Caribbean Multi-disciplinary Perspective*. Kingston, Jamaica: Ian Randle Publishers, 1997.

Balutansky, Kathleen M., and Marie-Agnès Sourieau, eds. *Caribbean Creolization: Reflections on the Cultural Dynamics of Language, Literature and Identity*. Gainesville, FL: University Press of Florida, 1998.

Banham, Martin, Errol Hill, and George Woodyard, eds. *The Cambridge Guide to African and Caribbean Theatre*. London: Cambridge University Press, 1994.

Barnes, Natasha. *Cultural Conundrums*. Ann Arbor, MI: University of Michigan Press, 2006.

Barrow, Christine, ed. *Caribbean Portraits*. Kingston, Jamaica: Ian Randle Publishers, 1998.

——. "Charting Futures." *Gender: A Caribbean Multi-disciplinary Perspective*. Edited by Barbara Bailey, et al. Kingston, Jamaica: Ian Randle Publishers, 1997.

Basch, Linda, et al. *Nations Unbound: Transnational Projects, Postcolonial Predicaments and Deterritorialized Nation-States*. Langhorne, PA: Gordon and Breach Science Publishers, 1994.

Baucom, Ian. *Specters of the Atlantic: Finance Capital, Slavery and the Philosophy of History*. Durham, NC: Duke University Press, 2005.

Beckles, Hilary. *Centering Woman: Gender Discourses in Caribbean Slave Society*. Mona, Jamaica: Ian Randle Publishers, 1998.

Bell, Beverly. *Walking on Fire: Haitian Women's Stories of Survival and Resistance*. Ithaca, NY: Cornell University Press, 2001.

Bellegarde, Dantes. "Alexandre Pétion: The Founder of Rural Democracy in Haiti." *Caribbean Quarterly*, vol. 3, no. 3 (December 1953): 171.

Benítez-Rojo, Antonio. *The Repeating Island: The Caribbean and the Postmodern Perspective.* Durham, NC: Duke University Press, 1992.

Berlant, Lauren. *The Queen of America Goes to Washington City: Essays on Sex and Citizenship.* Durham, NC: Duke University Press, [1997] 2002.

Besson, Jean, and Karen Fog Olwig. *Caribbean Narratives of Belonging: Fields of Relation, Sites of Identity.* Oxford, UK: Macmillan Publishers Limited, 2005.

Blouet, Olwyn M. *The Contemporary Caribbean.* London: Reaktion Books, 2007.

Boal, Augusto. *Theatre of the Oppressed.* Charles A. and Maria-Odilia Leal McBride, trans. New York: Theatre Communications Group, 1979.

"Booker's Empire." Accessed May 2013. http://www.guyana.org/features/guyanastory/chapter112.html.

Braziel, Jana Evans. "Remembering Défilée: Dédée Bazile as Revolutionary *Lieu de Memoire*." *Small Axe*, vol. 9, no. 2 (2005): 57–85.

Brizan, George. *Grenada—Island of Conflict: From Amerindians to Peoples' Revolution, 1498–1979.* London: Zed Books, 1984.

"Brown." Personal interview. July 17, 2011.

Brown, Karen McCarthy. *Mama Lola.* Berkeley: University of California Press, 1991.

———. *Tracing the Spirit: Ethnographic Essays on Haitian Art.* Seattle: University of Washington Press, 1995.

Brown, Kimberly Nichele. *Writing the Black Revolutionary Diva: Women's Subjectivity and the Decolonizing Text.* Bloomington: Indiana University Press, 2010.

Brown, Vincent. *The Reaper's Garden.* Cambridge, MA: Harvard University Press, 2008.

Burnett, Paula. "'Where Else to Row, but Backward?' Addressing Caribbean Futures through Re-Visions of the Past." *Ariel*, vol. 30, no. 1 (January 1999): 11–37.

Burnham, Forbes. *A Destiny to Mould: Selected Speeches.* C. A. Nascimento and R. A. Burrowes, comps. New York: African Publishing Corporation, 1970.

Burton, Richard D. E., and Fred Reno, eds. *French and West Indian: Martinique, Guadeloupe, and French Guiana Today.* Charlottesville: University Press of Virginia, 1995.

Bush, Barbara. *Slave Women in Caribbean Society, 1650–1838.* Bloomington: Indiana University Press, 1990.

Butler, Judith. "Critically Queer." *A Journal of Lesbian and Gay Studies*, vol. 1, no. 1 (1993): 17–32.

———. *Undoing Gender.* London: Routledge, 2004.

Buyers, Christopher. "Haiti Monarchy." Accessed May 2012. 4dw.net/royalark/haiti.php.

Carew, Jan. *Children of the Sun*. Boston: Little, Brown and Company, 1976.

Carpentier, Alejo. *The Kingdom of This World*. Harriet de Onís, trans. New York: Alfred A. Knopf, [1949] 1957.

Cauvin, Marie-Hélène. *Vers un destin insolite sur les flots bleus de la Mer des Antilles*. Painting, 2002. Retrieved July 10, 2010. http://mariehelenecauvin.com/.

Césaire, Aimé. *The Tragedy of King Christophe*. Ralph Manheim, trans. New York: Grove Press, 1969.

Chagnon, Napoleon A. *Yanomamö: The Fierce People* (Case Studies in Cultural Anthropology). New York: Holt, Rinehart, and Winston, 1968.

Chancy, Myriam J. A. *Framing Silence*. New Brunswick, NJ: Rutgers University Press, 1997.

———. *From Sugar to Revolution: Women's Visions of Haiti, Cuba, and the Dominican Republic*. Waterloo, ONT: Wilfrid Laurier University Press, 2012.

———. *Searching for Safe Spaces*. Philadelphia: Temple University Press, 1997.

———. "Subversive Sexualities: Revolutionizing Gendered Identities" *Frontiers: A Journal of Women's Studies*, vol. 29, no. 1 (2008): 51–75.

Chatland, Jan. "Descriptions of Various Loa of Voodoo." Accessed April 2, 2013. http://www2.webster.edu/~corbetre/haiti/voodoo/biglist.htm.

Cheyfitz, Eric. *The Poetics of Imperialism: Translation and Colonialism from The Tempest to Tarzan*. Philadelphia: The University of Pennsylvania Press, 1997.

Chierci, Rose-Marie. "Caribbean Migration in the Age of Globalization: Transnationalism, Race, and Ethnic Identity." *Reviews in Anthropology*, vol. 33 (2004): 43–59.

Clark, VèVè A. "Haiti's Tragic Overture." In *Representing the French Revolution*. James A. W. Heffernan, ed. Hanover, NH: University Press of New England, 1992.

———. "Developing Diaspora Literacy and *Marasa* Consciousness." *Theatre Survey*, vol. 50, special issue 01 (May 2009): 9–18.

Cliff, Michelle. "Caliban's Daughter: The Tempest in the Teapot." *Frontiers: A Journal of Women*. vol. 12, no. 2 (1991): 36–51.

Colchester, Marcus. *Guyana Fragile Frontiers*. Washington, DC: Latin America Bureau, 1995.

Collins, Merle. *Angel*. Leeds, UK: Peepal Tree Press, [1987] 2011.

Collins, Patricia Hill. *Black Feminist Thought*. London: Routledge, 1990.

Conquergood, Dwight. "Performance Studies: Interventions and Radical Research." *The Drama Review*, vol. 46, no. 2 (Summer 2002): 145–156.

Cooper, Carolyn. *Noises in the Blood: Orality, Gender and the "Vulgar" Body of Jamaican Popular Culture*. Durham, NC: Duke University Press, 1995.

———. *Sound Clash: Jamaican Dancehall Culture at Large*. New York: Palgrave Macmillan, 2004.

Cosentino, Donald J., ed. *In Extremis: Death and Life in 21st-Century Haitian Art*. Los Angeles: Fowler Museum at UCLA, 2012.

———. *Sacred Arts of Haitian Vodou*. Los Angeles: Fowler Museum at UCLA, 1995.

Coughlin, Dan, and Kim Ives. "WikiLeaks Haiti: Let Them Live on $3 a Day." *The Nation*, June 1, 2011. Accessed May 2013. http://www.thenation.com/article/161057/wikileaks-haiti-let-them-live-3-day.

Craps, Stef. "Learning to Live with Ghosts: Postcolonial Haunting and Mid-Mourning in David Dabydeen's 'Turner' and Fred D'Aguiar's *Feeding the Ghosts*." *Callaloo*, vol. 33, no. 2 (Spring 2010): 467–475.

Crichlow, Michaeline. "Making Waves: (Dis)Placements, Entanglements, Mo(ve)ments." Conference presentation, *The Sea Is History* exhibit, Duke University, April 2009.

Crichlow, Michaeline, with Patricia Northover. *Globalization and the Post-Creole Imagination*. Durham, NC: Duke University Press, 2009.

Crosley, Reginald, MD. *The Vodou Quantum Leap: Alternative Realities, Power, and Mysticism*. St. Paul, MN: Llewellyn Publications, 2004.

D'Aguiar, Fred. *Feeding the Ghosts*. Hopewell, NJ: Ecco Press, 1997.

Daly, Vere T. *The Making of Guyana*. London: Macmillan Press, 1974.

Danticat, Edwidge. *Create Dangerously: The Immigrant Artist at Work*. New York: Vintage Contemporaries, 2011.

———. *The Farming of Bones*. New York: Soho Press, 1998.

———. *Krik? Krak!* New York: Soho Press, 1995.

Danticat, Edwidge. "A Wall of Fire Rising." In *Krik? Krak!* New York: Soho Press, 1995.

Danticat, Edwidge, and Jonathan Demme. *Island on Fire: Passionate Visions of Haiti from the Collection of Jonathan Demme*. London: Kaliko Press, 1997.

Das, Mahadai. *Bones*. Leeds, UK: Peepal Tree Press, 1988.

Dash, J. Michael. "The Disappearing Island: Haiti, History and the Hemisphere." The Fifth Jagan Lecture and the Third Michael Baptitsta Lecture at York University, March 20, 2004. York, ONT: CERLAC, 2004.

———. *The Other America: Caribbean Literature in a New World Context*. Charlottesville, VA: The University of Virginia Press, 1998.

Davis, Annalee, dir. *On the Map*. Barbados, Manipura, Inc., 2008. 32 min.

Davis, Ossie. "Afterword." *The Autobiography of Malcom X*. New York: Ballantine Books, 1999.

Dayan, Joan. *Haiti, History, and the Gods*. Berkeley: University of California Press, 1995.

deCaires, Denise Narain. "Body Talk: Writing and Speaking the Body in the Texts of Caribbean Women Writers." In *Caribbean Portraits*. Christine Barrow, ed. Kingston, Jamaica: Ian Randle Publishers, 1998.

"Declaration of the Rights of Man and of the Citizen." Accessed July 2004. http://www.hrcr.org/docs/frenchdec. html.

DeLoughrey, Elizabeth. *Routes and Routes: Navigating Caribbean and Pacific Island Literatures*. Honolulu: University of Hawai'i Press, 2009.

Desruisseau, Rose-Marie. *The Ceremony at Bois Caïman*. Painting, 1986. In *La Rencontre des Trois Mondes*. Paris: Editions Henri Deschamps, 1992.

———. *Vodou Ceremony*. Painting, 1986. Accessed August 5, 2011. http://www.martellyartgallery.com/artists/rmdesruisseaux.htm.

Di Cenzo, Maria, and Susan Bennett. "Women, Popular Theatre, and Social Action: Interviews with Cynthia Grant and the Sistren Theatre Collective." *Ariel*, vol. 23, no. 1 (January 1992): 82.

Dubois, Laurent. *Avengers of the New World*. Cambridge, MA: Harvard University Press, 2004.

Dubois, Laurent, and John D. Garrigus, eds. *Slave Revolution in the Caribbean 1789–1804: A Brief History with Documents*. New York: St. Martin's Press, 2006.

Edmondson, Belinda. *Making Men*. Durham, NC: Duke University Press, 1999.

Eisenstein, Zillah R. *The Color of Gender: Reimagining Democracy*. Berkeley: University of California Press, 1994.

Ellwood, Wayne. *The No-Nonsense Guide to Globalization*. Toronto: New Internationalist/Between the Lines Press, [2001] 2003.

Eze, Emmanuel Chukwudi, ed. *Race and the Enlightenment: A Reader*. Oxford: Blackwell Publishers, 1997.

Falk, Richard A. "The Making of Global Citizenship." In *The Condition of Citizenship*. Bart van Steenbergen, ed. London: Sage, 1994.

Fanon, Frantz. *Black Skin, White Masks*. Charles Lam Markmann, trans. New York: Grove Press, [1952] 1967.

———. *The Wretched of the Earth*. Richard Philcox, trans. New York: Grove Press, [1961] 2005.

Farmer, Paul. *The Uses of Haiti*. Monroe, ME: Common Courage Press, [1994] 2006.

Faul, Michelle. "Haiti's Ruler Chides World for Disinterest." *Guardian of London*, October 23, 2004.

Fick, Carolyn. *The Making of Haiti: The Saint-Domingue Revolution from Below*. Knoxville: University of Tennessee Press, 1990.

Field, Tory, and Beverly Bell. "Farmers and Consumers versus Monsanto: David Meets Goliath." *Other World*, April 8, 2013. Accessed July 2013. http://truth-out.org/news/item/15601-farmers-and-consumers-vs-monsanto-david-meets-goliath.

Fleurant, Gerdès. *Dancing Spirits: Rhythms and Rituals of Haitian Vodun, The Rada Rite*. Westwood, CT: Greenwood Press, 1996.

Forbes, Curdella. *From Nation to Diaspora: Samuel Selvon, George Lamming and the Cultural Performance of Gender*. Mona, Jamaica: University of the West Indies Press, 2005.

Ford-Smith, Honor. "Ring, Ding, Ding in a Tight Corner: Sistren, Collective Democracy, and the Organization of Cultural Production." In *Feminist*

Genealogies, Colonial Legacies, Democratic Futures. M. Jacqui Alexander and Chandra Talpade Mohanty, eds. New York: Routledge, 1997.

Forte, Maximilian C. "Caribbean Indigeneity, Resurgent Indigenism." Accessed July 2012. http://openanthropology.org/za/.

———. "We Are Not Extinct: The Revival of Carib and Taino Identities, Internet, and the Transformation of Offline Indigenes into Online 'N-digenes.'" Sincronía 2002. Accessed May 2012. http://sincronia.cucsh.udg.mx/Cyber-Indigen.htm.

Fox, Desrey. "Continuity and Change among the Amerindians of Guyana." In *Ethnic Minorities in Caribbean Society.* Rhoda Reddock, ed. St. Augustine, Trinidad and Tobago: University of the West Indies, 1996.

———. 1989 interview. Transcript. Georgetown, Guyana: Banyan Productions. January 15, 2005. http://www.pancaribbean.com/banyan/ desrey.htm.

Francis, Donette. *Fictions of Feminine Citizenship.* New York: Palgrave Press, 2011.

Frías, Maria. "Building Bridges to the Past: An Interview with Fred D'Aguiar." *Callaloo,* vol. 25, no. 2 (Spring 2002): 418–425.

Fuentes, Marisa J. "Power and Historical Figuring: Rachael Pringle Polgreen's Troubled Archive." *Gender & History,* vol. 22, no. 3 (November 2010): 564–584.

Fusco, Coco. "Miranda's Diary." In *English Is Broken Here: Notes on Cultural Fusion in the Americas.* New York: The New Press, 1995.

Gant-Britton, Lisbeth. "The Question of Power in *Monsieur Toussaint* and *The Tragedy of King Christophe.*" *Paroles gelées,* vol. 14, no. 1 (1996): 43–61.

Garraway, Doris. *The Libertine Colony: Creolization in the Early French Caribbean.* Durham, NC: Duke University Press, 2005.

Gaspar, David Barry, and David Patrick Geggus, eds. *A Turbulent Time.* Bloomington: Indiana University Press, 1997.

Gatsby, Meredith. *Sucking Salt: Caribbean Women Writers, Migration and Survival.* Kansas City: University of Missouri Press, 2006.

Geggus, David P. "The Haitian Revolution." In *The Modern Caribbean.* Franklin W. Knight and Colin A. Palmer, eds. Chapel Hill: University of North Carolina Press, 1989.

———. *The Impact of the Haitian Revolution in the Atlantic World.* Columbia: University of South Carolina Press, 2001.

George, Ian. "Grenada's Underwater Sculpture Park Unveils New Sculpture." October 27, 2010. Accessed June 2011. http://www.barnaclegrenada.com/index.php/component/content/article/17-travel-a-tourism/1773-grenadas-underwater-sculpture-park-unveils-new-sculpture.

Gibson, Philip. "Cruising in the 21st Century: Who Works While Others Play?" *International Journal of Hospitality Management* 27 (2008): 42–52.

Gilroy, Paul. *The Black Atlantic: Modernity and Double Consciousness.* Brooklyn: Verso, 1993.

Girvan, Norman. "Reinterpreting the Caribbean." In *New Caribbean Thought.* Brian Meeks and Folke Lindalhl, eds. Kingston, Jamaica: University of the West Indies Press, 2001.

Glissant, Édouard. *Caribbean Discourse: Selected Essays.* Michael Dash, trans. Charlottesville: University of Virginia Press, 1992.

———. *Monsieur Toussaint: A Play.* J. Michael Dash, trans. Boulder, CO: Lynne Rienner Publishers, 2005.

———. *Poetics of Relation.* Betsy Wing, trans. Ann Arbor: University of Michigan Press, 1997.

Goodison, Lorna. *Lorna Goodison Reading from Her Poems.* CD. London, The Poetry Archive, 2012.

Gordon, Avery. *Ghostly Matters: Haunting and the Sociological Imagination.* Minneapolis: University of Minnesota Press, [1997] 2008.

GRAIN. "Haiti's Farmers Call for a Break with Neoliberalism" *Seedling,* July 13, 2010. Accessed May 2013. http://www.grain.org/article/entries /4056-haiti-s-farmers-call-for-a-break-with-neoliberalism.

Green, Sharon L. "Sistren Theatre Collective: Struggling to Remain Radical in an Era of Globalization." *Theatre Topics,* vol. 14, no. 2 (2004): 473–495.

Greenblatt, Stephan. *Marvelous Possessions: The Wonder of the New World.* Chicago: University of Chicago Press, 1991.

Gregoire, Crispin, et al. "Karifuna: The Caribs of Dominica." In *Ethnic Minorities in Caribbean Society.* Rhoda Reddock, ed. St. Augustine, Trinidad and Tobago: University of the West Indies, 1996.

Guyana National Development Policy. "Chapter 22: Amerindian Policies." October 15, 1996. Accessed October 13, 2004. http://www.guyana.org/ NDS/chap22.htm.

———. "Current Policies toward Amerindians." Accessed January 2007. http:// www.guyana.org/NDS/chap22.htm.

Haiti Grassroots Watch. "Monsanto in Haiti." May 5, 2011. Accessed July 2013. http://www.truth-out.org/news/item/917:monsanto-in-haiti.

"Haitian Migrants Apprehended." June 3, 2013. *Nassau Guardian.* Accessed June 20, 2013. /index.php?option=com_content&view=article&id=39606:h aitian-migrants-apprehended&catid=3:news&Itemid=27.

Harris, Wilson. *The Infinite Rehearsal.* London: Faber and Faber, 1987.

———. "Judgment and Dream." In *The Radical Imagination: Lectures and Talks.* Alan Riach and Mark Williams, eds. Liège, Belgium: Université de Liège, 1992.

———. *The Womb of Space: The Cross-Cultural Imagination.* Westwood, CT: Greenwood Press, 1983.

Hartman, Saidiya. "Seduction and the Uses of Power." *Callaloo,* vol. 19, no. 2 (1996): 537–560.

Henry, Paget. "Philosophy and the Caribbean Intellectual Tradition." Caribbean Studies Association Conference Paper. Antigua, 1998.

Hill, Errol. "The Emergence of a National Drama in the West Indies." *Caribbean Quarterly*, vol. 18, no. 4 (1972).

Hinds, David. "Power Sharing: Towards a New Political Culture." Guyana-Caribbean Politics. Accessed May 28, 2004. http://www.guyanacaribbean-politics.com/commentary/hinds_ps.html.

———. *Race and Political Discourse in Guyana: A Conversation with African Guyanese in the Presence and Hearing of Indian Guyanese.* Georgetown, Guyana: Guyana-Caribbean Politics Publications, 2004.

Hitchcock, Peter. "Revolutionary Violence." *Symploke*, vol. 20, nos. 1–2 (2012): 9–19.

Hodge, Merle. "Challenges of the Struggle for Sovereignty: Changing the World versus Writing Stories." In *Caribbean Women Writers.* Selwyn Cudjoe, ed. Wellesley, MA: Calaloux Publications, 1990.

———. "The Shadow of the Whip." In *Is Massa Day Dead?* Orde Coombs, ed. New York: Doubleday, 1974.

———. "We Kind of Family." In *Gendered Realities.* Patricia Mohammed, ed. St. Augustine, Trinidad: University of West Indies Press, 1998.

Hoffman, Larry G. *Haitian Art: The Legend and Legacy.* Ann Arbor, MI: Davenport Art Gallery, 1985.

Høgsbjerg, Christian, ed. *Toussaint Louverture: The Story of the Only Successful Slave Revolt in History: A Play in Three Acts.* Durham, NC: Duke University Press, 2013.

Holloway, Karla. *Private Bodies, Public Texts: Race, Gender, and a Cultural Bioethics.* Durham, NC: Duke University Press, 2011.

Hopkinson, Nalo. *The Salt Roads.* New York: Warner Books, 2003.

"How Does Empathy Make Us Uniquely Human?" Frank Stasio and Shawn Wein. *The State of Things with Frank Stasio.* WUNC Radio, January 16, 2013.

Hulme, Peter. *Colonial Encounters: Europe and the Native Caribbean, 1492–1797.* London: Routledge, [1986] 1992.

Hulme, Peter, and William H. Sherman. *"The Tempest" and Its Travels.* Philadelphia: University of Pennsylvania Press, 2002.

Hume, David. "Of National Characters." In *Race and the Enlightenment: A Reader.* Emmanuel Chukwudi Eze, ed. Oxford: Blackwell Publishers, 1997.

I is a Long Memoried Woman. Video. Frances-Anne Solomon, dir. Leda Serene Films, 1990.

Indian Immigration Fund (Guyana). Accessed March 14, 2005. http://beerbhajan.com/Guyana. htm.

Jackson, Shona N. *Creole Indigeneity: Between Myth and Nation in the Caribbean.* Minneapolis: University of Minnesota Press, 2012.

James, C. L. R. "The Artist in the Caribbean." In *The Future in the Present: Selected Writings.* London: Allison & Busby, 1977.

———. *The Black Jacobins*. In *A Time and a Season: Eight Caribbean Plays*. Errol Hill, ed. Trinidad and Tobago: School of Continuing Studies, the University of the West Indies, 1993.

———. *The Black Jacobins: Toussaint L'Ouverture and the San Domingo Revolution*. New York: Vintage Books, [1938] 1989.

Jenkins, Lee M. *The Language of Caribbean Poetry: Boundaries of Expression*. Gainesville: University Press of Florida, 2004.

Johnson, Howard, and Karl Watson. *The White Minority in the Caribbean*. Kingston, Jamaica: Ian Randle Press, 1998.

Jones, Civ. "'The Vicissitudes': An Underwater Sculpture that Honors the African Ancestors Lost at Sea during the Middle Passage." March 23, 2012. Accessed July 6, 2012. http://magicbaltimore.com/3278378/the-vicissitudes-an-underwater-sculpture-that-honors-the-african-ancestors-lost-in-the-sea-during-the-middle-passage/.

Joseph, May. "The Scream of Sycorax." In *Nomadic Identities: The Performance of Citizenship*. Minneapolis: University of Minnesota Press, 1999.

Juste, André. "Review of *Saving Grace* Exhibition." In *Haiti Liberté*. Accessed April 23, 2013. http://www.haiti-liberte.com/archives/volume4-24/Saving%20Grace.asp.

Kant, Immanuel. "On National Characteristics." In *Race and the Enlightenment: A Reader*. Emmanuel Chukwudi Eze, ed. Oxford: Blackwell Publishers, 1997.

Kempadoo, Kamala. *Sexing the Caribbean: Gender, Race, and Sexual Labor*. New York: Routledge, 2004.

King, Bruce. *Derek Walcott and West Indian Drama*. New York: Oxford University Press, 1995.

King, Nicole. *C. L. R. James and Creolization: Circles of Influence*. Jackson, MS: University Press of Mississippi, 2001.

———. "Double or Nothing: The Two *Black Jacobins*." In *C. L. R. James and Creolization: Circles of Influence*. Jackson: University Press of Mississippi, 2001.

King, Rosamund. "Notes on the Invisibility of Caribbean Lesbians." In *Our Caribbean: A Gathering of Lesbian and Gay Writing from the Antilles*. Thomas Glave, ed. Durham, NC: Duke University Press, 2008.

Klein, Ross. "High Seas, Low Pay: Working on Cruise Ships." *Our Times: Canada's Independent Labour Magazine*. Accessed May 2011. http://www.cruisejunkie.com/ot.html.

Knight, Franklin W., and Colin A. Palmer. *The Modern Caribbean*. Chapel Hill: The University of North Carolina Press, 1989.

Koff, Clea. *The Bone Woman: A Forensic Anthropologist's Search for Truth in the Mass Graves of Rwanda, Bosnia, Croatia, and Kosovo*. New York: Random House, 2004.

Kurlansky, Mark. *A Continent of Islands: Searching for the Caribbean Destiny*. Reading, MA: Addison-Wesley Publishing Company, 1992.

Lamming, George. *The Pleasures of Exile*. Ann Arbor: University of Michigan Press, [1960] 1992.

Lara, Ana-Maurine. *Erzulie's Skirt*. Washington, DC: Red Bone Press, 2006.

Largey, Michael. *Vodou Nation: Haitian Art, Music, and Cultural Nationalism*. Chicago: University of Chicago Press, 2006.

Layng, Anthony. "The Caribs in Dominica: Prospects for Structural Assimilation of a Territorial Minority." In *Caribbean Ethnicity Revisited*. Stephen Glazier, ed. New York: Gordon and Breach Science Publishers, 1985.

Leclerc, George-Louis. "The Geographical and Cultural Distribution of Mankind." In *Race and the Enlightenment: A Reader*. Emmanuel Chukwudi Eze, ed. Oxford: Blackwell Publishers, 1997.

Levine, Daniel. "Migration from the Caribbean: Issues for the 1990s." In *Journal of the International Institute*, vol. 3, no. 1 (Fall 1995). http://hdl.handle.net/2027/spo.4750978. 0003.106.

Lewis, Gordon K. "Emergence of National Society: Guyana." In *The Growth of the Modern West Indies*. New York: Modern Reader Paperbacks, 1968. 257–288.

———. *The Growth of the Modern West Indies*. New York: Modern Reader Paperbacks, 1968.

———. *Main Currents in Caribbean Thought*. Baltimore, MD: Johns Hopkins University Press, 1983.

Lewis, Linden. "Caribbean Masculinity: Unpacking the Narrative." In *The Culture of Gender and Sexuality in the Caribbean*. Gainesville: University Press of Florida, 2003.

Long, Richard A. "Artists of Haiti: Reflections on a Narrative." In *Caribbean Visions: Contemporary Painting and Sculpture*. Alexandria, VA: Art Services International, 1995.

Lopez, Iris. *Matters of Choice: Puerto Rican Women's Struggle for Reproductive Freedom*. New Brunswick, NJ: Rutgers University Press, 2008.

Lorde, Audre. "The Uses of the Erotic." In *Sister Outsider*. Freedom, CA: Crossing Press, 1984.

Lovelace, Earl. *The Dragon Can't Dance*. New York: Persea Books, 1979.

———. *Salt*. New York: Persea Books, 2004.

Mamdani, Mahmood. *When Victims Become Killers: Colonialism, Nativism, and Genocide in Rwanda*. Princeton, NJ: Princeton University Press, 2002.

Manley, Robert H. *Guyana Emergent: The Post-independence Struggle for Nondependent Development*. Cambridge, MA: Schenkman Publishing Company, 1982.

Manne, Robert. "The Colour of Prejudice." Accessed March 15, 2002. *storage.canalblog.com/27/55/486154/31404396.doc* .

Marshall, Paule. *Praisesong for the Widow*. New York: Plume, [1983] 1984.

McAlister, Elizabeth. "Haiti Mobs Lynch Voodoo Priests over Cholera Fears." *BBC World News*, December 24, 2010. Accessed July 2012. http://www.bbc.co.uk/news/world-latin-america-12073029.

———. "Voodoo's View of the Quake." *Washington Post*, January 15, 2010. Accessed July 2012. http://newsweek.washingtonpost.com/onfaith/guest-voices/2010/01/voodoos_view_of_the_quake_in_haiti.html.

McClintock, Anne. "'No Longer in a Future Heaven': Women and Nationalism in South Africa." *Transition* 51 (1991).

McKinley, Catherine E. *Indigo: In Search of the Color That Seduced the World.* New York: Bloomsbury, 2011.

Meehan, Kevin. *People Get Ready: African American and Caribbean Cultural Exchange.* Jackson: University of Mississippi, 2009.

Meeks, Brian. "Envisioning Caribbean Futures." Caribbean Studies Association Conference, Belize City, Belize, 2003.

———. *Narratives of Resistance: Jamaica, Trinidad, the Caribbean.* Kingston, Jamaica: University of the West Indies Press, 2000.

Meeks, Brian, and Folke Lindhal, eds. *New Caribbean Thought: A Reader.* Kingston, Jamaica: University of the West Indies Press, 2001.

Mehta, Brinda. *Notions of Identity.* New York: Palgrave Macmillan, 2009.

Melville, Pauline. "The Caribbean Experience in London." Informal lecture for "The Caribbean Experience in London" class. University of North London, August 2001.

———. *The Ventriloquist's Tale.* London: Bloomberg, 1997.

Mintz, Sidney. *Sweetness and Power: The Place of Sugar in Modern History.* New York: Penguin Books, 1986.

Mintz, Sidney, and Michel-Rolph Trouillot. "The Social History of Haitian Vodou." In *Sacred Arts of Vodou.* Donald J. Consentino, ed. Los Angeles: UCLA Fowler Museum, 1995.

Mohammed, Patricia. "Writing Gender into History." In *Engendering History.* Barbara Bailey et al., eds. New York: St. Martin's Press, 1995.

Mohammed, Patricia, and Catherine Shepherd, eds. *Gender and Caribbean Development.* Kingston, Jamaica: Canoe Press, [1988] 1999.

Moitt, Bernard. *Women and Slavery in the French Antilles, 1635–1848.* Bloomington, IN: Indiana University Press, 2001.

Mordecai, Pamela, and Betty Wilson. *Her True-True Name: An Anthology of Women's Writing from the Caribbean.* London: Heinemann, 1989.

Morrison, Toni. *Beloved.* New York: Alfred A. Knopf, 1987.

Murphy, Joseph M. *Working the Spirit: Ceremonies of the African Diaspora.* Boston: Beacon, 1994.

Naimou, Angela. "'I Need Many Repetitions': Rehearsing the Haitian Revolution in the Shadows of the Sugar Mill." *Callaloo*, vol. 35, no. 1 (2012): 173–192.

Nicholls, David. "Economic Dependence and Political Autonomy: The Haitian Experience, 1974." In *Libète: A Haiti Anthology.* Charles Arthur and Michael Dash, eds. London: The Latin American Bureau, 1999.

Nichols, Grace. *I is a Long Memoried Woman.* London: Karnak House, 1983.

———. *Whole of Morning Sky*. London: Virago Press, 1986.

Nunez, Elizabeth. *Prospero's Daughter*. New York: Ballantine Books, 2006.

O'Callaghan, Evelyn. *Woman Version*. New York: St. Martin's Press, 1993.

Olmos, Margarite Fernández, and Lizabeth Paravisini-Gebert, eds. *Creole Religions of the Caribbean*. New York: New York University Press, 2003.

———. *Sacred Possessions: Vodou, Santería, Obeah, and the Caribbean*. New Brunswick, NJ: Rutgers University Press, 1997.

Olwig, Karen Fog. *Cultural Adaptation and Resistance on St. John: Three Centuries of Afro-Caribbean Life*. Gainesville: University of Florida Press, 1985.

Omolade, Barbara. "Hearts of Darkness." *Rising Song of African American Women* (1994): 3–22.

Oxford English Dictionary. www.oed.com.libproxy.lib.unc.edu.

One Million Bones Project. Accessed April 2013. http://www.onemillionbones.org/the-project/.

———. "One Million Bones Storytelling Grant Highlights." Accessed March 2013. http://www.comptonfoundation.org/grants-awarded/grant-highlights/storytelling-grant-highlights/.

Paravisini-Gebert, Lizabeth. "Decolonizing Feminism." In *Daughters of Caliban*. Consuelo Lopez Springfield, ed. Bloomington: Indiana University Press, 1997.

———. "The Haitian Revolution in Interstices and Shadows: A Re-reading of Alejo Carpentier's *The Kingdom of This World*." *Research in African Literatures*, vol. 35, no. 2 (Summer 2004).

Patullo, Polly. *Last Resorts: The Cost of Tourism in the Caribbean*. London: Latin American Bureau, 2006.

Payne, Anthony, and Paul Sutton. *Charting Caribbean Development*. Gainesville: University Press of Florida, 2001.

Peabody, Sue. *"There Are No Slaves in France": The Political Culture of Race and Slavery*. New York: Oxford University Press, 1996.

Pearce, Lynne, ed. *Devolving Identities: Feminist Readings in Home and Belonging*. Aldershot, UK: Ashgate, 2000.

Philip, M. Nourbese. *Zong!* Middletown, CT: Wesleyan University Press, 2008.

"The Pill." *American Experience*. Chana Gazit and David Steward, dirs. Public Broadcasting Service, February 17, 2003.

Poupeye, Veerle. *Caribbean Art*. New York: Thames and Hudson, 1998.

Powell, Patricia. *The Pagoda*. Boston: Mariner Books, 1999.

Puri, Shalini. *The Caribbean Postcolonial: Social Equality, Post-nationalism and Cultural Hybridity*. New York: Palgrave Macmillan, 2004.

Reddock, Rhoda. *Ethnic Minorities in Caribbean Society*. St. Augustine, Trinidad and Tobago: University of the West Indies, 1996.

———. *Women, Labour and Politics in Trinidad and Tobago: A History*. London: Zed Books, 1994.

Renda, Mary A. *Taking Haiti: Military Occupation and the Culture of U.S.*

Imperialism, 1915–1940. Chapel Hill: The University of North Carolina Press, 2001.

Retamar, Roberto Fernández. *Caliban and Other Essays.* Minneapolis: University of Minnesota Press, 1989.

Rice, Alan J. *Radical Narratives of the Black Atlantic.* New York: Continuum, 2003.

Rodman, Selden. *Where Art Is Joy—Haitian Art: The First Forty Years.* New York: Ruggles de Latour, 1998.

Rodney, Walter. *A History of the Guyanese Working People, 1881–1905.* Baltimore, MD: Johns Hopkins University Press, 1981.

Rosenberg, Leah Reade. *Nationalism and the Formation of Caribbean Literature.* New York: Palgrave, 2007.

Roth, Walter E. *An Inquiry into the Animism and Folk-lore of the Guiana Indians.* London: Johnson Reprint Company, [1915] 1970.

Rouse, Irving. *The Tainos: Rise and Decline of the People Who Greeted Columbus.* New Haven, CT: Yale University Press, 1992.

Saunders, Patricia Joan. *Alien-Nation and Repatriation.* Lanham, MD: Lexington Books, 2007.

Scarry, Elaine. *The Body in Pain: The Making and Unmaking of the World.* New York: Oxford University Press, 1985.

Schutzman, Mady, and Jan Cohen-Cruz. "Introduction." In *Playing Boal: Theatre, Therapy, Activism.* Mady Schutzman and Jan Cohen-Cruz, eds. London: Routledge, 1994.

Schwarz-Bart, André. *A Woman Named Solitude.* Ralph Manheim, trans. New York: Atheneum, 1973.

Schwarz-Bart, André, and Simone Schwarz-Bart. *In Praise of Black Women: Heroines of the Slavery Era.* Vol. 2. Madison: University of Wisconsin Press, 2002.

Scott, Helen. *Caribbean Women Writers and Globalization.* Burlington, VT: Ashgate Publishing, 2006.

Senghor, Leopold Sedar. "Negritude: A Humanism of the Twentieth Century" (1966). In *I Am Because We Are: Readings in Black Philosophy.* Fred Lee Hord and Jonathan Scott Lee, eds. Amherst: University of Massachusetts Press, 1995.

Senior, Olive. *Arrival of the Snake-Woman and Other Stories.* London: Longman Caribbean, 1989.

———. *Working Miracles: Women's Lives in the English-speaking Caribbean.* Bloomington: Indiana University Press, 1991.

Sheller, Mimi. *Citizenship from Below.* Durham, NC: Duke University Press, 2012.

———. *Consuming the Caribbean.* London: Routledge, 2003.

Shemak, April. "Alter/Natives: Myth, Translation and the Native Informant in Pauline Melville's *The Ventriloquist's Tale.*" *Textual Practice*, vol. 19, no. 3 (2005): 253–372.

———. *Asylum Speakers: Caribbean Refugees and Testimonial Discourse.* New York: Fordham University Press, 2010.

Shepherd, Verene A. "Gender, Migration and Settlement: The Indentureship and Post-indentureship Experience of Indian Females in Jamaica, 1845–1943." In *Engendering History: Caribbean Women in Historical Perspective.* Verene A. Shepherd, Bridget Brereton, and Barbara Bailey, eds. New York: St. Martin's Press, 1995.

———. *Maharani's Misery: Narratives of a Passage from India to the Caribbean.* Mona, Jamaica: University of the West Indies Press, 2002.

———. *Women in Caribbean History.* Kingston, Jamaica: Ian Randle, 1999.

Shinebourne, Jan. *The Last English Plantation.* Leeds, UK: Peepal Tree Press, 1988.

Shirley, Tanya. *She Who Sleeps with Bones.* London: Peepal Tree Press, 2009.

Sitrin, Marina. *Horizontalism: Voices of Popular Power in Argentina.* Oakland, CA: AK Press, 2006.

Sizer, Nigel. *Profit without Plunder: Reaping Revenue from Guyana's Tropical Forests without Destroying Them.* Washington, DC: World Resources Institute, 1996.

Skloot, Rebecca. *The Immortal Life of Henrietta Lacks.* New York: Broadway Books, 2011.

Smith, Katherine. "Genealogies of Gede." In *In Extremis: Death and Life in 21st-Century Haitian Art.* Donald J. Cosentino, ed. Los Angeles: Fowler Museum at UCLA, 2012.

Smith, Faith L., ed. *Sex and the Citizen: Interrogating the Caribbean.* Charlottesville: University of Virginia Press, 2011.

Smyth, Heather. "'Roots beyond Roots': Heteroglossia and Feminist Creolization in *Myal* and *Crossing the Mangrove.*" *Small Axe*, September 12, 2002, 1–24.

"Solitude Exhibit" at La Médiathèque Caraïbe of the General Council of Guadeloupe. Basse-Terre, Guadeloupe. Under the aegis of Maison Schwarz-Bart. Maison des Illustres, May 2012.

Sperry, Todd. "Cruise Ship Rescues 23 Cubans at Sea," April 6, 2012. Accessed April 10, 2012. http://www.cnn.com/2012/04/06/travel/cruise-ship-rescue/.

Spillers, Hortense. "Mama's Baby, Papa's Maybe: An American Grammar Book." *Diacritics*, vol. 17, no. 2 (Summer 1987): 64–81.

Stebich, Ute. *A Haitian Celebration: Art and Culture.* Exhibition catalog. Milwaukee, WI: Milwaukee Art Museum, 1993.

Sullivan, Shannon. *Living Across and Through Skins: Transactional Bodies, Pragmatism, and Feminism.* Bloomington: Indiana University Press, 2001.

Swan, Michael. *The Marches of El Dorado.* London: Jonathan Cape, 1958.

Tann, Mambo Chita. *Haitian Vodou.* Woodbury, MN: Llewellyn Publications, 2012.

Taylor, Diana. *The Archive and the Repertoire: Performing Cultural Memory in the Americas.* Durham, NC: Duke University Press, 2003.

Taylor, Jason deCaires. "Jason deCaires Taylor." Accessed April 30, 2011. http://www.underwatersculpture.com/pages/gallery/grenada.html.
——. "Interview with author." May 22, 2012.
Tinsley, Omise'eke Natasha. "Black Atlantic, Queer Atlantic: Queer Imaginings of the Middle Passage." *GLQ*, vol. 14, nos. 2–3 (2008): 191–215.
——. *Thiefing Sugar: Eroticism between Women in Caribbean Literature.* Durham, NC: Duke University Press, 2010.
Torres-Saillant, Silvio. *Caribbean Poetics.* New York: Cambridge University Press, 1997.
Trouillot, Evelyne. *Rosalie L'infâme.* Paris: Éditions Dapper, 2003.
Trouillot, Michel-Rolph. *Silencing the Past.* Boston: Beacon Press, 1995.
Turner, J. William. *The Slave Ship.* Tate Museum, London. Accessed May 25, 2011. http://www.tate.org.uk/art/artworks/turner-the-slave-ship-t06374.
Turner, Mary, ed. *From Chattel Slaves to Wage Slaves: The Dynamics of Labour Bargaining in the Americas.* Kingston, Jamaica: Ian Randle, 1995.
"Underwater Sculpture Park Action Group Strategy and Plan: Investing in the Future." Report. St. George's, Grenada: Underwater Sculpture Park Regeneration Project, 2011.
Vega, Ana Lydia. "Cloud Cover Caribbean." In *Her True-True Name.* Mark McCaffrey, trans. Pamela Mordecai and Betty Wilson, eds. London: Heinemann, [1982] 1989.
Velez, Diana. "We Are (Not) in This Together: The Caribbean Imaginary in 'Encancaranublado' by Ana Lydia Vega." *Callaloo*, vol. 17, no. 3 (1994): 826–833.
Walcott, Derek. "The Antilles: Fragments of Epic Memory." Nobel lecture. New York: Farrar, Straus & Giroux, 1992.
——. "The Caribbean: Culture as Mimicry?" *Journal of Inter American Studies and World Affairs*, vol. 16 (February 1974).
——. *The Haitian Earth: A Trilogy of Plays.* New York: Farrar, Straus & Giroux, 2002.
——. "The Muse of History." In *Is Massa Day Dead?* Orde Coombs, ed. New York: Doubleday Books, 1974.
——. *Star-Apple Kingdom: Poems.* New York: Farrar, Straus & Giroux, 1983.
Wallace, Belinda. "'I Will Pay for This Fearlessness': Post-colonial Rebels and Revolutionary Lyricism in the Works of Dionne Brand." Unpublished manuscript.
Walvin, James. *Black Ivory.* London: Blackwell Publishers, [1992] 2001.
——. *The Zong.* London: Yale University Press, 2011.
Warner, Marina. *Indigo.* London: Random House, 1993.
——. "Siren/Hyphen; or, the Maid Beguiled." In *Caribbean Portraits: Essays on Gender Ideologies and Identities.* Christine Barrow, ed. Kingston, Jamaica: Ian Randle Press, 1998.

stories of the community spoken and sung in call-and-response fashion. The Priyè Ginen is followed by the Priyè Afriken, which, in contrast to the Priyé Ginen, is sung in a combination of Kreyol and words from various African languages, referred to as *langaj*: "Some of the first Kreyol words that can be made out include the often-repeated phrase *zo-a li mache li mache, li manche* [the bones are walking, walking, walking], a reference to the ancestors, and the history continues."[44] At sunset, these prayers are followed by communal dancing, the invocation of the three families of *loa* (Rada, Petro, and Gede), and possible possession by the *loa*.[45]

These basic ceremonial components are present in Desruisseau's painting: the *pòto-mitan*, the singing, dancing, and the invocation of the spirits who hover above the ritual. The phrase "the bones are walking" reiterates the nature of bones, which is to shape and tell stories, to remind and memorialize, to incriminate (as Clea Koff would put it), and to connect. These walking bones likewise call to mind D'Aguiar's *Feeding the Ghosts* (as discussed in chapter 1), in which Mintah thinks of the slave children dumped into the sea and if and how their bones will find their way home. Referring to a little girl thrown overboard off the *Zong*, Mintah contemplates "[h]er small bones adding to a sea of bones."[46] Ritualizing the history, as Dayan suggests, is one way of rehearsing it. The systemic invocation is the constant reminder and physicality of ancestral suffering connected to that of the worshippers.

Vodou Ceremony has no recognized heroes, no stars; it is not a citadel built around and unto a single person. Instead, it celebrates and commemorates the presence of everyday men and women as active participants. This is belonging steeped in the masses, and it is this concept that Desruisseau celebrates. These nameless—even androgynous—people, draw together toward a single light, struggle side by side for a liberty with seemingly meager resources. In an interview, Desruisseau positioned herself within that struggle: "I feel like a miserable little woman confronted by these great moments of history . . . while nonetheless rewriting it [by] revealing the socio-cultural forces that were part of the Haitian struggles against slavery."[47] In this rewriting, the artist rehearses both the revolutionary aspects of quotidian struggles and the method by which the people, who were and are the source of revolutionary struggle, can rehearse them: Vodou. This rewriting is Dédée Bazile's struggle. Counter to other representations of the Haitian Revolution, Desruisseau places the mass of the people at the center when she imagines Haiti's past. Furthermore, she calls our attention to the realities of the community and its economic station—through their torn and tattered clothes and simple environment, and their political will to rise up and fight.

A second painting by Desruisseau, *Ceremony at Bois Caïman* (1986), is a representation of the famed 1791 religious ceremony that marked the beginning of the Revolution, narratives of which are largely mythical. The panel features rebelling slaves and two central figures: a dancing woman and a shirtless man in red pants with a red scarf tied about his head. They are presumably the *manbo* (priestess) Fatiman and the *hougan* (priest) Boukman. Encircled by a large crowd that extends deep into the woods and beyond the frame, Cécile Fatiman dances in a bright red dress, a knife held aloft in her right hand while a slaughtered black pig lies in the foreground. The multitude in the forest holds torches while lightning flashes in a background in shades of dark blue, representing the deep darkness of the night, the mystical nature of the endeavor, and the indigo plants enslaved workers produced for the plantation economy. The mouths of the figures are open, as in *Vodou Ceremony*, and the women and men in striped pants and vibrant headscarves, both genders bare-chested with breasts exposed, indicate Desruisseau's belief in the indistinguishable nature of all the participants—men and women, old and young, the healthy and the infirm—as part of Haiti's quest for freedom. The dress of enslaved people mark them as a unit, their troubles the same. Some hands are in the air, and some are dipped into the pig's blood contained in a bowl held by the *hougan*; they are taking the oath to live free or die.

Desruisseau's inclusion of women as essential participants in both paintings rejects the role of weeping maternal victim as described by McClintock. Female bodies are vital in both the ritual and the representation of it, both as leaders and as members of the extensive crowd;[48] leadership is shared between the sexes, and participation is equal. The use of androgynous figures reinforces the idea of rethinking and revising gender politics.[49] In both paintings, by using this visual language in the twentieth century, Desruisseau rehearses the idea that struggle—direct physical and spiritual resistance—is central to creating an independent and sustainable Haiti.

The originating moment for Desruisseau's rehearsal in *Ceremony at Bois-Caïman* is the fusion of legend and history in the story of this event. Dayan cautions that Haiti's enemies, who were invested in bloody and gothic renderings of Haiti's story, may have imagined this ceremony. However, she concedes that Haitians themselves have found the story "necessary [and] continue to construct their identity not only by turning to the Revolution of 1791, but by seeking its origins in a service quite possibly imagined by those who disdain it."[50] Laurent DuBois notes that various accounts indicate that Boukman—driver, coachman, and priest—along with Cécile Fatiman, healer and *manbo*, presided over the swearing of a blood oath of secrecy and revenge: "Boukman apparently proclaimed: 'The god of the white man calls him to commit crimes; our god asks only good works of us. But this god who is so good orders revenge! He will direct our hands; he will aid us. Throw away the image of the god of the whites who thirsts for our tears and listen to the voice of liberty that speaks in the hearts of all of us.'"[51] Boukman's prayer—whether real or imagined—conveys the idea that eradicating white or European religion was as critical as overthrowing the political and economic system of the plantation. The prayer consecrates several transformative ideas: rupturing psychological ties were as critical as severing physical ties; equally critical was disturbing the hierarchy of European justification from God to the master to the enslaved, as was creating a distinct moral universe in which "our god asks only good works of us." Yet this god understands and demands justice. "Our" god does not require passivity and tears in the face of oppression; in fact, this god will help us fight—"he will direct our hands"—possibly through spiritual leaders.

Other accounts suggest that the *manbo* was Maroon leader Maya-nèt,[52] but both of Desruisseau's paintings feature unknown people. In fact, Desruisseau creates an environment similar to the one in *Vodou Ceremony*, filled with physical and spiritual bodies that extend beyond the frame, giving a limitless sense of who is involved in this rehearsal. While the second painting foregrounds leaders on one critical night, those leaders are not alone; they are embedded in community, just as they are embedded in the canvas. Boukman and Fatiman (or Mayanèt) had leadership roles because of their religious positions, yet this visual space is taken up by a mass of people, each face suggesting investment in the revolutionary process. Desruisseau's work reveals the tension in rehearsing the past, the apparent simplistic ease of memorializing individual heroes rather than remembering the thousands who participated and sacrificed so equally. By foregrounding Vodou as a communal, religious, and public ceremony valued by Haitians, she invites us to participate in the latter conversation. Desruisseau remembers both heroes sung and people forgotten, but she emphasizes the difference by removing leadership from an individual icon and distributing it among these ritual participants on their communal terrain.

Desruisseau's paintings of Haitian Revolution rehearsals show revolution at its most collaborative and communal. The paintings emphasize not only the relational nature of Vodou practice but the fierce determination of Haiti's men and women to transform their society and end slavery. Their determined faces and joyful dancing, coupled with weapons ranging from sticks to knives, reveal a version of the Revolution at its most domestic yet most dramatic. Women in both pieces are armed and visible, and they are central actors in the frame. They are on the forefront of the action because the systems of oppression—be they slavery or occupation—affect their lives. These images rupture the romance of the solitary messianic leader by painting broader tableaux of the actors involved.

Desruisseau's *Vodou Ceremony* and *Ceremony at Bois Caïman* illustrate the transactions made between religion, representation, and contemporary sensibilities. Carolyn Fick contends that "voodoo provided a medium for the political organization of the slaves, as well as an ideological force, both of which contributed directly to the success of what became a virtual blitzkrieg attack on the plantations across the province."[53] The paintings expose the negotiations made during this struggle for physical, political, and spiritual emancipation. While these images, particularly *Vodou Ceremony*, are not quite images of the Crusades and the Knights Templar, they clearly link the religious to the martial. Vodou as a spiritual practice is imagined as part of the struggle from the start. Revolutionary figures, including Boukman and Georges Biassou, were said to be Vodou practitioners, if not *hougans*. As an initiate herself, Desruisseau depicted these rituals in historical tableaux, thus promoting the links between Vodou and the formulation of the Haitian nation. By foregrounding the feminine in these pieces as Vodou adepts and as fighters, Desruisseau's representations do not cede ground to the overwhelmingly male representations of the Revolution that emphasize the triumph of the individual male. Additionally, the indistinct gender of some of the figures ruptures the ease of characterizing revolutionary action as masculine or feminine. Instead, by rehearsing the Revolution in these two pieces, Desruisseau recalibrates the gender hierarchy that has prevailed, particularly in historic and artistic renderings of the Revolution. Desruisseau's characters, like Défilée, or perhaps Dédée, reconfigure the nation in emotionally moving yet less singular terms. Défilée not only offered visibility for Dessalines's body and, in a sense, her own body, which is also memorialized in the Haitian national imagination, but the ritual aspects of her hearseness are embedded in Desruisseau's work.

Watson, Hilbourne A. "Caribbean Options under Global Neoliberalism." In *The Caribbean: New Dynamics in Trade and Political Economy*. Anthony T. Bryan, ed. Coral Gables, FL: North-South Center, University of Miami, 1995.

Webb, Barbara. *Myth and History in the Caribbean*. Amherst: University of Massachusetts Press, 1992.

Wekker, Gloria. "One Finger Does Not Drink Okra Soup: Afro-Surinamese Women and Critical Agency." In *Feminist Genealogies, Colonial Legacies, Democratic Futures*. M. Jacqui Alexander and Chandra Talpade Mohanty, eds. New York: Routledge, 1997.

Welsh, Sarah Lawson. "Pauline Melville's Shape-Shifting Fictions." In *Caribbean Women Writers*. Selwyn Cudjoe, ed. Wellesley, MA: Calaloux Publications, 1990.

Welter, Barbara. "The Cult of True Womanhood: 1820–1860." *American Quarterly*, vol. 18, no. 2 (1966): 151–174.

West-Durán, Alan. *African Caribbeans: A Reference Guide*. Westport, CT: Greenwood Press, 2003.

Whitehead, Neil L., and Robin Wright. *In Darkness and Secrecy: The Anthropology of Assault Sorcery and Witchcraft in Amazonia*. Durham, NC: Duke University Press, 2004.

Williams, Brackette F. *Stains on My Name, War in My Veins: Guyana and the Politics of Cultural Struggle*. Durham, NC: Duke University Press, 1991.

Williams, Raymond. "Structures of Feeling." In *Marxism and Literature*, 128–135. Oxford: Oxford University Press, 1977.

Wilson, Samuel. *The Indigenous People of the Caribbean*. Gainesville: University Press of Florida, 1997.

Wilson-Tagoe, Nana. *Historical Thought and Literary Representation in West Indian Literature*. Gainesville: University Press of Florida, 1998.

Wynter, Sylvia. "Beyond Miranda's Meaning: Un/Silencing the Demonic Ground." In *Out of Kumbla*. Carol Boyce Davies and Elaine Savory Fido, eds. Trenton, NJ: Africa World Press, 1990.

———."Rethinking 'Aesthetics': Notes towards a Deciphering Practice." In *Ex-Iles: Essays on Caribbean Cinema*. Mbye Cham, ed. Trenton, NJ: Africa World Press, 1992.

Zabus, Chantal. *Tempests after Shakespeare*. Hampshire, UK: Palgrave Macmillan, 2002.

Index

Panama, 6, 172, 173
Paravisini-Gebert, Lizabeth, 73, 81–85
Pascal-Trouillot, Ertha, 90
Patullo, Polly, 37, 181n49
Peasant Movement of Papay (Haiti), 65, 68
Péralte, Charlemagne, 98
performance theories, 14–16. *See also* feminist rehearsals
Pétion, Alexandre, 61, 65; art schools and, 94; Césaire on, 67–70; death of, 186n60; as president, 187n68
Philip, Marlene NourbeSe, 33–35, 181n42
plantation system, 18; Barrow on, 120; Benítez-Rojo on, 120, 179n10; in British Guiana, 147; after emancipation, 142–143; gendered norms in, 27–28, 60–61, 120, 132–133; for indigo, 130; motherhood and, 126–129, 133–134, 142–143; rape and, 27–28, 90, 92, 115, 118; Schwarz-Bart on, 118–119. *See also* slavery
Platt Amendment, 6
Pocahontas, 200n60
pòto-mitan, 97, 99, 131, 191n39. *See also* Vodou
Poulier, Jacky, 115–116, 119, 120
Powell, Patricia, 196n94
Price, Lucien, 93
"primitive" Haitian artists, 93, 190n19
Princess cruise ships, 37
Puerto Rico, 3, 6, 40, 173
Puri, Shalini, 177n47

race, 2, 13–14, 18–22, 67, 157; gender and, 129, 132–138, 142–143, 184n5, 196n94; hybridity and, 12, 149–150, 152, 177n47; identity and, 25–26, 39; immigrants and, 43–45; masculinity and, 54–59; mixed, 69–72, 75, 118, 131, 135–139, 145, 150–155, 197n2; nationalism and, 165; Vodou and, 80, 84, 95, 102
Racine, Jean, 76
rape: on cruise ships, 37, 182n59; during Middle Passage, 30, 49, 116, 118; and plantation system, 27–28, 90, 92, 115, 119; in Shakespeare, 136
Rastafarianism, 39
Raynal, Abbé de, 67
Rediker, Marcus, 49

rehearsal. *See* feminist rehearsals
Retamar, Roberto Fernández, 137
Rhys, Jean, 123, 136
Robertson, Pat, 103, 192n55
Robeson, Paul, 56
Rochambeau, Count of, 66, 90
Rodó, José Enrique, 122
Rodrigues, Basil, 197n14
Rosenberg, Leah, 11
Roth, Walter, 161
Royal Caribbean cruise ships, 37
Rupununi Uprising, 153–154

The Salt Roads (Hopkinson), 21, 114, 130–131, 133–142, 188n91
Sam, Vilbrun Guillaume, 72
Santería, 41
Saunders, Patricia, 11
Savain, Pétion, 93, 94, 98
Scarry, Elaine, 4
Schwarz-Bart, André, 114, 115, 118–120
Scott, William, 94
Seaton, Margot, 39
Senghor, Léopold Sédor, 60–61
Shakespeare, William. *See The Tempest*
Sheller, Mimi, 142, 176n25
Shemak, April, 41, 182n66, 198n17
Sistren Theatre Collective, 15
Sitrin, Marina, 176n35
Skloot, Rebecca, 3–4
slavery, 40, 55, 111, 118, 170; abolition of, 6, 62–63, 65, 69, 102, 139, 171, 193n4; Code Henri and, 71–72, 187n69; gendered norms in, 28, 60–61, 68, 74–75, 132–133, 143; indentured servants and, 17–18, 28, 37, 133, 142, 146, 170; *Zong* massacre and, 23, 28–35, 50, 99, 133, 181n42. *See also* Middle Passage; plantation system
slavery rebellions. *See* Maroons
Smith, Faith, 142
Society of King Cristophe's Friends, 71
Solitude (Poulier), 115–117
Soulouque, Faustin, 72
Spanish-American War, 6
Spillers, Hortense, 5–6, 7
St. Kitts and Nevis, 138
steel drums, 148
Stonewall Rebellion (1969), 140
Sullivan, Shannon, 17

Nick Nesbitt, *Universal Emancipation: The Haitian Revolution and the Radical Enlightenment*

Doris L. Garraway, editor, *Tree of Liberty: Cultural Legacies of the Haitian Revolution in the Atlantic World*

Dawn Fulton, *Signs of Dissent: Maryse Condé and Postcolonial Criticism*

Michael G. Malouf, *Transatlantic Solidarities: Irish Nationalism and Caribbean Poetics*

Maria Cristina Fumagalli, *Caribbean Perspectives on Modernity: Returning the Gaze*

Vivian Nun Halloran, *Exhibiting Slavery: The Caribbean Postmodern Novel as Museum*

Paul B. Miller, *Elusive Origins: The Enlightenment in the Modern Caribbean Historical Imagination*

Eduardo González, *Cuba and the Fall: Christian Text and Queer Narrative in the Fiction of José Lezama Lima and Reinaldo Arenas*

Jeff Karem, *The Purloined Islands: Caribbean-U.S. Crosscurrents in Literature and Culture, 1880–1959*

Faith Smith, editor, *Sex and the Citizen: Interrogating the Caribbean*

Mark D. Anderson, *Disaster Writing: The Cultural Politics of Catastrophe in Latin America*

Raphael Dalleo, *Caribbean Literature and the Public Sphere: From the Plantation to the Postcolonial*

Maite Conde, *Consuming Visions: Cinema, Writing, and Modernity in Rio de Janeiro*

Monika Kaup, *Neobaroque in the Americas: Alternative Modernities in Literature, Visual Art, and Film*

Marisel C. Moreno, *Family Matters: Puerto Rican Women Authors on the Island and the Mainland*

Supriya M. Nair, *Pathologies of Paradise: Caribbean Detours*

Colleen C. O'Brien, *Race, Romance, and Rebellion: Literatures of the Americas in the Nineteenth Century*

Kelly Baker Josephs, *Disturbers of the Peace: Representations of Madness in Anglophone Caribbean Literature*

Christina Kullberg, *The Poetics of Ethnography in Martinican Narratives: Exploring the Self and the Environment*

Maria Cristina Fumagalli, Bénédicte Ledent, and Roberto del Valle Alcalá, editors, *The Cross-Dressed Caribbean: Writing, Politics, Sexualities*

Philip Kaisary, *The Haitian Revolution in the Literary Imagination: Radical Horizons, Conservative Constraints*

Jason Frydman, *Sounding the Break: African American and Caribbean Routes of World Literature*

Tanya L. Shields, *Bodies and Bones: Feminist Rehearsal and Imagining Caribbean Belonging*